I'll Be the
Parent,
You Be the
Child

I'll Be the Parent, You Be the Child

Encourage Excellence, Set Limits and Lighten Up

PAUL KROPP

FISHER
BOOKS™

The author thanks the following for granting permission to reprint extracts of their work in this book:
I'd Swore I'd Never Do That! by Elizabeth Fishel © 1991. Reprinted by permission of Conari Press, Inc.
Extract from a column by Linwood Barclay © 1997 by the Toronto Star Syndicate. Reprinted by permission of the author.
Extract from column by family psychologist John Rosemond, the author of *Family of Values* (Andrews and McMeel). Reprinted by permission of the author.

Note: All the families and incidents described in this book are real, but names and details have been changed to disguise specific identities. The author has drawn on many friends by way of example and would like to keep at least a few of them after publication.

Cover design by Suzanne Heiser
Text design by Tonya Hahn
Set in 11-point Janson by Perseus Publishing Services

First published in 1998 by Random House Canada.

A CIP record for this book is available from the Library of Congress.

ISBN 0–55561–323–3

Fisher Books is a member of the Perseus Books Group.
Find us on the World Wide Web at http://www.fisherbooks.com

Fisher Books' titles are available at special discounts for bulk purchases in the United States by corporations, institutions, and other organizations. For more information, please contact the Special Markets Department at HarperCollins Publishers, 10 East 53rd Street, New York, NY 10022, or call 1–212–207–7528.

First printing, April 2001
1 2 3 4 5 6 7 8 9 10—04 03 02 01 00

Acknowledgments

To begin, thanks and admiration must be extended to three well-known writers on the parenting of children: Burton White, Judy Dunn and Penelope Leach. Thanks are due also to the many people who offered advice and information, looked at the rough text or provided material used in the book: Helena Aalto, Emma Adam, Gale Bildfell, Russell Brown, Priscilla Galloway, Linda Granfield, Joan Grusec, Virginia Hamilton, Andrea Wayne von Konigslow, Claire Mackay, Patty Papas, Patricia Quinlan, Shari Siamon and Bruce Steele. And then there are thanks to the many families who let the author into their lives, at least for a while: the Allens, Atkinsons, Cappons, Collins, Crockatts, Drinnans, Georges, Gullands, Hertzes, Machlachlans, Moorhouses, Muirs, Paquins, Rhodes, Tumblins, Whishes and many others who won't be named here.

I am indebted, of course, to my own children and stepchildren who have taught me much about being a parent and provided some of the examples in this book: Jason, Justin and Alex Kropp and Emma and Ken Adam. I owe a great debt to Linda Lewis and the *Today's Parent* staff who sometimes let me explore, in print, those parenting issues that interested me. Appreciation always goes to my editor at Random House of Canada, Sarah Davies, who believes in what I write and ensures that the words make reasonable sense when they get into print.

Finally, let me thank my own parents, Marjorie and Lloyd Kropp, who managed to tackle real-life parenting with conviction and love—two important ingredients needed by anyone to wants to be a parent.

Paul Kropp

Contents

Introduction

It's shortly after Christmas, and my wife, youngest son and I are on our way to visit the Archers at their cabin near the ski slopes north of our city. We have come equipped with gifts for the kids and a mandatory bottle of wine for the adults. When we arrive, Brad Archer has a roast in the oven; Irene is creating some of her famous ratatouille and their children are cheerfully playing a game of board hockey, although 7-year-old Kevin clearly outmatches 3-year-old Christine. We all smile as we enter, as if we'd been looking forward to this for months. Actually, there was some question about how well the seven of us would get along for a long weekend in a relatively small cabin.

With the Archers, we all got along very well. The presence of all three kids added a lot to our time together. Little Christine, whose biggest demand was to have one *more* book read aloud to her, did much more than the wine to warm up the adults. The older child, Kevin, not only helped out with his sister, but seemed to enjoy being with the adults for part of dinner and then playing Clue with us before his bedtime. My own sometimes surly, sometimes delightful teenage kid consistently offered the nicer side of his personality.

When we left the next afternoon, my wife and I were both enthusiastic about the time everyone had spent together: "The food was great . . . "; "the kids were wonderful . . . "; "everybody got along so well. . . ." Even my teenage son declared that the Archers were "cool," verging on "way cool."

As every parent knows, family visits don't always go so well. Two weeks later, we were called on to make a weekend visit to a family I'll call the Zacharies, a visit that quickly turned into the proverbial Weekend from Hell. Not that the Zacharies themselves are Stephen King horrors, by any means. Bill and Francine are a thirtyish couple, both college educated, well read, creative and articulate people. They have two children, cute as the clichéd buttons, but the parents' notions about parenting are quickly turning the kids into monsters and their family life into an ongoing *Simpsons* episode.

On this weekend, our mostly grown children were busy at their own enterprises, so we made the five-hour drive to the Zacharies' remodeled farmhouse on our own. We were slightly dazed on arrival. Maybe that's why I wasn't ready for their 5-year-old, Freddy, who raced into me, knocking his head into my crotch. "Uncle Paul! Uncle Paul!" he shouted as I fought to get my breath back.

The Zacharies' second child, Sally, was just over two years old and not so forthcoming. She was busy hiding behind Francine until we took off our coats. That's when she began to cry, for reasons that probably made good sense to a 2-year-old but were lost on the rest of us.

"She's a crybaby!" Freddy said triumphantly. "Crybaby! Crybaby!"

"Freddy, please . . ." his father warned.

"Crybaby! Crybaby!" Freddy went on, deaf to his father's words and unappreciative of his tone of voice.

At this point, Francine spoke sympathetically to her daughter. "Sally, you know it makes me unhappy when you cry like that."

Great, I thought to myself, now *two* of them are unhappy. At least Freddy had let go of my leg. He was too busy chanting, "Crybaby, crybaby!" to pay further attention to me.

Sally, irritated by her failure to get instant attention and her brother's successful if unmusical chant, decided to take a swing at Freddy. It worked. Her little fist connected with his face and Freddy started crying. We were up to three unhappy people, not counting ourselves. The casualty list was mounting.

Bill looked sternly at his family, perhaps trying to figure out how to impose some discipline. He looked at triumphant Sally, crying Freddy and unhappy Francine. Then he turned to us with a sheepish expression. "I guess we're not having a good day."

The night proved no better. The Zacharies do not believe in a fixed bedtime for their kids. Instead, they wait for the children to expire. Only then do they tuck the still-warm but now pliable bodies into bed.

"It's more natural," Francine explained to us at ten o'clock, "for kids to go to bed when they're tired."

With a full day of arguing, crying, whining and complaining behind them, one might expect both children to be quite tired. But the only people who seemed exhausted at that point were the adults. Certainly I was tired of the kids fighting, yelling, crying and throwing things. I was tired of Francine's repeated, "You know I'm not happy when you do that," and Bill's desperate efforts to distract the kids from various dangerous or unpleasant behaviors. I kept looking at my watch, wondering whether it would be socially acceptable for me to go to bed.

Finally Sally expired in front of the TV and was carried to bed by her father. Apparently she often woke up screaming as she was slipped into bed and, according to Francine, the only way to get her back to sleep was for dad to sing along with a Barney tape as it played on the children's tape recorder. When the rest of the adults went to bed at eleven o'clock, dad was still singing and Freddy had taken over the TV to watch a video.

The next day, my wife and I felt the urge to leave early. This was a shame, really, because with both kids sleeping that morning, we found our time with the parents to be fairly pleasant. But I confess I had a certain dread of the day to come, when the kids would be at it again and the parents would start behaving like the idiot adults in *Home Alone*. It was the dread that sent us packing.

So we left, or fled, depending on how you look at our retreat, mumbling phrases to each other like "well, one visit down," and "the kids are at a difficult age" and "maybe we're getting too old for this." Running through the back of our minds were visions of these out-of-control children and foolish parents who had made it unbearable to stay any longer.

The problem with the Zacharie household was not that Francine and Bill didn't want to be good parents. The problem is that they followed the current dogma in parenting *much too closely*. They read all the parenting magazines, knew how important it was to be child-focused, had mastered the "12 Easy Ways to Distract Your Disruptive Child" articles, worked desperately to maintain the children's self-esteem, and tried so hard to be friends to their kids that it became virtually impossible for them to act like parents.

I'm sympathetic to the Zacharies' situation. After three kids and two stepkids of my own, I have to be. I know perfectly well that it has never been easy to be a parent—not in the year one, with the Pharaoh causing problems, or in the year 1001, with limited opportunity for job promotion around the manor; nor in the year 2001, with unpredictable economic change and massive social confusion.

These days, I often see young couples like the Zacharies who are simply too tired and distracted themselves to be parents. They are overworked by the demands of the outside world and unsure what's "right" in dealing with their own children. Not many of these young families are being helped much by their own parents or by a society that gives little support for the vital business of raising children. Even worse, many young people who read popular writers on parenting emerge with clever techniques on how to survive the years with their children but too many wrong-headed concepts on how to raise kids to become reasonable human beings in the twenty-first century.

> They . . . tried so hard to be friends to their kids that it became virtually impossible for them to act like parents.

Frankly, parenting shouldn't be that hard.

So I decided to undertake this book, to investigate what we know and don't know about parenting, where today's parents may be smarter than my generation was, and where they may be off course. This is a hazardous proposition for anyone to undertake, especially if some of the views expressed do not jibe with contemporary thought. There are other books on the shelves that are wonderful manuals on childhood ailments, or speak eloquently of children's needs, or look deeply into child development. Any young parent should have a copy of Dr. Spock's *Baby and Child Care* for reference, Penelope Leach's *Children First* for its philosophy and Burton

White's *The First Three Years of Life* for its insights on early development. Yet I think it's past time for a new book that offers some serious thought and a little historical perspective on the hot-button topics in raising children—on what works and what doesn't, on what's true and what isn't, on what's politically correct and what's *really* correct.

The chapters in *I'll Be the Parent, You Be the Child* can be read in any order, although I think the first two chapters provide good background for subsequent reading on particular issues. The boxes simply encapsulate the basic ideas in a handy format for people who like to browse books by thumbing from the back. Obviously the topics treated here are enormous—child development, discipline and punishment, child psychology, demographics, pharmacology, education, modern sociology and economics as it affects families—and all of them have received treatment in whole books if not on entire library shelves. None of these topics is going to be definitively treated in a book of this size. But there is a need, I feel, to bring together contemporary thought, solid research and real-life experience in a style and format that's accessible to most parents. *I'll Be the Parent, You Be the Child* doesn't pretend to offer the last word on these issues, but to survey the available research, do a reality check up and down neighborhood streets and then take a stand on what parents should be doing.

I've spent the last three years haunting libraries, studying research literature, attending parenting workshops and classes, watching families in real life and on video, consulting with college professors and psychologists, and otherwise seeking out the material for the book that's in your hands. Some of what I found is encouraging: We really do have a body of research that should make parenting today more intelligent than it was thirty years ago, when I first became a father. But some of what I see in both popular and professional writing depresses me: opinions dressed up as research, untested notions presented as tried techniques, unreasonable

> Good parenting . . . calls for tough decisions, consistent day-to-day discipline and often financial sacrifice.

fears and dumb suggestions trotted out as the latest wisdom. It seems to me that today's parents deserve better.

The overall theme of *I'll Be the Parent, You Be the Child* is that good parenting is a serious responsibility—it calls for tough decisions, consistent day-to-day discipline and often financial sacrifice. Our kids will not grow and thrive if we abdicate decision making to them, or substitute the latest electronic marvel for our time and attention, or allow drug companies to modify their attention spans. Our kids need us to take on the role of parent so they can be free to be kids. Anything less cheats them—and us—of what ought to be the most wonderful relationship in our lives.

Chapter 1

Styles of parenting . . .
and what *really* makes us the parents we are

How do we end up becoming the parents that we are? There is a couple across the road who have thrown out the television and always put their kids to bed at eight; parents down the street whose kids are glued to the tube and go to bed at all hours; parents who act like Ward Cleaver of *Leave It to Beaver* and parents who seem more negligent than the Bundys on *Married . . . with Children.* All of us undertake the enterprise of raising children differently, making up much of what we do as we go along, but somehow defining our own style in the process. Lately this concept of "parenting styles" has become very trendy, indeed.

There used to be only two parenting styles: Parents were either "strict" or "permissive." Strict parents adhered to certain codes of conduct that required children to behave in socially approved ways. Their children didn't dare wiggle at church, talk back to the teacher at school or refer to adults without a "sir" or "ma'am" attached to the sentence. The way in which strict parents usually elicited such behavior involved a combination of regular spanking and considerable emotional distance between child and adult. The results of these techniques were too often children who acted like flawless angels in public and ruthless little devils in private.

The other style of parenting was "permissive," from the Latin *permissio*, which suggests that the parents have "let go" of their children or at least taken a more hands-off approach than have other parents. Dr. Spock was widely accused of having foisted permissive parenting on the world, but such charges came mostly from political conservatives in the sixties who were upset that members of the first Spock generation were burning draft cards and growing their hair too long. The conservatives accused Dr. Spock of "permissiveness"—which was nonsense to anyone who actually read Spock—but the label stuck and the word achieved some force.

Strict and permissive are really two poles on a single continuum in parenting, a pretty linear way of approaching a very complex phenomenon. Recent writers have attempted to make this line somewhat more three-dimensional.

More and more and more styles

The number of parenting styles increased from two to three or four as time went on and various writers looked at parenting in more complex ways. Some of this expansion goes back to work done when educator Bernice McCarthy began working with McDonald's—a company so serious about selling hamburgers that it has its own "university" at which to study the business. McCarthy's project was to find the most effective way to train employees. She devised a theory of learning styles to explain how similar concepts need to be presented in different ways to different people. In education, learning styles quickly flipped into teaching styles so that, in the 1980s and '90s, teachers were constantly being reminded to vary their lesson plans in order to accommodate the different ways in which kids learn.

Parenting books became stylish, if you'll pardon the pun, shortly after that. One of the best known is Barbara Coloroso's *Kids Are Worth It*. Coloroso, a teacher and consultant in Denver, is a popular presenter at teachers' conferences. Her talks are punchy, practical and leave audience members smiling with the sense that they have something new for first period Monday morning. Her book offers much of the same for parents. There is excellent material on dumb things that some parents do, on how to talk to kids effectively, and important statements about maintaining dignity for both parent and child. But Coloroso also believes in styles, and she draws on earlier academic work by psychologist Diana Baumrind to separate parents into three groups: "brick-wall" parents, "jellyfish" parents and "backbone" parents.

Brick-wall parents don't listen to their kids and have all the flexibility a wall suggests. Jellyfish parents give in to a child's every whim and then wonder why the child turns into a monster. Backbone parents are the good guys—us, presumably—who manage to deal with difficult situations in child rearing without resorting to beating or rolling over and playing dead.

Taking the "styles" approach one step further is Elizabeth Fishel, an editor of *Child* magazine. Her provocatively titled book, *I Swore I'd Never Do That!*, offers four differently labeled parenting styles: Traditionalists, Rebels, Compensators and Synthesizers. For Fishel, the operating modes of parents aren't established by their own wonts but in reaction to the way they grew up. Traditionalists, then, embrace the parenting style of their own parents and try to replicate it in raising another generation. Rebels swear to do the exact opposite of what their parents did, defining their parenting by opposition. Compensators are anxious to give their kids "what I didn't have when I was growing up." And Synthesizers are the good guys—presumably us—who make conscious parenting choices, either repeating the best of the past or adopting the best of the new.

Fishel does an intelligent critique of her four styles, exercising her penchant for psychological insight into parenting as part of the commentary. She says of traditionalist parents, for instance, that adolescent separation tends to be a difficult issue because "boundaries are fuzzy and enmeshed." She notes, too, that the glowing memories that traditionalist parents cherish may be difficult to achieve in today's changed circumstances. Ward Cleaver on *Leave It to Beaver* and Dr. Jim Anderson on *Father Knows Best* made plenty of money, all by themselves, to pay 3% mortgages on $15,000 houses and still look after their families in fine style. Parents today don't have it quite so easy.

Fishel's Rebels, the opposite of Traditionalists, are ironically unaware of how much their behavior is dictated by the very parents whose style they are trying to reject. Again, she notes, "Rebels are sometimes excessively tied to their children, particularly their negative attributes." Such parents sometimes permit their children to do their own acting out, producing kids who can be real terrors. Fishel's Compensator parents use all sorts of imagination and fantasy to conjure up an ideal world for their own children. This fantasy world tends to be delivered in very material ways, especially around Christmas, and can lead to children whose concept of parental love and approval is much too connected to their receipt of a new Lego set or computer game.

Fishel is justifiably critical of the first three types of parents and only abandons her arched eyebrow when she comes to the good guys:

> The Synthesizer is likely to have a stack of books by her bed on families and child raising. After the last child has been tucked in she will settle down and savor the stories of family life, noting different families' choices and approaches the way other people might relish the quirks of character in a good novel. She reads not for answers or directions but for the pleasure of sharing kinship with fellow travelers on the parenting journey.

Sigh! It is possible to be a good parent after all.

The attraction of books that discuss styles of parenting is their Aha! factor—*Yes, there are other parents like me.* We acknowledge, at a certain level, that part of us may be a jellyfish or a rebel, but mostly we pride ourselves in being the synthesizer-backbone parent so approved of by the authors of the books. By and large, people who read books on parenting are already capable parents and looking for ways to do a somewhat better job. Child abusers, wife beaters, kid haters, alcoholics and negligent parents tend not to shell out twenty dollars for a book that will make them feel worse about themselves. At a deep level, they feel pretty lousy already. It is to the "high-functioning" parent that the idea of parenting styles appeals. Like those fashion mirrors with flattering lights, these books make us look good to ourselves.

The Five Most Powerful Influences on Our Parenting

1. Subconscious memories of our own childhood
2. Conscious memories, examples set by our parents, whispers and overheard conversations when we were growing up
3. Images of what parenting should be—from television, movies, books
4. Standards, expectations of friends and community
5. Advice from various sources

Nonetheless, "parenting style" is probably a misnomer. The suggestion is that we *have* a style, as we might have curly hair, or that we *choose* a style, as we might tell a hairdresser how to cut our bangs. In parenting, this is not entirely true. A fair amount of research in the 1980s showed that most parents used many different parenting styles—at least for discipline—depending on the nature of their kids and exactly what the children had done. Many parents used physical punishment when their kids broke something, "power assertion" for offenses such as lying and stealing, and reasoning for complex social issues such as cooperation in the playground. Real parents, it seems, are far more varied than the slots that writers create for us. And the most powerful influence on real parents is not any style or theory; it is our own past.

Ghosts in the nursery, ghosts in our heads

In 1974, three staff members at the Child Development Project at the University of Michigan—Selma Fraiberg, Edna Adelson and Vivian Shapiro—wrote an article called "Ghosts in the Nursery" that has since become famous in psychological literature. The three authors write with a power and poetry unusual in their profession. They begin:

In every nursery there are ghosts. They are the visitors
from the unremembered past of the parents, the uninvited
guests at the christening.

Indeed, there are always such metaphorical ghosts. As parents,
we carry them with us. When we are weak, or unthinking or lost in
our parenting, the ghosts can take over.

First, whatever "style" of parenting we think we've embraced,
chances are that most of what we actually do is determined by what
our parents did. We carry the ghosts of our parents' child rearing in
our heads. These specters haunt us unconsciously, in how we feel,
and consciously, in many of the small, day-to-day dealings we have
with our kids.

Fraiberg and her colleagues, who worked with severely
dysfunctional families, dealt primarily with the most tenacious of
ghosts: those in the unconscious. One of their most powerful stories
is that of Mary, a baby who was with their program for almost two
years. Mary's depressed mother, Mrs. March, gave her baby only
cursory child care. Her neglect was so apparent that the diagnostic
team had a hard time controlling their urge to intervene. In one
excruciating videotape, Mary screams for five minutes while mom
looks off into the distance, unconcerned. This led the therapists to
ask each other the central question: "Why doesn't this mother hear
her baby's cries?"

The answer had nothing to do with parenting style; it lay in
Mrs. March's unconscious. Her own mother had attempted suicide,
so Mrs. March was reared by an aunt and then a grandmother, with
occasional visits from a mostly absent father. Connected to this was
the mother's depression—an anger and grief she had turned against
herself. After a few weeks, the therapeutic team came up with a
treatment hypothesis: "When this mother's own cries are heard, she
will hear her child's cries." To do that, they needed to form a bond
between the principal therapist and Mrs. March, a bond of trust that
the mother had never known before.

The hypothesis turned out to be better than that—it was a real
treatment plan. As Mrs. March was able to open up with the
therapists and "feel" her own past neglect, she was also able to
become a better mother.

And then, one day, still within the first month of treatment, Mrs. March, in the midst of an outpouring of grief, picked up Mary, held her very close, and crooned to her in a heartbroken voice. And then it happened again, and several times in the next sessions. An outpouring of old griefs and a gathering of the baby into her arms. The ghosts in the baby's nursery were beginning to leave.

For parents who are haunted by such terrible ghosts, specters whose names cannot even be spoken and memories too awful to be felt, there is little choice but psychotherapy. Only by opening up and working with the memories can unconscious repetition be avoided.

However, not every child who was abused or neglected in growing up will become abusive or neglectful as a parent. The resilience of the human spirit is such that many such people will, most of the time, keep the ghosts at bay and become reasonably competent parents themselves. Psychology presents us only with tendencies, not necessities. Thank goodness for that.

Experience, on the other hand, suggests that our parents' parenting has enormous influence even on our conscious choices. As Elizabeth Fishel rightly points out, many of us actively model our parenting on how we were brought up. Many others vigorously attempt to reject those memories, thereby making our child rearing into funhouse mirror reflections of our own past.

This became obvious to me while listening to a group of moms and dads at a parenting class. These are mostly competent parents, looking for ways to be better yet. So they sit in the school library, drinking coffee from Styrofoam cups and turn to the topic of discipline.

"She kept crying," begins one mother, "so I said, if you keep making that noise, I'll have to put you outside."

"What happened?" asks the instructor.

"She kept it up, so I put her outside." The mom looks at her hands and hesitates a little before going ahead. "I put her outside in the backyard. Then I locked the door."

"What happened then?"

"She started banging on the door." The mom looks up, feeling guilty. "Maybe I should have tried something else."

The instructor nods. "Why did you lock her out?"

"Well, it's what my mom used to do when I bugged her."

"Did your mom's technique work for you?" the instructor asks.

"Well, it was plenty good enough for *my* parents," a dad chimes in.

"But did it work for you?" the instructor repeats.

"Well, no."

"So why did you do the same thing to your own child?" asks the instructor.

"It's all I could think of," says the first mom emphatically. "That's why I'm here, so I can think of something else."

That mom is exactly right. So much of what happens in parenting happens immediately, without thought or planning. As parents, we feel like we are making up the script to this real-life drama as we go along. The only cue cards we have seem to pop up from our own past history. We may not know what an ideal parent does, or what a good parent would do, or even how our neighbors might handle a given situation. But we can remember what our mom and dad did.

Parenting classes at least provide a chance to think about what we're doing and suggest a different set of impromptu responses than the ones we remember from our own childhood. Thought and inventiveness don't solve all the problems of being a parent, but they do help.

Ridding ourselves of the ghosts

Psychology tells us that the most powerful influence our parents had on us goes back to memories we don't even remember. This irony is the basis of psychoanalysis. By working through the unremembered memories, a person brings the unconscious into the conscious mind where the ghosts are less powerful and certainly less scary. When memories stay unremembered, a person simply repeats them in unconscious ways.

The problem in being a parent with invisible ghosts whispering advice all the time is that our supposedly rational choices aren't really rational. Instead, we repeat some actions of our parents, which may well go back to actions of their parents, and on and on. Our kids end up on the receiving end of this psychological sludge-pile and then, if they're lucky, realize it and change their behavioral patterns. If they're not lucky, they carry the sludge forward another generation.

I remember a dinner party at our house that we gave for a few people visiting from a distant university. I was anxious to impress the visitors, for reasons I can't recall any more, and a sit-down dinner for ten is always a pretty harried event even among the best of friends. The food for the dinner went okay, conversation was reasonably pleasant and everyone seemed to have a good time except for one of my sons, who had settled into a blue funk. Such a large teenager sitting at the table, morose and silent, was hard to ignore. All right, maybe it was just hard for *me* to ignore. Here I was, trying to impress these people and be a gracious host and listen attentively and not drink too much—and my kid was sitting at the table like a surly adolescent.

I fumed, dinner went on, the guests left and I ended up driving the son in question to the subway fairly late that night. I lit into him, using words and expressions that embarrass me to this day. He responded, as that particular son tends to, by falling into a sullen, pouty silence that made me even more irate. Fortunately, the subway isn't far from the house so my tirade probably didn't go on for more than five minutes before he slammed the door and went off to see the girlfriend who had brought on the blue funk in the first place.

The next morning, I felt lousy and confessed to my wife.

"He wasn't that bad," she said. "I don't think anybody really noticed."

"He *was* that bad," I maintained. "He didn't say a word all evening. He kept rolling his eyes when Dr. Jones talked about statistical analysis. He brooded."

"Paul, everybody rolls their eyes when Dr. Jones talks about statistics. And teenagers *do* brood. He got dumped by that girl what's-her-name, you know?"

"Really?"

"It was brief," she explained. "They made up."

"Well, I'm still not going to have a kid of mine sitting like that at a table when there's company in the house. He can at least be civil."

She looked at me. "Paul, what's the problem? The *real* problem?"

"It's the kid."

"No, it's not," she said. "The *you* who lit into him in the car isn't the *you* we usually see. Who is it?"

At that moment, I had a quick image of my father, back when I was 13. He was red in the face with anger. My dad almost never got angry, not in my memory, but there was this one time. It was a company party. The crew from work had shown up at the house. My mother was desperately trying to be charming and witty and keep the snack trays full. My father was busy pouring drinks. My brother was being his delightful 11-year-old self. And I was a hunk of 13-year-old, obnoxious adolescence, somehow stuck in a blue funk.

Midway through the party, my dad came back to the bedroom where I had gone to mope and lit into me. Because I deserved it, I was especially shocked and embarrassed. So much so that I buried that moment for more than thirty years . . . until I acted out the scene with my own child. It was my child who paid the price for my embarrassment way back then.

To conclude the story, let me say that I did not immediately undertake a personal analysis; instead, I apologized to my son. He responded graciously, "It's okay, dad. I knew you were nuts."

As parents, we're all nuts upon occasion. One of the many advantages of having two parents is that they are rarely nuts in exactly the same way. My wife may be irrationally fixated on seat belts, use of dental floss and unchipped glassware; I may have irrational problems with messy rooms, fingerprints on windows and collections of spiders kept in alcohol. But our nutty areas only rarely overlap. When they do, the kids had better watch out, because such overlaps can really distort the definition of reality in the household.

> For most of us, a little conscious reflection on our goals as parents will do wonders to improve our handling of day-to-day crises.

For parents who carry real emotional scars from childhood—people who were beaten or abused or shunned as kids—the initial response to anyone who comes close to the memories is aggressive defense. Freud called this *resistance*. Resistance is why you can't fix deep psychological problems by

Five Ways to Beat the Ghosts

1. Thought and discussion in sane moments, before the next crisis, work wonders.
2. Pray that your partner balances out your personal foibles rather than mirrors them.
3. Create alternatives: Invent new family traditions to crowd out the old ones.
4. Choose your clichés: Instead of repeating your parents' old clichés, invent your own. They might be an improvement.
5. Psychoanalysis: You don't beat terrible ghosts by naming them, you've got to work your way past them.

chatting with your golf buddies or having a discussion with your wife. A dad who was regularly taken to the woodshed by his father and now occasionally wallops his own kids is not going to get over his tendency for child abuse because he reads an article on "timeout" or remembers cowering in the woodshed thirty years ago. A real fix takes time and often some professional help.

But most of us don't carry such baggage. For most of us, a little conscious reflection on our goals as parents will do wonders to improve our handling of day-to-day crises and may even help us when major stress-filled disaster comes along. Elizabeth Fishel suggests we write up a list of parenting techniques our parents used, then break down the list into techniques we want to keep and things we want to do differently. For people who actually keep to their New Year's resolutions, such a list might just do the trick. For the rest of us, it's at least a start.

The other big influence on our parenting: TV

While we all mimic our own parents in dealing with our kids, each generation does bring some new ideas to the task of bringing up children. We read, we think, we observe trends, we find out what works for friends—but above all, we *see*. And the place where we see the greatest number of families dealing with kids isn't at school, or in the playground, or on the street—it's on television.

For the generations before us, images of ideal family life were drawn from earlier forms of media: books, plays and movies. Clarence Day's *Life with Father*, for instance, gave a good image of upper-middle-class family life just after the turn of the century. This extended family revolved around Father, who was depicted as a bumbling but kindly man, successful in business but awkward with both his wife and his children. Mother was far brighter than Father, but in a seemingly subservient position in terms of family and social power. That she invariably got her way by using her superior intelligence and social skills is sometimes forgotten by critics, but it may well be indicative of how families actually operated at the time. Men were nominally in charge; women mostly ran the operation.

In a story entitled "A Holiday with Father," son Clarence tells Father that he wants to grow up to be a cowboy. The older Mr. Day pooh-poohs the idea. Clarence recalls, "Father briefly explained that their lives, their food and their sleeping accommodations were outlandish and 'slummy.' 'Put your cap on straight,' he added. 'I am trying to bring you up to be a civilized man.'"

Young Clarence immediately adjusts his cap and continues walking with his father, not daring to whine or complain. But his thoughts are his own. "The more I thought about it, the less I wanted to be a civilized man. . . . What with fingernails and improving books and dancing school, the few chocolate eclairs that a civilized man got to eat were not worth it."

Obviously, Father is no modern parent. He is unconcerned about his son's self-esteem; has no intention of being his son's buddy; and actually thinks he has some idea what it means to be a civilized man. There are some disadvantages to such arbitrary parenting, but the advantage for young Clarence is that there's plenty of room in the father-son relationship for a kid to be a kid. That's why Clarence can so easily hold on to his cowboy dream.

Of course, many real parents and children did not quite measure up to such charming depictions, or else we would never have had the plays of Ibsen, Eugene O'Neill or Tennessee Williams. But popular entertainments did not ordinarily represent the seamier sides of family life. The major problem for Dorothy in *The Wizard of Oz* was not her absent parents, the perhaps iffy relationship of Auntie Em and Uncle Henry, or the covertly sexual looks of the three hired men. No, Dorothy's problem was a tornado and the difficulty of getting back to Kansas. At the end of the film, when the Good Fairy of the North asks her what she's learned, Dorothy replies brightly, "If I ever go looking for my heart's desire, I won't be looking further than my own backyard." The media ideal used to be as simple as that.

Early television reflected some of the worldview of the films and plays that preceded it: the family as a solid, safe, reassuring spot in a somewhat mad world. The major change in the 1950s was the elimination of the traditional extended family that had included grandparents, uncles, aunts and servants. These were replaced with a new extended family of neighbors, a change that reflected the rise of the suburban single-family home after the end of World War II. The roles of uncle and aunt in *I Love Lucy* are not taken by relatives but by Fred and Ethel Mertz, who live down the hall. Lucy and Desi themselves live in an apartment so small that neither grandparents nor indigent uncles could be accommodated.

This smaller, mostly nuclear family could be found in many of the TV shows of the late 1950s: *Ozzie and Harriet, Burns and Allen, Leave It to Beaver, Father Knows Best.* None of these households had financial problems of any kind, nor did they reflect any of North America's growing racial and ethnic diversity (*Amos 'n' Andy* and *The Goldbergs* were dropped by American networks early in the 1950s). Like the families in earlier forms of media, these TV families were stable: Nothing really changed week to week or season to season. Little Ricky wanted to grow up, go to college and become . . . just like Big Ricky.

Until 1960. That was the year Lucy filed for divorce from Desi in real life, just like millions of other North Americans in what was becoming a liberated age. Television—and perhaps the institution of the family—would never recover from the trauma. But it took another ten years for the image of the family on television to begin to reflect the changed life of most North American families. In 1971, *All in the Family* became a hit by featuring an out-of-tune, working-class, urban household, one that was dominated by real-life problems and generational conflict. Archie Bunker, the character America loved to hate or hated to love, had virtually nothing in common with Rob Petrie of *The Dick Van Dyke Show* or Ward Cleaver of *Leave It to Beaver*. But the program was a tremendous success because it reflected the new reality of an America divided along generational lines. It was no accident that when Mary Tyler Moore returned to television in the 1970s, she was no longer a New Rochelle housewife but a single woman working for a Minneapolis television station.

Was television reflecting change or creating change? When African Americans began rioting in 1967, commentators said that their frustration stemmed from the difficulty of achieving the economic quality of life they saw on TV. If so, television had begun to define a normality as much as to reflect what was really there. Sometimes, television and real life began to interconnect with each other in surreal ways, as in Archie Bunker's line: "Y'know, there are three great moments in a man's life. He buys a house, a car . . . and a new color TV. (audience laughter) That's what America's all about."

> Was television reflecting change or creating change?

To some extent, the image of "father" in *All in the Family* was simply an enlargement of the image of Father in *Life with Father*. Bumbling had turned to stupidity. Social awkwardness had turned to boorishness. Conservative opinion had turned to bigotry. In both cases, mom ruled the house—although Edith Bunker was considerably less adept than Vinnie Day. Parents in the popular media, who had always been verging on the foolish, were now verging on idiocy. Children in the media, who had previously accepted the value systems of their elders, now challenged them.

So we got . . . lip.

In the 1980s, adult parents were still reasonable enough to be able to turn around childish "lip" and maintain some semblance of control. The amazing Huxtables of *The Cosby Show* were remarkably adept at this, more than Kate or Allie or the ex-hippie parents of *Family Ties*. But by the 1990s, the image of adult parents on television was reduced to its lowest common denominators: Homer

Simpson and Al Bundy. The children on *The Simpsons* and *Married
. . . with Children* are not only intellectually superior to their parents,
but use their quick wit to demonstrate their parents' stupidity and
ineffectiveness. In *Life with Father*, Clarence Day Sr. is in a position
to tell Clarence Day Jr. that "I am trying to bring you up to be a
civilized man," presumably because the father has some idea of how
to raise children and what civilization means. It's hard to imagine
this from current TV parents. Homer Simpson would never tell
Bart to put his cap on straight, or if he did, Bart's one-liner response
would reduce Homer to his characteristic line: "D'Oh!"

What's wrong with TV images of parenting

As a dad, I confess I dislike seeing fathers on television portrayed as
bumbling idiots. But the effect of television on parenting is really
much more pervasive than the way it depicts any single player in the
family. What's scary is the kind of normality television defines—a
normality that is frequently accepted by kids and sometimes even by
their parents:

- Fathers are stupid or menacing, or both.
- Mothers are sweet and comforting, unless troubled by
  a stupid, menacing father.
- Children are inordinately wise, clever and capable of
  looking after themselves.
- Discipline of children can be handled with a cheery
  "Hey-hey-hey!" or occasionally by a stern, "Now, son."
- Almost all family problems are neatly resolvable within
  22 minutes.
- Individual and family situations have no relationship
  to social policy or political issues.
- The ultimate goals of life are not spiritual, emotional
  or philosophical, but revolve around the acquisition of
  consumer goods.

Intelligent adults all know that television is guilty of these
distortions. For children, our schools are now offering media
literacy courses to teach them why the world they see on the tube

doesn't resemble the household where they wake up in the morning and munch their bowl of breakfast cereal. But our collective immersion in these images has had an effect, chronicled by Douglas Coupland in his novels and any number of social scientists in their academic works. We parent differently now because our ideas of normality are drawn less from real life, less from church and community ideals, and more from a medium that primarily exists to sell us consumer goods.

> Our families have to deal with some big issues . . . that are not reflected on the television screen.

In one notable television commercial, Bill Clinton declared that being a parent is a tougher job than being President of the United States. Such hyperbole echoes the feelings of many parents, 80 percent of whom tell pollsters that parenting is the hardest job they know. Actually, parenting isn't that tough—but television makes it seem that way. While most parents I know do quite a reasonable job, and frequently make many sacrifices for their children's benefit, no one manages to parent with the continuing ease and good humor of the Huxtables or the parents on *The Brady Bunch*. It's not that most of us are bad parents, just that we can't measure up to the impossible ideals of televised family life.

This is not to suggest that our real-life parenting is always wonderful as is, but that we'd better stop looking at TV for models if we want to improve it. Our families have to deal with some big issues, right now, that are not reflected on the television screen. As parents, we have to find a balance between praising our children and engaging in verbal fraud, between occasional distraction and much-needed discipline, between listening to children and idealizing them, between looking after the kids at home and somehow meeting the mortgage payment. In the larger world that affects our families, social inequalities are growing, young families are more transient and less connected to their own parents, and there is less time available to be a parent than ever before. None of these situations can be resolved by a 22-minute television show or will be discussed on *Oprah* or *Jenny Jones*, but they deserve attention from parents and the general public.

Chapter 2

Kids can be born rotten . . .

and grow up even worse if we help them

In the school playground, I watch the children at recess. There are supposed to be two teachers, a principal and perhaps a parent volunteer keeping an eye on things, but the supervision roster has come up short today. Only one teacher is actually on duty, off in one corner, and she seems busy with a first-grader who is crying.

The other children are scattered about the playground:

- three groups of girls are busy playing a game, fairly cooperatively;
- two groups of boys are playing ball, noisily at times, but they're peaceful enough until one boy fouls another on a lay-up;
- three boys are watching the ballplayers, perhaps waiting to be asked to play—and they will wait a very long time;
- a dozen children are playing on the monkey bars, near the distracted teacher, perhaps because they feel safer with an adult close by;

- one upper-grade boy has taken another boy's ball; the "owner" is complaining and then threatening; the "borrower" is laughing derisively;
- one fifth- or sixth-grade girl has jabbed another girl in the back with her pen, but pretends she's done nothing;
- one boy, hidden from the teacher's view, is kicking a smaller boy who was sitting on the ground reading a book; I cannot determine the cause for this.

This is an ordinary suburban playground, a playground anyone might observe who stopped to take the time. Mostly we don't stop to take the time—the world of childhood, especially while the kids are at school, gets little attention from adults. But the variety of behaviors we see in a playground have much to say about the various personalities of children.

Why is the one boy kicking the other? Why is the "kickee" accepting the punishment rather than running for help? What is it that makes one child so aggressive and another so masochistic?

Is it nature or nurture?

This is a basic philosophical question, lately much explored by psychologists, geneticists and medical researchers as well. The answers to it are of real importance to parents in determining how we deal with our children. Liberal parents, for instance, must assume that children are innately good, basically compliant and easily moved by reasonable argument. Authoritarian parents may feel that children are innately evil, born into their vile personalities and fit to live in the world only after considerable and frequent punishment. Neither view is entirely correct, but sorting out what's true and not true is important if we're going to make intelligent choices in raising our kids.

Hobbes, Rousseau, Freud and today's monster children

The glorified image we have of children today is a relatively new development, dating roughly from the days of Shirley Temple in her 1930s movies. For most of human history, children have either been ignored or seen as creatures who are as nasty as any adult. The Catholic concept of original sin, in which children are born guilty of the transgression of Adam and Eve and purified only through baptism and other rites, certainly does not suggest that children are innately sweet and innocent. The British philosopher Thomas Hobbes used the phrase "nasty, brutish and short" not to describe children specifically but to define the essential nature of human life. For Hobbes and his Puritan colleagues, children were in need of strong punishment to overcome their basic willfulness. Regular abuse of children with rods, belts and other brutal instruments has been part and parcel of child rearing for more than two millennia, always justified because "it's for their own good."

It was the eighteenth-century French philosopher Jean-Jacques Rousseau who first maintained the opposite, that children are innately good. Rousseau wrote that "everything is well when it leaves the Creator's hands, everything degenerates in the hands of man." Rousseau's concept, largely developed in opposition to the church of his day, led him to write the remarkable novel *Emile*. In that book, Rousseau describes the ideal education of a young child in order to show the wondrous results that a wise, kind and thoughtful parent can achieve with a coherent philosophy of education and child rearing. That Rousseau never actually undertook such a project with a real child is a mild technical flaw—in the eighteenth century, neither novelists nor philosophers were expected to engage in anything as mundane as research—but his ideas had tremendous impact nonetheless.

By the nineteenth century, children were seen as either corrupt or angelic, and sometimes both at once. One British minister preached to his parishioners "as innocent as children seem to be, they are young vipers!" This was a popular view. Of course, this was also an age when Queen Victoria's personal physician could declare that rocking babies and singing them lullabies was a "miserable and depressing performance" for parents. Actually kissing babies, according to childcare authority Dr. Emmett Holt in his 1895 *Care and Feeding of Children*, was a sign of parental weakness. Far better that the children be purified with an hour-long cold bath or with healthy doses of cod-liver oil. Regardless, parents were urged to understand the "extreme necessity of a daily action from the bowels" as recommended by the Society of Orificial Surgeons. Impurity was everywhere and it began at birth.

This is the image we sometimes get in the media of our century. Those dastardly children in Lillian Hellman's *The Children's Hour* were obviously evil from birth. The kids in Arthur Miller's *The Crucible* were shaped by their times, but still quite evil and vindictive at heart. And then there was Linda Blair in *The Exorcist*, who, born innocent, was obviously overwhelmed when possessed by an evil spirit. In real life, of course, we do not believe in evil spirits, and we have increasing difficulty acknowledging that there may be evil people. Instead, we tend to blame upbringing. We look to the parents of serial murderers, for example, point the finger and say that *they* produced the human monster. Increasingly, research shows that this isn't fair.

Kids are born different

We all know the hospital-visit routine with the new baby . . .

"His eyes are just like grandpa's."

"His mouth is just like yours."

"He sleeps just like you did when you were a baby."

Some of these observations are undoubtedly true (especially the one that goes, "He's so cute"), but many are merely projections from a hopeful set of relatives. Thanks to genetics, some physical characteristics of some babies do resemble their parents'. For other babies, your husband's parents may walk away, whispering about your marital fidelity.

The random nature of genetics—just which information is carried by whose DNA—leads to a pretty random assortment of kids at birth. But our children do carry a genetic destiny. The destiny is what we see later on, when we look at photos of grandad and dad and junior, all at age ten, thirty or fifty. That's when the real physical similarities show up: the big ears you didn't want, the tuft of hair that always sticks up, the left bicuspid that's been crooked for at least three generations. From this, it's possible to conclude that genetics plays an important part in who we become . . . but wait a minute.

Genetics is obviously a considerable factor in determining what we look like, but mostly because there is very little intervention in our society to shape or alter our physical appearance. Where families and societies do intervene, genetics loses importance. In pre-twentieth-century Japan, for instance, a genetic predisposition toward large feet would not, for an upper-class woman, make any difference. Women's feet were bound through childhood. Similarly, African tribes can induce lengthened necks or extended lips by physical means throughout the growing years. In our society, orthodontists make their living by altering genetic destiny and have given us an adult generation with the most evenly spaced teeth in human history. Whether this is worth the money or the discomfort involved is beside the point: Humans can frustrate the physical aspects of our genetic heritage when they want to.

If we look at slightly more complex physical phenomena, such as speech, we find that virtually every child is born with the genetic capacity to learn every language on the planet, from romantic French to guttural German to the amazing !Kung tongue of central Africa. But each individual child grows up in a family and culture that supports one set of language sounds, and our kids gradually lose the capacity to produce the others. The fact that a child speaks English reasonably well, struggles with French despite persistent efforts in French class and will likely never master either !Kung or Japanese isn't the fault of his genes; it's because we raise him that way.

So how important, then, is genetics in determining personality? Since we have yet to clone human beings, most of what science tells us on the matter comes from "separated twin" studies. These compare personality aspects of identical and fraternal twins raised by different families. Scientists use statistical tools to calculate how much of a twin's personality is genetic and how much has been determined by the way the twin was raised. In the academic papers, this is referred to as the impact of "temperament" (nature) versus "development" (nurture).

Depending on just who crunches the numbers and which aspects of personality are being considered, it's fair to say that between one third and one half of human personality comes to us from temperament. It's a given—from birth. The remaining portion of our child's personality is developed and shaped by the environment in which he grows up. That's where parenting and family life make a difference.

What does this mean in real life? Plenty. When our kid goes off to summer camp and has to decide whether to risk her neck by doing a swan dive off the cliff into the lake, her decision is based on temperament, upbringing and environment. Some kids are simply more fearless than others, even within the same family, so they will see the dive as a challenge. Kids who are fearless by temperament will seek out situations to display the quality. Kids who are more fearful will try harder at boondoggling. These general traits are present right from birth.

But whether a child dives off the cliff depends not just on her temperament. Complicating the decision is what she's learned from us ("A gutsy kid tries anything once, even if it seems stupid—that's what dad always says"), the environment she's in (whether the camp counselors are asleep or have actively encouraged the traditional Camp Koochewachee thrill dive) and the social situation ("If you don't do it, Joanie, you're a wuss!"). Regardless of the genetic predisposition we pass on to our children—about which we can do nothing—what our kids do in a given situation has a great deal to do with our parenting and the environments we create for them.

Parenting is important, especially in the first two or three years

Parenting counts. If your baby is strong, cheerful and resilient, it probably doesn't count as much as if your baby is weak, colicky and prone to distress, but parenting still counts. As Burton White observed, "It is truly remarkable how some babies from loving homes, having shown typical euphoric and endearing behavior when they were four months old, become chronic malcontents by two years of age, while others become incredibly happy about their lot in life." Actually, it's not that remarkable—it's mostly in how we treat the kids.

Lately, even experimental science has tended to emphasize the importance of early upbringing. Researcher Stephen Suomi of the National Institute for Child Health and Human Development works with monkeys who have been bred to be either "inhibited" or "uninhibited" in terms of their behavior. Suomi found that when an "inhibited" baby monkey is raised by a bold foster mother, the young monkey not only develops her lifestyle but also changes his body chemistry (noreprinephrine shows up in saliva) to match his new uninhibited behavior. Experiments on rats by Philip Gold and other neuroscientists show that seven or eight days of

> What happens to kids in early childhood reverberates throughout their lives.

consecutive stress early in life (they used small electric shocks) were sufficient to permanently change both a rat's adult behavior and the way the genes in its brain functioned.

Alice Miller, a German psychologist, has written a number of books tracing the effects of early childhood experience on famous adults. She makes a persuasive case, for instance, that a large influence on Picasso's adult art stems from early artistic encouragement by his parents and the emotional trauma of an earthquake when he was three years old. She's tried a similar analysis of many other historic figures—Adolf Hitler, Kathë Kollwitz, Friedrich Nietzsche—and may well be right about her basic premise. What happens to kids in early childhood reverberates throughout their lives.

In Canada, Fraser Mustard of the Canadian Institute for Advanced Research will sometimes load up his color slides and present his talk about the importance of the early parenting of children. His case is persuasive: Any intervention by society to help families in the first three years of their children's lives pays big dividends in the long term. Among the studies Mustard cites is the famous Perry Preschool program, one of the precursors of the nationwide Head Start program. Perry Preschool served mostly low-income African-American families in Ypsilanti, Michigan. Half the families were led by single mothers and only one parent in five had finished high school. In the experiment, the disadvantaged 3- and 4-year-olds from these families were sent, at random, either to a control group or to an enriched daycare program. The kids did not seem terribly bright to start with (IQs ranged from 60 to 90) and initially the program was seen as a failure because the children's tested intelligence did not significantly improve. But fifteen years later, the *real* results came in. At age nineteen, the kids who had come out of the enriched program were twice as likely to have jobs, 30 percent *more* likely to have graduated from high school and 40 percent *less* likely to have been arrested. If good daycare can have this much effect, imagine how important good parenting can be.

Even a good kid can get screwed up by lousy parents

Thirty years of experiments with monkeys have shown that negligent parenting can produce an adult monkey who functions in a bizarre fashion. In human history, we've been doing similar experiments on children for thousands of years through war, famine, plague and family dysfunction. But in our human experiments, we've found that stress and negligence only sometimes produce adults who function in a bizarre or antisocial fashion. The good news, then, is that human babies have personalities that are harder to damage than monkey babies. The bad news is that, if we work at it hard enough, we can damage the kids anyhow.

Let's look at the good side first. Almost everyone would agree that among the worst things adults can do to young children is to physically or sexually abuse them. A 1995 study of maltreated adolescents, for instance, finds that physically abusive parenting leads to adolescents who are six times more likely to run away from home than kids from nonabusive households. Kids who suffer sexual abuse are six times more likely to think about committing suicide. Those who witness spousal violence are eleven times more likely to abuse drugs. Two solid studies say that physical abuse while growing up also leads to long-term repetition of the abuse. As the generalization goes, children of parents who were abused are most at risk of being abused themselves.

But how much risk? Cathy Spatz Widom, a professor of criminal justice and psychology at the State University of New York at Albany, looked at the criminal records of 1,575 people, two-thirds of whom had suffered physical or sexual abuse as children. She found that 27 percent of the abused children were later arrested as juveniles, versus 17 percent of the general population. The newspaper headlines could rightly say, then, that childhood sexual abuse increases the likelihood of becoming a young offender by

60 percent—and that's a terrible truth. What the headline doesn't give us is the good news: that almost three-quarters of abused children do *not* become teenage offenders. Similarly, the portion of Widom's study group who suffered sexual abuse as children were no more likely to be arrested for sex crimes as adults than the population at large. Undoubtedly, childhood sexual abuse had an impact on this group—but how that impact gets expressed in later life is not entirely clear.

Thankfully, the human personality is remarkably resilient. Our children are shaped by their genetics, their upbringing and the millions of other factors that affect their lives. But the first and most important influence on their lives is us—their parents.

This becomes clear not so much in looking at the biographies of successful adults—because these vary greatly—but in looking at the converse, at the upbringing of sociopaths. Society has always been somewhat confused about what qualities it values in a successful adult, whether we want warriors (as the Spartans did) or shrewd merchants (as the Hanseatic League did) or philosophers (as Plato suggested) or happy, well-adjusted proletarians (valued by both Mao Zedong in his *Little Red Book* and Bobby McFerrin in "Don't Worry, Be Happy"). As a result, we are equally confused about how a successful adult should be raised and whether education should involve training with a broadsword or courses in conflict mediation. Generalizing becomes difficult in the midst of such confusion.

On the other hand, our society has reached a consensus on what we *don't* want. We call these people criminals and define the worst of their number as sociopaths, criminals without even a conscience. Looking at the upbringing of sociopaths—the Paul Bernardos and Jeffrey Dahmers—may not tell us how to be good parents, but it will give some indication on how not to be a bad parent.

On the basis of the best research we have, it seems that sociopaths are produced by four factors: physical abuse, childhood neglect, sexual molestation and parental inconsistency. In the case of sociopath Paul Bernardo, for instance, we have a young man who was beaten as a child, perhaps sexually molested by his own father and forced to grow up in a self-righteous middle-class family that masked in-house horrors with the outward appearance of propriety.

Years later Bernardo became the Scarborough rapist and the murderer of at least two teenage girls, but he steadfastly maintained his innocence right through the trial, causing still further grief to the families of his victims. A sociopath, by definition, feels no guilt.

There are, of course, other adults who suffered similar kinds of abuse and turned out to be a credit to their society. Individuals such as T. E. Lawrence, Jerzy Kosinski and Marilyn Monroe all had childhood horror stories but still managed to become successful adults—admittedly with some substantial psychological scars. And we have accounts from individuals such as Lionel Dahmer, the father of cannibal-murderer Jeffrey Dahmer, who maintains adamantly that it wasn't his fault; that he really doesn't know why Jeffrey turned out the way he did.

Nonetheless, it seems clear that certain parenting practices are wrong because they are very likely to damage a child's development. It's possible, from these, to develop some simple advice: Don't beat up your kid. Don't molest your child. Make sure there's something for the child to eat. Try not to say one thing and do another.

Every parent would agree that we should try to avoid these mistakes. As in medicine, the first rule must always be "do no harm."

The important question, however, is "How do we help?" Here the answers are not nearly as clear—and the closer we get on specific points, the fuzzier the research becomes.

Raising a great kid

There are no perfect parents; nor does striving for perfection tend to lead to excellent parenting as much as it does to parental anxiety. The famous British psychologist D. W. Winnicott suggests that our goal should not be perfection but to become a "good-enough" mother or father. We must be good enough to do what is needed, not so wonderful that we take over the space where our children must grow. The half-dozen rules that follow from this are fairly straightforward:

Love our kids. It's difficult, for people who don't much love their kids, to begin loving them simply because somebody says it's a good idea. In fact, it's virtually impossible in today's society for any parent to admit, even to themselves, that they can't love their kids all of the time. "Whaddya mean, of course I love my kid!" is what comes back with an angry glare. The trouble, of course, is that kids are sometimes quite unlovable and that some of us, for whatever reason, have real problems extending love to them or to other people. Such relationship difficulties don't stop people from *having* kids, so perhaps it would be better to suggest that we love our kids as much as we can. Then when we make mistakes in our parenting—and we all do—at least they will have been done with affection.

Know who we are. As the title of this book indicates, you're the parent, the child is the child. Our children do not want us to be children (except sometimes, like when we're wrestling on the floor or playing Scrabble and not trying too hard to win). Kids need a real parent, not a childish one. They especially need some very adult qualities in us: consistency, support, authority, a good role model. All of us, at times, are somewhat deficient in these qualities, and it does no good to blame our inner child or our own parents for these failings. We should try to do the best we can for our children regardless.

Have some goals for your child. This does not mean determining, at birth, that young Sally will become a brain surgeon. It does mean having a goal that Sally will become an honest, confident, competent and caring adult. It also means, ironically, having some respect for whatever kind of person Sally starts to become. Goals that are reasonable have to be connected to the real child, not to some failed goal of our own. Some parents, unfortunately, push goals on their kids far too aggressively and the results backfire. For every Earl Woods—who gave baby Tiger a golf club to hold in his crib and spent twenty more years nurturing his son to golfing stardom—there are too many other parents who have simply pushed their kids into drugs, depression or personal destruction.

Yet goals are essential. As parents, we should never forget that ultimately our kids are going to become grown-ups; in fact, it's their job to become grown-ups. It's *our* job to help them along with at least one eye on the adult who is in process. One problem with being a parent is that too much of what takes place with our kids happens right now, on-the-spot, immediate decision required. Unless we have some goals for our children as they move toward being grown-ups, our reactions will all be impromptu—we'll make up the lines as we go along. This is lousy. For most of us, there is no rehearsal for parenting. There is no script we can buy to make it easy. But we should take the time to think through the outlines with our partner long before we're called upon to make key decisions for the kids.

Have a sense of humor. Our kids are pretty clear on this: Mom and dad should lighten up. Not everything a child says is dreadfully serious, nor does every family melodrama have to be played with Wagnerian music playing in the background. Kids are fun and funny; so is much of family life if we can just ease up and enjoy it.

Parents enjoy significant bonuses from smiling more and yelling less. Discipline tends to be much more effective. Sibling rivalry and attention-getting decreases. Levels of tension in the whole family decline. Besides, people who laugh a lot tend to live longer—we can make our kids wait for their inheritance.

Stay close and leave room. I realize these are contradictory statements, but so is much of good-enough parenting. A parent must be close to the child and pay careful attention to what the child really needs. Infants make sure this happens through a clever alternation of smiles and cries; older children may be less successful at getting the closeness they require. Then it's up to us. There is so much to be said for kissing, hugging and mussing hair that parents, despite increasingly vociferous objections from their children, should continue such behavior until their children have children of their own. At that point, we can transfer some of this attention to the grandchildren.

At the same time, there must be room for kids to be kids and for kids to grow up. Children do not need adult playmates, but they need adults nearby when the game gets too rough. Children do not particularly want to hear the adult "voice of experience," but they need us as role models and persons with experience in the real world. Older children, especially, do not want us to be cool, or interact too much with their friends, or do anything besides drive them where they need to go. That's as it should be. Hug them goodbye; wait up till they get home.

The distance a parent should keep is always changing as a child grows older. While there's probably every reason to pick up a crying

6-month-old, there are definitely times when a 3-year-old should be allowed to wail away. While we should help a 6-year-old assemble a model plane, we shouldn't help her tie her shoes. A great parent for a baby can be a so-so parent for a school child and a miserable parent to a teenager: The parent hasn't changed, but the child's needs certainly have. Our kids need flexibility *and* consistency; and that, of course, is another contradiction.

Give children our time, not our wallets. Children need time, lots of time, especially early on. As each year passes, they need less of our time but may start demanding more of society's substitute—cash. That's a poor trade-off. When our children are young, we should take off our watches and give them all the time in the world. When our children go to school, we can put our watches back on and give them a small allowance. Parents who try to replace themselves with their wallets or what the wallet contents can buy are deluding themselves; this isn't parenting and it's not what our kids need. They need *us*.

With a little attention to basic principles, parenting is neither so difficult nor so complex that most of us can't do a good-enough job. Dr. Spock's basic premise was that parents should trust themselves, and for fifty years he has been shown to be largely correct. Again and again in history, we find that parents' natural instincts are denied, only to be proven correct a generation later. This doesn't mean that we are all, automatically, good parents or that there is nothing for parents to learn. Humility remains a virtue in our goal of being good-enough parents as long as it doesn't make us doubt who we are and what our goals are. Just to be clear, we are the parents and our goal is to raise great children. These two items interconnect.

Chapter 3

The "family conference" and other cases of adults acting like children . . .

and children forced to act like adults

My colleague Joe is an excellent father who listens to his kids, finds as much time as he can for his family and usually understands pretty well his role in the family structure. He understands what it means to be firm, to set limits and how important it is to be a parent so that children can get on with their job of being kids. But even a solid parent like Joe can get caught up in trendy foolishness, as I discovered the other day.

"You and Jean decide on spring vacation yet?" I asked him.

He gave me a look of despair. "Orlando again."

"I thought you went last year," I said. "Do you really enjoy Disney World that much?"

"I hate the whole thing," he groaned. "Disney World, MGM, they're all so crowded over the break. Feels like you're paying $100 at the gate just to stand in lines all day. Jean thinks it's a kind of living hell for adults."

I asked the sensible question. "So why are you going again?"
Joe looked at me sheepishly. "We had a family conference."
"So?"
"Jean and I were out-voted."
I was probably caught with my mouth open, astonished.

My friend Joe, who very much enjoys the national park system, and his wife, Jean, who has a fondness for theater, both felt doomed to a vacation in Orlando. Again.

I am not about to protest the Disney World/MGM/Orlando "experience," which has become as ubiquitous as the Walkman for today's young people. I frankly like Disney World, kitsch and all, but I'd hate to be dragged there *every* year.

What bothers me is the way Joe and his family reached their decision. They obviously used a family conference, which combines the very good idea of listening to your kids with the very good idea of democracy. Logically, combining two good ideas should produce an even better one, but the resulting concept of family democracy might well be a contradiction in terms.

The family conference

The family conference is supposed to go like this: Mom, dad and the kids agree to have a meeting at a particular time, say right after dinner, to talk about a few items of concern. The meeting itself is usually run as a kind of democratic collective, which means there is no chairperson. Somebody who has an issue brings it up and makes a case for some action or change in family policy. Then everyone talks through the issue and a decision is reached through compromise and consensus.

At least, that's how it's *supposed* to work.

In my own experience, family conferences work best when the kids bring up an issue of concern where a decision can be reached by reasonable deliberation as opposed to emotional badgering. When my kids were growing up, for instance, they were allowed to ride their bikes and play relatively unsupervised within a "radius" of blocks around the house. Every year or two, the kids would want their radius expanded and we'd have a family conference, complete with street maps, to figure out what the new limits would be. It worked, at least until one son decided his radius included Switzerland, but that's another story.

The family conference really can be a wonderful forum for listening, discussing and exchanging of views. Even when it works imperfectly, a family conference is a much better means at arriving at decisions than arbitrary rulings by parents that involve neither listening nor talking. Kids, especially older kids, respond poorly to such dictatorial parenting.

But the family conference is an easy forum to subvert. I've been guilty of some of this myself, because parents frequently use family conferences as a means of manipulation. This isn't fair, but we do it.

"We're having a family conference after supper tonight," I recall telling my 10-year-old son.

"Why? What did I do?" he asked.

"Nothing. Well, not much."

"So I *did* do something."

"Okay, you did. We've got to talk about it."

"So why don't you just talk to me about what I did instead of calling a family conference? Give me a break!"

> Even when it works imperfectly, a family conference is a much better means at arriving at decisions than arbitrary rulings by parents that involve neither listening nor talking.

He was right. I wasn't really calling a family conference, I was intending on a public discipline session. I didn't really want to listen to what everybody else had to say on the issue, I wanted to mete out punishment. As my son suggested, if that's all I really had in mind, I should do it one-on-one rather than embarrass him in front of the rest of the family. Like many parents, I was guilty of hijacking the family conference to reach a predetermined destination. This happens far too often and it's certainly not fair.

But parental manipulation wasn't Joe's problem. He had gone in the other direction. Joe had let his family conference overpower the adults, and he had done so out of some misguided sense of the role of democracy in the household. To be clear, democracy is usually a good thing, but it requires a certain level of equality among the *polis*, as the ancient Greeks would say. In today's real-life families, however, mom and dad usually have all the money and most of the experience. The kids usually have no money and experience limited to their age group, which can be substantial in terms of computer games and nonexistent in terms of balancing the family checkbook.

Ordinarily, mom and dad should have some long-term goals for the family and for the children. The kids, especially younger ones, often have very few goals that extend much beyond next week. The consequences of a family decision can fall on either the parents or the children, though no one—thanks to the democratic process—bears responsibility for the decision that was reached. Unlike political democracies, nobody can vote mom or sister Samantha out of office because her voting record was dumb or self-serving or inconsistent.

Some families have tried to get around these problems of inequality through a system of weighted voting. This can be quite elaborate: Mom and dad get two votes each because they're old; brother John gets a half vote because he's little, sister Susie gets a three-quarters vote until she hits age 12 and one-and-a-half after. I suppose such a system would have helped Joe get a vacation at Yellowstone rather than Disney World, but vote allocation often becomes as loaded a topic as electoral vote counts.

> Your child cannot know the future benefits of piano lessons or a newspaper route or entering the science fair.

Nonetheless, family conferences work well on issues where the whole family really can discuss an issue as disinterested *people*. This involves stepping outside our parent and child roles and responsibilities and taking on the mantle of a democrat: wise, objective, interested in the good of everyone. In our house, I can recall such family meetings on issues related to birthday celebrations, computer software purchases and bicycle replacement. I cannot imagine such discussion on issues that are more contentious: piano lessons, whether Ellen and her boyfriend can make out on the front porch, cleaning the house and family vacations. In these latter cases, the parents are either manipulating the conference to avoid decision making or else they are

---

Five Handy Phrases for Parents

Worthy of practice until mastered . . .

1. "I need time to think about that."
2. "Have you run the idea by your mother/father?"
3. "Sorry, I've thought more about that and I have to change my mind."
4. "Exactly which part of 'no' don't you understand, the 'n' or the 'o'?"
5. "Of course I love you, but I don't like it very much when you do something like that."

---

abdicating their role as parents and handing decision making to the kids. Both are poor moves.

A parent is ordinarily twenty or thirty years older than the kid, has ten more years of education and a vastly wider experience in the world. Of the three places on earth your child knows, Disney World may rate very highly. But of the 200 places of which *you* know something, it could be you'd like to show your child Washington, D.C., Mexico City or the serpent mounds in Ohio instead. Experience and information really do count. Moreover, a parent ordinarily has some kind of vision of what family life should be like, how a kid should act and what the long-term goals are for both family and child. Your child cannot be expected to balance the virtues of a new car against paying down the mortgage. Your child cannot know the future benefits of piano lessons or a newspaper route or entering the science fair. An important part of being a parent is looking ahead for your children.

When the kids get older, their most hurtful condemnation of our parenting usually takes the form of, "When I was little, why didn't you make me . . ." and then they fill the blank with virtually anything—learn to swim, practice my trombone, and so on. A certain amount of decent decision making, early on, can save us guilt trips later.

Our inner child should stay inner

Parents sometimes have deep psychological reasons for abdicating their decision-making role in the family. Among fathers, for instance, there may be some difficulty in admitting that we're no longer the "wild and crazy guy" we once were. It really doesn't matter that most of us weren't wild and crazy guys to begin with. Once we take on the mantle of fatherhood—and the weight of mortgages, car payments and diaper changing—a certain resistance sets in. While we're prepared to accept our socially defined paternal roles 90 percent of the time, there's an urge to pretend that part of us hasn't changed, that inside our hearts is a James Dean or Sean Penn just waiting to burst free.

The question comes down to what to do with our inner child in the context of our families? The sensible answer is simple: Keep what's inner, inner.

I realize this is an uncool response, but I'm speaking here on behalf of the children. Children may enjoy parents who are fun— they may laugh like crazy at that "wild and crazy guy" when dad starts dancing around the kitchen—but most of the time they want us dull as dishwater. In fact, they *need* us to be dull as dishwater. They want us to drive them in the car, tell the appropriate corny jokes, nag them about eating vegetables and otherwise behave like Ward and June Cleaver. When parents become too interesting, we can overwhelm our kids and really interfere with their growing up.

Parents who are interesting all the time—Hollywood stars, borderline psychotics and intense artistic folks, for example—tend to produce unhappy, maladjusted children. One need only look at the biographies of Gloria Vanderbilt, Mackenzie Phillips and Carrie Fisher to see the fate of such kids. Fortunately, many people who are truly interesting often have the deep good sense to partner with someone who is emotionally rock solid, providing at least one parent on whom a child can depend throughout life. Picasso, for instance, was a pretty erratic father to his various kids and a mostly miserable partner despite seven tries at forming a stable relationship, but his fairly sensible wives and mistresses still managed to raise some fairly sensible children.

One of the most "interesting" times for parents, and most traumatic for kids, is the period surrounding separation, divorce and re-partnership. Because this seems to be an experience for more than half of today's families, it's worth noting. This period between marriages is probably the only period when dad's wild and crazy guy actually manages to come out more than once a week; it's also the only period when mom—ordinarily as sexual as the kitchen sink in the eyes of her kids—suddenly becomes a *femme fatale*. Children respond to this sudden surge of interesting parental personality by becoming anxious and depressed, suffering lower grades in school and sometimes requiring weekly psychological counseling sessions. If all the family upset associated with divorce weren't bad enough, these suddenly interesting adults are taking up too much of the kids' mental and emotional space.

The problem with parents being too interesting is the same as parents being too involved in a kid's life: We take up emotional room. Kids, when they find their emotional room crowded with adults, will either punch out the walls or move elsewhere emotionally to find a little space for themselves.

I have a friend, for instance, who has recently become obsessed with long-distance bicycling. This began innocently enough when his son, Nathan, became old enough to ride from one end of our city's bicycle paths to the other without having to make five bathroom stops along the way. One of my kids and I would sometimes go along on a portion of these outings, though we were never gung-ho enough to ride the whole distance.

Initially, Nathan welcomed his dad's involvement. Having dad along expanded Nathan's radius to include the whole city, and it meant a pleasant car ride at the end to get home. But gradually, dad began to take over Nathan's territory. It began with the new bikes—bikes so expensive they had to be watched every moment of the trip rather than left propped against a wall so Nathan could play on a swing. Next came the new equipment—the odometers, cycling shoes and special packs that dad felt made the riding more fun. Finally, the trips became truly expansive, stretching across 35, 50 and 125 miles of rugged terrain, along with camping overnight beside the bike trail.

A while ago, I had a phone call inviting me to join one of the weekend outings. "It'll be great, Paul, scenery, easy riding, just your speed."

"I guess," I said. "Are we taking kids on this? What about Nathan?"

"Don't think so," his dad replied.

"How come?"

"He doesn't seem that interested lately," his dad said. "Spends all his time with this band and their gawdawful music. I think he's playing at a concert or something."

"What a shame," I said.

I was actually referring to the whole process rather than the bike trip. By taking over bicycling, my friend had helped crowd his son out of the sport. Nathan has some tiny chance of someday becoming a great drummer for a rock band, but what a shame that he can't also enjoy doing long-distance biking.

Kids beyond age five can be quite jealous of their territory and don't particularly want us in it. Your 6-year-old will proudly announce, "I can tie my own shoes, Mom," when you try to help, but a 12-year-old may say nothing when you decide to tag along with her and her girlfriends on an outing to the local theme park. She will simply be mortified for life when you emerge sick to your stomach from a wild ride on the Thriller-Killer Roller Coaster. As our kids get older, they would prefer not to pay much attention to us if they don't have to. This naturally satisfactory situation will become unbalanced only if parents make it a point to intrude.

We shouldn't. We should give the kids plenty of room to be kids. This means, of course, that we have to make every effort to be reasonably adult, at least in their eyes.

Confessions are not for our children's ears

Another kind of childish parental behavior often seen in the process of divorce is that of confession. This is not confession as we know it in the Catholic Church, where one's sins are told to a priest and appropriate expiation and prayers are set in response. No, this is the questionable habit of some adults to confess misdeeds to their own children. This can happen in any family where the parents are under the misguided notion that their children are their best friends. In divorce scenarios, this is compounded by a perverse urge of some parents to point out the misdeeds of the other.

To put the matter simply, your kids' need-to-know requirements do *not* include

- details of your affair with Joan or John;
- details of your partner's affair with Bill or Jill;
- detailed statements of your financial circumstances;
- stories of disgusting things you did as an adolescent; or
- your inner fantasy life or your current sexual frustration/enthusiasm.

In other areas, parental honesty is a very good thing. It's helpful for kids to know that parents have feelings, regrets and anxieties. It's probably better for you to admit, straight out, that you're nervous about being fired rather than having the kids figure it out from the way you're behaving around the house. Kids have built-in emotional radar: They know at a very early age when you're in trouble. Briefly discussing the trouble makes it more concrete and less threatening to your kids. Moreover, kids often respond to such opening-up in a very helpful way by asking that key question, "What's the worst thing that can happen?" Usually the worst thing isn't nearly as awful as either we or our children have been busy imagining.

> Children are not priests, therapists or confidants.

Children are not priests, therapists or confidants. Parents who are looking for confession, psychotherapy or a best friend should approach the appropriate people in an adult way: Kneel, pay the fee or buy the beer. Leave the kids alone. If we are having trouble dealing with divorce or family stress, don't imagine it's any easier for the kids and try to dump our problems on them.

Give 'em a break: Don't leave big decisions in the kids' hands

Part of being an adult, of course, is making decisions. "That's why they pay me the big bucks," goes the standard business joke (wryly funny these days as middle-management income keeps dipping).

Nonetheless, people in business and professions are paid to make tough calls, to take the resultant glory or stand the heat.

Parents, too, have to make the tough calls. We cannot hide behind tissue-thin democracy, nor can we shrug our shoulders and say, "Well, whatever . . ." in response to serious questions from our children. We don't have the option of abdicating decision making, because our kids will keep pushing us on the subject until we're forced to make one.

The most outrageous examples of this occur in adolescence as kids desperately look for boundaries and otherwise nice parents find that boundaries do not self-generate. I know a couple who were determined to avoid the autocratic parenting style they had both grown up with. As children of stern German parents, they were brought up following the tenets of "Spare the rod and spoil the child" and "Children should be seen but not heard." As adults, they decided their own children would have a much freer upbringing.

Free it was. When their son Jamie was thirteen, he became—as the phrase goes—sexually active. Jamie was told, "It's your decision," and the parents provided him with condoms.

When Jamie was fifteen, he wanted to have sex with his current girlfriend in the parents' house. "It's your decision," the parents said, reasoning that he'd be less likely to get the girl pregnant if the sex was at home than in the back seat of a car.

When Jamie was sixteen, he had built up a large collection of video pornography that he kept in the basement recreation room. His parents told friends, "Jamie's coming to terms with pornography."

Apparently Jamie had finished coming to terms with it the very next year. His parents arrived home from work one day to find Jamie videotaping his own pornography in the recreation room. This was too much. The parents told Jamie to take his video camera and his girlfriend and get out. Jamie did, and has been gone for three years. The parents wonder if they were too judgmental and repressive.

The real problem, of course, is that they became judgmental *too late*. After a lifetime of being told, "It's your decision," Jamie couldn't accept the simple truth that families and societies place limits on behavior. Children will push against whatever limits we set, whatever boundaries there are, until they find where the real limits are located.

Smart parents establish those limits ahead of time. Once those limits are set, the most important thing for us to do is to hold fast to what we've said. Inconsistent and unpredictable parenting is among those factors that correlate most strongly with kids ending up in prison, doing drugs and otherwise messing up their lives. Yet kids are remarkably adept at making us inconsistent, or setting parents at war with each other or otherwise manipulating limits for their own ends. This talent starts early. Babies, for instance, are known to influence parental behavior through smiles and crying from the age of eight months. By two years, they have figured out how to read our moods, the surrounding situation and the likely success or failure of any attention-getting ploy they might have at their disposal. Knowing this, they invariably act up when we're out shopping, or trying to impress Aunt Martha or the new client who's just popped in for coffee.

> Children will push against whatever limits we set . . . until they find where the real limits are located. Smart parents establish those limits ahead of time.

By age three or four, most kids are perfectly capable of playing mom against dad or vice versa. By five or six, many kids are as effective as World War II submarines, seeking out the weakest boat in the fleet, sending out the emotional torpedoes and putting the whole convoy in disarray.

Try as we might, all parents can be suckered in. When dad's little buddy sidles up to suggest that maybe, just maybe, a new computer CD-ROM would be a great thing, and he just knows mom doesn't want to hear this, but dad, dear dad, will understand—dad's being played for a sucker. When mom's little darling, the baby of the family, says that those new rollerblades are just essential for her acceptance in the neighborhood and mom, dear mom, will understand—mom's taken the bait.

The kids are always smart enough not to bring these issues up at dinner, where the parents can talk or present a united front. They get us alone, watching TV or peeling potatoes, and hit us with arguments so precisely attuned to our hidden desires and buried psychological flaws that we would have a better chance dealing with a professional con man.

Later on, we get trapped by our nice-guy acquiescence.

"But Mom said the rollerblades would be a good idea," your daughter declares.

You look at each other with a sinking feeling.

"I just thought . . ." she begins, feeling guilty and foolish.

"I thought we decided . . ." you say, trying to remember what you two had come up with in a more sober moment.

And your daughter might as well be off shopping with the family credit card.

The divide-and-conquer technique was perfected historically by Caesar but psychologically it's mastered by most children as soon as they reach school age. Parents become vulnerable whenever they lose sight of long-term objectives for the family and the kids. And we lose the battle whenever we forget to say, "Let me talk to your mom/dad about this."

Rule number one for any parents in the process of raising children is to talk to each other *first*, before making any significant decision on what the kids can do. When we don't, the kids will skewer us on our own urge for personal consistency. While consistency is important for parents—we can't keep changing the rules day after day—we can too easily get caught by kids who come back with a direct quotation: "But you said . . . "

In consumer affairs, most states have legislated a 24-hour cooling-off period in which we can simply change our mind on a major purchase. "No, I don't like that chair, take it back." "Nah, this car is a lemon, I don't want it." Perhaps as parents we need to demand something similar: a 24-hour period to check with our partners to make sure that whatever we agreed to in the afternoon wasn't entirely idiotic by the time we watch the evening news.

> We lose the battle whenever we forget to say, "Let me talk to your mom/dad about this."

The family conference, of course, is one way to avoid divide-and-conquer. It tends to work well on issues like the rollerblade purchase because the issue is reduced to rational rather than emotional terms. Even better, though, is the parent-to-parent conference, actually talking with our partner about the children, what we expect and what's likely to come up. Forty years ago, when Father made the half-dozen big decisions and Mother made almost all the others, parents didn't have to talk so much; they could issue edicts. These days, a real partnership requires lots of talking by mom and dad, some careful listening to the kids, and the wisdom to separate one method from the other.

Five Tips on Family Decision Making

1. **Set limits and make decisions.** You're the parent and have a lot more experience than your children.
2. **Listen.** Any parental decision should come up for review periodically; listening makes that review more intelligent.
3. **Don't usurp.** Kids deserve to have the world of childhood for themselves; they don't need you butting in or taking over.
4. **Don't confess, at least to your kids.** Priests, doctors, ministers and psychologists are equipped to listen to your problems, but your kids have better things to do.
5. **Don't let children divide and conquer.** The kids will seek out the "weakest" parent, alone, and use any concession as a lever against the other.

Chapter 4

Praise-junkie kids:
Too much self-esteem can be dangerous to our kids' mental health

The young mother on my television screen stares slightly to the left of the camera toward the unseen interviewer.

"It was terrible growing up like that," she says. "You can't imagine." The camera zooms in close so her eyes are at the top of the screen and her quivering mouth at the bottom.

I have tuned in late to the program, my channel flicking stopped by the caption at the bottom of the screen. This is a show about parenting and it's on an *educational* channel, at that, so I settle back on the couch and take out my notebook.

". . . Whatever I did, whatever I said. Well, I'm not raising my kids like that. They're not going to suffer the way I have."

The camera pulls back to show the woman's two children, one of them staring right at the lens, the other one climbing over the back of the couch. The voice-over tells us that Tina is a single mom, trying hard to get by, despite her difficulties.

I begin to wonder what those difficulties were. The problem of flipping through channels is that the channel flipper is never quite sure what the topic is when his channel flipping stops. Was Tina an abused child? Was she sexually assaulted? Does she have AIDS? Cancer?

"All my life I've had to suffer from what my parents did to me. It's their fault I'm like this . . . that I have to take classes to get over it."

A-ha! I think, an *it*! But it can't be a disease, because she's taking classes to get over the problem. Surely her parents are guilty of some heinous abuse.

"They destroyed it," she cries. "They destroyed my self-esteem!"

Quickly the visual changes to show Tina in a discussion group that will, presumably, build her self-esteem back to a functional level. I close my notebook and begin to wonder. Television always has the tendency to make situations either silly or melodramatic, but what of this "self-esteem" issue we see raised so frequently in the media? Where did it come from and how important is it, really, for our children?

The self-esteem movement . . . and the self-esteem industry

The self-esteem movement, like so much else in our self-absorbed culture, goes back to the 1970s, when lack of self-esteem was first seen as a kind of emotional vitamin deficiency leading to cringing behavior in adults. Gloria Steinem, the feminist celebrity, apparently summed up a prevailing feeling when she wrote, "Self-esteem may not be everything, but without it you have nothing." This is the kind of comment that left many adults suffering from fear of sudden emotional poverty. To the rescue came any number of self-help books and educational programs—an entire self-esteem industry.

By the 1980s, self-esteem development had become a hot topic at educational conferences. Back then, too many traditionalist teachers had the unfortunate tendency to use the put-down phrase rather than the build-up comment. Professional development for these teachers was probably a good thing for them and for their students. But then the self-esteem industry spilled over into medicine, psychology and how we rear children. Now we have hundreds of books with titles like *101 Ways to Improve Your Self-Esteem* and *The Self-Esteem Repair and Maintenance Manual*, workshops, Internet sites and even board games.

Self-esteem advocates urge parents to bolster their children's self-esteem using a number of clever techniques. Jean Illsley Clarke wrote an early book in the field, one with cheerful line drawings and charts with titles such as, "What You Stroke Is What You Get." Louise Hart's more recent book, *The Winning Family: Increasing Self-Esteem in Your Children* offers many examples of children who would have been successful if only their families had ladled out more praise. Another example of the genre is *101 Ways to Make Your Child Feel Special* by Vicki Lansky. It's a picture book, though addressed to adults, with a number of reasonable parenting ideas, from hugging your kids to getting them library cards. But occasionally Lansky goes overboard with her suggestions on how to build a child's self-esteem. She suggests, for instance, that parents send an anonymous note to their child from "a secret admirer" and then not admit to being the sender. Or, she advises, "Tell your child how nice he or she looks this morning (and every morning)—even if plaid pants are being worn with a striped shirt." It's with suggestions like these that Lansky asks parents to cross the line from simply praising their children to engaging in downright fraud.

At what point is a child's self-esteem so important that a parent should blatantly lie to support it? In real life, I admit such moments do occur. When your teenage daughter has just been dumped by her boyfriend and is convinced that she is ugly, stupid and has bad hair, a wise parent will tell her that she is beautiful, brilliant and has hair befitting a shampoo commercial . . . at least while the tears are still flowing. It's not possible in a world of emotional defeats and social politeness to tell the truth *all* the time, but systematic lying does no one any good.

Some years ago, I taught a young man named Mark who was being torn apart by his parents' demands and his consistent sense of personal failure. He was a gangly, red-headed boy who showed many of the physical manifestations of too much stress: psoriatic skin, nervous tics, a slight stutter. His parents, two physicians who had laid their family hopes squarely on the head of their only son (their daughter, interestingly, had very few expectations placed upon her), consistently told Mark that he was not "measuring up to his potential." Mark's "potential" had been certified by IQ tests, psychologists and even coerced teachers, though I find it ironic how often "potential" just happens to coincide with parental expectations rather than with a child's actual achievement.

Mark's high-school grades were a disappointment to everyone. The family actually took some advice, including mine, and got into counseling arranged through the local medical center. I think the parents were looking for a quick fix that would get their son on the college track; I was just hoping that Mark wouldn't end up an emotional basket case before the end of the school year.

> Both too *little* praise from parents and too *much* praise from parents create problems later.

At the counseling sessions, the parents learned how to praise Mark for his achievements and keep their mouths closed over the disappointments; they learned to talk rather than lecture; and they became aware of what their expectations were doing to their son. The results of the therapy were wonderful for Mark, at least initially. His skin improved, the facial tics disappeared and his grades went up to a B level. But the heaping of praise went to his head.

"Where are you planning to apply for college?" I asked him about a year after things had begun to improve.

"I'm going to go to Juilliard."

"Juilliard," I said. "In New York?" I probably raised an eyebrow, the kind of thing I do in disbelief.

"Yeah," Mark told me. "I'm going to study piano there. I'm real good at piano."

"Real good," I repeated. "Do you have any idea how good you have to be to get into Juilliard?"

"Oh, I'm good enough. My mom was telling me just the other night how good I was." He smiled, his eyes brimming with newfound confidence.

The bell rang and we both had to get to class, which was a good thing for me because I find it awkward to talk "real world" to kids who are living in never-never land. Of the approximately five thousand students I have taught in twenty years, at least one hundred have told me they were going to Harvard. Only one kid actually got there. Mark, incidentally, ended up in the local college jazz program, where he's done very well—more power to him.

Does it hurt a kid to aim for admission to Harvard or Juilliard or the Air Force Academy? In most cases, definitely not. There's never any point in shooting *down* a goal. But for a kid who's struggling to get Cs, too much self-esteem polishing can get in the way of real-life planning.

The problem for Mark and kids like him, of course, is that both too *little* praise from parents and too *much* praise from parents create problems later. The former devalues and depresses young people, the latter pumps them full of unrealistic expectations and makes real achievement too dependent on how it appears to others.

Praise junkies

The problem the self-esteem industry created is this: It has inadvertently defined the idea of self-esteem as a quality that is determined by praise or criticism from other people. If your mom says you're good, you'll feel good about yourself and you'll have good self-esteem—or so the theory goes. If only real life were that simple!

While it is true that praise from parents is an important part of children developing a sense of self-esteem, what our kids think of themselves should never depend entirely on whether they're praised by us. Self-esteem, when the word was first coined, was attached to the idea of good and ennobling behavior, not whether mom and dad were going to applaud you for finishing your soup at dinner. All parents want their children to grow up with a confident sense of themselves. But we don't want them to become praise junkies, dependent on a parent, a boss or a lover for the next verbal stroking that will make them feel good.

Recently, I visited two friends and was asked to look at a piece of writing done by their 7-year-old son.

"It's Geoffrey's first book," dad announced.

"We've already told him how wonderful it is," mom explained to me, with the implied *hint, hint, nudge, nudge.*

"Well, I'm impressed," I said, even before I looked. "May I see it?"

Geoffrey was holding the book behind his back while doing a strange tap dance with his feet. Finally, he handed over the book, shyly, then tried to hide behind his mother's skirt. I have met enough wannabe-writers to know that this particular urge is not unusual, though adults rarely bring their mothers with them to the public library's creative writing workshops.

"I like the title," I said, even if *The Fairy's Toothbrush* wasn't the most original I'd run across.

"My dad did it," Geoffrey mumbled.

"It's better than *Goo in Your Mouth* or whatever you wanted to call it," his father replied.

By now I was on page two. "I like the way the boy in the story doesn't really want to brush his teeth," I said. Obviously even a person who grudges the whole concept of self-esteem development will sometimes lavish praise on young children.

"Yeah, that's like me," Geoffrey piped up. "Dad made me change the name."

"Well, the drawings are excellent. I really like the big tooth."

"Mom did that."

"*I helped*, Geoffrey," mom threw in. "*You* drew it."

I kept turning pages and offering comments until I reached the end of the book. Then I concluded, "Geoffrey, you must be really proud of yourself."

"Nah," Geoffrey said.

"Of course you are," I said, a typical adult refusing to listen. "And are you working on another story?"

"Nah," Geoffrey told me. "That one's perfect. If I did another one, I'd just mess up."

Geoffrey's achievement, sadly, was not his own. He had satisfied his mother and his father, produced the requisite product and received more than the appropriate amount of praise—but it had done nothing for him. Everyone—including me—had gone through the motions that should have bolstered his self-esteem, but the fraud underlying it all made the exercise valueless.

> Instead of *helping*, mom and dad ended up *doing*.

How had the parents gone wrong? I suspect that the project wasn't Geoffrey's idea to start with or, if it was, that mom and dad had quickly taken it over. I suspect that instead of *helping*, mom and dad ended up *doing*. And I suspect that the sum total of dozens of little errors and encroachments by the parents ended up making *The Fairy's Toothbrush* something that brought Geoffrey no real pride. That he should get praise for this—and have to seek further praise from his parents' friend—must have rubbed salt into the wound.

Given too much praise in childhood for too little real achievement, a kid will naturally grow to expect the same from the rest of the world.

The first lasting encounter that many young people have with the real world is school, where the kindergarten teacher may not appreciate their gifts and genius nearly as much as mom and dad. But teachers, thanks to the self-esteem movement, have been pressured for many years now to replace criticism with gentle nudges, and evaluation with dollops of verbal praise. Thus the old-style F connoting failure has been replaced on report cards by NI for "needs improvement," and the traditional bell curve for grade distribution has been replaced by report cards that tell us that the *middle* student in a particular twelfth-grade history class garnered a B-plus. No wonder parents are demanding report cards that tell us, honestly, how hard our child worked and how he stacks up against his peers.

> **False praise from parents does not build self-esteem but insecurity.**

Children who have become praise-junkies at home are quick to transfer this addiction to school. These are the ones who so frequently come up to the teacher's desk, work in hand, to seek verbal approval. They are not brown-nosing or currying favor. Instead, they are soothing their anxiety by continually looking to an adult to praise their work. Schools, for their part, have gone overboard emphasizing "process" in everything from creative writing to researching biology, so the poor teacher ends up looking at the same piece of work in various stages, over and over, long before giving the effort a grade. I'm not sure this process helps the anxious praise-junkie.

"Is it better, Mr. Kropp?"

"Yes, Melissa," I reply.

How to Spot a Praise-Junkie Kid

1. He's anxious.
2. He asks what you would think of a project even before he starts.
3. He asks for your opinion more often than your help.
4. He's more worried about what the essay/project looks like than what it says.
5. He values your approval more than his own achievement.

"I fixed the spelling this time."

"I see that."

"You like it, don't you?"

"It's coming along nicely." I have mastered noncommittal phrases for these situations.

"It'll be worth an A for sure, right?"

"I hope so. When it's finished."

"But you do like it," Melissa goes on, looking vaguely hurt. "I'm doing my best."

"I'm sure you are."

And Melissa goes off, frustrated, because I won't say that her scribbled rough notes on *Wuthering Heights* are worthy of the Pulitzer Prize.

If Melissa does not get an A, her teachers will have to deal with pouting, anger, accusations of incompetence and perhaps a visit from mom. Is it any wonder that so many have thrown in the towel and hand out As like Marie Antoinette tossing coins to the peasants?

Melissa and Geoffrey's problem, like that of other praise-junkie children, is that false praise from parents does not build self-esteem but insecurity. While it is important for moms, dads and teachers to praise the efforts of young people, such praise is meaningless unless it is based on a foundation of truth. Your child may do a wonderful job playing Mozart's C Major piano sonata, but that doesn't mean he's ready to tour with the New York Philharmonic. Praise built on falsehood is like a house whose foundation rests on sand—you always have to worry about a future flood.

Self-esteem and self-confidence

In the last few years, the self-esteem industry increasingly has tied itself to images rather than substance. Thus we have books on maintaining one's self-esteem despite obesity, for example. Such books suggest that the problem lies not with the obesity, but in how society perceives these things and how that perception makes a person feel. It's a neat argument, and has some truth to it. But the effect of an increasing emphasis on appearances has been to open the self-esteem movement to an accusation.

The accusation is narcissism, and the accusation is correct.

The problem of narcissism comes from the superficiality implied in the word "esteem." "Esteem," literally, is to be held in high respect by others. This respect might be completely unrelated to the deep merit of an individual, because it is really a measure of superficial appearances. An individual might be esteemed for his art collection, his successful career or his shrewd investments—yet be surreptitiously defrauding the government or his clients. The esteem, then, is ultimately based on appearances and not on deep truths. A child may be a fine student and have a strong sense of commitment to his family, his siblings and his own future, but he will have little esteem from his peers in some classrooms if he wears *déclassé* sneakers. Esteem can be quite superficial.

Esteem can be quite superficial.

Self-esteem takes this superficiality and puts it in front of a mirror. Rather than deeply examine our character, our efforts and our personality against the highest standards, we need only consider how others see us. This leads not to self-improvement but to behaviors that curry favor.

Far better for our children to concentrate on those other "self" words—"self-confidence," "self-reliance" and "self-worth." Here are qualities that have deeper roots and greater utility, wholly independent of whatever passing fashion brings popularity in the short term. It is this kind of deep self-valuing that Emerson discusses in his famous essay, "Self-Reliance."

> Few and mean as my gifts may be, I actually am, and do not need for my own assurance or the assurance of my fellows, any secondary testimony. What I must do is all that concerns me, not what the people think. This rule, equally arduous in actual and in intellectual life, may serve for the whole distinction between greatness and meanness.

Of course Emerson's essays are no longer taught in schools. They've been replaced by pamphlets with names such as *Celebrate Yourself—Six Steps to Building Your Self-Esteem*. Emerson wrote of independence, courage, principles and encountering real life. Self-esteem pamphlets describe "learning to love yourself again," "making loving yourself a habit" and learning to describe one's character with upbeat adjectives ("awesome" is suggested).

> Far better for our children to concentrate on those other "self" words—"self-confidence," "self-reliance" and "self-worth."

In parenting, efforts to bolster self-esteem seem like covering up cracked plaster with wallpaper rather than putting in the time and labor to fix the real problem. Sure, wallpaper works, but not for long. Paste-on improvements in self-esteem are of little value if a child grows up without self-confidence, self-reliance and self-worth.

Building those other "self" qualities will always require more work and more time, but the rewards come in an older child who does not have to grovel for approval because she can honestly evaluate her own worth. The rules for building these "selfs" are simple to write down, yet hard to practice day after day, year after year:

- Pay attention to what your child does and says—you don't have to agree, but you do have to listen.

- Find plenty of time to work together on projects, keeping the child's real abilities in mind.
- Remember that activity and success build the self, not phony praise.

My middle son, Justin, was a plastic-model builder from age six or so, when kids first get excited about that kind of thing. His initial efforts were pretty crude, even he will admit. The first models ended up with splattered paint, glue-fingerprints and all the other hallmarks of a 6-year-old trying to produce a plastic B-52 bomber. Those first efforts also required a fair amount of dad-input, especially because Justin's reading and small-motor skills were still rudimentary.

His mom and I always applauded the models, as parents do, but never suggested that he automatically had a future in aircraft or automobile assembly. Nonetheless, each model was better than the last: There was less glue on the wings and in his hair, straighter lines of paint, fewer decals stuck to the table. The kits got more elaborate (and expensive) as Justin's skills grew. By age eight he was as good as

How to Build Your Child's Self-Confidence

1. **Include the child in what you're doing.** Not every nail in the backyard deck has to be straight.
2. **Don't set the hurdles too high.** Kids have to build a birdhouse before they tackle a grandfather clock.
3. **Don't rescue too soon.** Give your child a chance to experience honest frustration first.
4. **Make sure there are real outside challenges.** Scouts, swim teams, music lessons.
5. **Praise the final results.** When you can see in your child's eyes that she thinks something is good, it's probably plenty good. Put it up on the real and the metaphorical refrigerator door.

his father in putting these things together; by age ten he had left me behind. Fifteen years later, the boy actually ended up a mechanical engineer, but it wasn't because I told him that glue smudges on a plastic fuselage were perfectly okay.

Praise does not, by itself, lead children to grow and seek new challenges. Nor does a word or two of criticism ("too bad there's a big thumbprint on this windshield") defeat a child who has his eyes on a goal and can take delight in his own achievements. Somewhere in between is where parents must position themselves. Finding and keeping to that spot, given the different moods and temperaments of our kids, is no small feat, but it's worth the effort.

Chapter 5

Quality time is such a beautiful sham

Early in the 1980s, before the final surge of conspicuous spending that closed that decade, writers began using the phrase "quality time" in reference to parenting. This was a real linguistic feat—cleverly breaking down all the hours spent together by a family into time that either had "quality" or didn't. The newly defined quality time was said to involve organized family activities, intense discussion and serious listening to the intellectual concerns of babbling children. Presumably, nonquality time meant that mom was busy doing paperwork, or dad was baking bread, and the kids were plopped in front of the TV. Obviously, quality time was the class act. It was quality time that got babies to talk, children to read, young students to do mental math and high-school kids into college.

Quality time just happened to fit neatly into a new economic regime where the earning and spending of money was deemed extremely important while raising children was sinking low on the charts. According to a 1985 study done by a University of Maryland sociologist, the amount of time parents spent with their children had dropped from 30 hours a week to 17 hours a week over the previous twenty years. Work had swallowed up the extra hours. Across North America, we're working longer hours than ever before. More than half of employees today average 45 hours a week—50 hours for professionals—and one worker in five is on the job 60 hours a week or more. Should it come as a surprise that there's no time left for the kids?

When "quality time" was coined, however, no one anticipated the degree of overwork that would follow. Back then, most people thought it was a wonderful thing for yuppie mom and dad to hold two high-powered jobs, drop the kids at the baby-sitter's before school and pick them up in the BMW after a long and busy day. Even with fast-food dinners or, better yet, a fine meal prepared by the housekeeper, there weren't many hours left between the cognac at the end of the meal and the hour the kids went to bed, but that time, according to the magazines, could be "quality time."

That popular image fell apart in the 1990s when the recession set in: Dad was downsized, the BMW was replaced by a minivan, and the kids had to sit at a neighbor's house until mom got home or, so much the worse, look after themselves. But even as the clichés changed, one concept remained: quality time. A certain portion of the time kids and adults spend together was somehow deemed significantly superior to time spent just hanging out together.

As a society, we've long felt this to be true. The conventional images of "good" parenting, from seventeenth-century woodcuts to Norman Rockwell covers for *The Saturday Evening Post*, always show mom and dad actively involved with the kids. Parents and children are depicted reading together, doing homework, playing a sport or fishing on a lazy summer's day (though dad seems to be asleep as Norman Rockwell illustrated it). In contrast, the documentary images and hidden camera videos we see of ordinary parents offer a very different depiction. There they are: Overweight mom on the couch, overweight dad in his chair, the three children eating potato chips on the floor, all of their eyes glued to the television set. Don't we all know which kind of family we want ours to resemble?

Yet I'm afraid the answer isn't as obvious as we are prone to believe.

Quality time and parental guilt

Dr. Alison Clarke-Stewart was among the first social scientists to support the idea of quality time. Dr. Clarke-Stewart, then an associate professor of education at the University of Chicago, used the phrase "quality time" to describe a style of parenting that should be "not only warm, loving and nonrejecting, but . . . stimulating and enriching." She based this on research she had done in the 1970s on working mothers and the quality of care they provided for their children. At the time, Dr. Clarke-Stewart was frequently cited in popular parenting magazines and new periodicals like *Working Mother*, though she says today that her research wasn't properly understood.

Regardless, the concept of quality time was quickly embraced by such child-rearing heavyweights as Dr. David Elkind and Dr. Stanley Greenspan. In fact, the latter is still a proponent of what he calls "floor time," where mom and dad spend 30 minutes a day literally on the floor, playing games or doing activities dictated by the child. "If she wants you to get down on all fours and bark like a dog, do it," Dr. Greenspan wrote enthusiastically in *Parents* magazine.

Reaction to such ideas set in fairly early, from columns in the *New York Times* to pieces in *Working Mother*, but the phrase "quality time" entered our language and the concept took on considerable power. Even parents who were at home all day looking after their children suddenly became afraid that the time they were spending with the kids lacked quality.

In retrospect, it's easy to see that the idea of quality time developed out of collective parental guilt as the number of families with two working parents grew in the 1970s. Today, with two-thirds of young families picking up two paychecks, with stay-at-home moms and dads on the defensive, it's difficult to understand where the guilt came from. But in the 1970s, the first baby boomers to have children themselves still felt they had to justify themselves to parents from the 1940s and 1950s. Those earlier parents had followed the Ward Cleaver/Dr. Jim Anderson parenting model: one employed dad, one stay-at-home mom. This older generation disapproved of families where both parents worked outside the home, though rarely enough to volunteer their time for baby-sitting services. Their children, the boomer parents, felt anxious about going back to work and putting the kids in day care—certainly anxious enough to seek intellectual support for what they felt they had to do.

Quality time provided that support. Psychologist Lois Hoffman of the University of Michigan was among the first to note "a more intense" mother-child interaction for employed mothers than for stay-at-home moms. Hoffman's theory was that the intensity was a way in which employed moms compensated for the additional hours stay-at-home moms spent with their children. As a concept, quality time provided an "out" for working moms, and later for overworked dads, who might have felt they were neglecting their children simply because they could not provide the same amount of family time as did the parents on *Leave It to Beaver*.

The activities suggested for quality time always involved one-to-one interaction, often using a game or activity as a mediator and stimulator. Among the activities suggested in various books and articles of the time, we find the following:

- baking cookies;
- going on family vacations;
- washing dishes together;
- playing sports together such as baseball, Frisbee, skiing;
- playing Monopoly, Scrabble, card games;
- working together on dad's hobbies, such as model rockets, car restoration;
- reading a book, talking about its story or illustrations; or
- joining in your child's dollhouse activity or other fantasy.

Quality-time activities were intense, interactive, verbal and one-on-one. It's probably a coincidence that the suggested time unit for "quality" interaction turned out to be exactly as long as the time required for a TV sitcom. It might also be coincidental that quality-time activities just happened to include the popular means of entertainment for parents and children during the pre-TV days of the 1940s and 1950s. Both nostalgia and economics are important factors affecting how we parent our kids.

I can speak now from a historical perspective about quality time, though our family was quite caught up with it back then. During the years when our double incomes were strong, we decided that skiing would be an excellent quality-time activity. It incorporated most of the key ingredients: one-on-one interaction, family discussion, physical activity and the great outdoors. Surely, we thought, such a worthwhile endeavor justified the outlay of a few dollars for secondhand skis and rope-tow tickets.

Over the years, however, the kids outgrew their secondhand skis and demanded new equipment often costing hundreds of dollars. As the bills mounted, I began to wonder whether this particular form of quality time was actually worth the cash outlay. I tried to reflect upon the significant family discussions we had had at the ski lodge, or in front of the open fire après-ski:

"I need new boots. My toes hurt."

"Can I have another hot chocolate?"

"You see how fast I took those moguls?"

"Oh, I hurt. I wiped out, like, hugely."

The only significant discussion I recall from a dozen years on the slopes occurred not while skiing, but while traveling in our station wagon stuffed full of kids, ski boots and bags of ski equipment. The talk was not about skiing. The discussion was about satire, irony and the capacity of song to convey significant social commentary. The inspiration for this particular discussion was not our day on the slopes but a rock-and-roll tape that one of the kids had brought along in his jacket pocket. We all listened; we all talked.

But that's the only quality time I can recall from a dozen years and thousands of dollars spent skiing. My hunch, alas, is that we might have enjoyed as much or more quality time had our family spent more hours playing Scrabble.

In praise of "dumb time" and quality moments

I am loath to refer to the obverse of quality time as "nonquality" or "low-quality" time because sometimes these moments are far more rewarding to both parents and children than anyone would expect. Let me, instead, call it "dumb time" because the phrase is easy to remember and it suggests the low-pressure approach that both parents and kids can enjoy during these periods.

Dumb time consists of all those moments parents and children spend in physical proximity to each other without engaging in any particular activity *together*. While quality time requires conversation, engagement and one-to-one interaction, dumb time requires only that parent and child are within earshot and eyeball distance of each other. A list of typical dumb-time activities could include

- parent ironing and child staring out the window;
- parent or child talking on the phone, the other nearby and eavesdropping;
- parent or child watching TV, perhaps even together;
- parent or child playing cards, the other staring blankly into space;
- parent making supper, child doing homework.

The simple truth, of course, is that much of the time families spend in each other's company has very little "quality" or even verbal interaction. Humans cannot continually be involved in serious conversation, or engaged in sporting activities, or even playing family games. We need dumb time to dawdle and meander and do nothing much at all, otherwise our dreams and ideas would grow too small and our fingernails would grow too long. In fact, I would say humans need dumb time as much as they need sleep.

So do families.

One problem with the idea of quality time is that it suggests parents can somehow force quality or improve what happens during the time they spend with children. But our capacity to create situations where quality moments will occur is actually quite limited.

We can no more bring on a quality moment than we can force creativity or enlightenment. Quality—like creativity and insight—has its own time schedule.

Quality time also makes the assumption that our agenda is the same as our child's agenda. This flows from a daytimer mentality where, if the time block between 7:00 and 8:00 is not otherwise filled, the busy parent can jot down "QT" and promptly engage in a quality-time pursuit with the child.

Children, at least until age eighteen or so, are rarely equipped with daytimers so it is difficult for them to tell parents that they have another pressing appointment in the 7:00 to 8:00 slot. They

> I would say humans need dumb time as much as they need sleep.

cannot say to an earnest and sincere parent ready to play backgammon, "Sorry, mom, I have an appointment to watch *The Simpsons* at Janey's house." Children know that such sentiments don't sit well with an overworked parent, so they will give in to our request for a quality-time activity, but not happily.

Parents should never forget that children do have their own timetables. Babies will eat and sleep at the darndest times; toddlers will play cheerfully or cry miserably following no discernible schedule; and older children will be subject to mood swings not entirely explicable by their ingestion of sugar products. A child who does not want to engage in serious discourse on, say, the real meaning of Christmas won't do it just because mom is reading Dickens' *A Christmas Carol* out loud. Nor will a child who really needs to discuss why Jimmy Jones wants to beat his head in be dissuaded somehow by the fact that it is his move in our quality-time game of chess.

In some thirty years of raising children, I have had significant conversations at the most unexpected times: on long car trips, watching (or staring) at TV, swinging on a hammock while trying to read a book, painting various rooms in the house, on the way to a movie or a ball game, making dinner and sitting in my office trying to write a book. Of course, significant conversation is only one aspect of quality time. One of the rewards of parenting is that there are also, unexpectedly, quality moments—points of time when we realize why we had these kids, why we pump thousands of dollars every year into their food and clothing, and why we voluntarily gave up the sports car/vacation/career of our dreams just to have a child who only pays attention to us when he needs cash, breakfast or a ride to the store.

Some years ago, my son Justin and I were busy re-shingling the porch roof. He was all of nineteen, physically bigger than I, but still just nineteen. Naturally, I was in charge of the project. It became apparent early on that the sub-roof boards would have to be replaced with plywood, so the four-by-eight sheets were ordered and carried up by the young apprentice carpenter. I

> Parents should never forget that children do have their own timetables.

proceeded to take the circular saw (my father's, actually, so there were three generations represented on that roof) and cut the line we had marked on the plywood.

"Dad, that's a lousy cut," Justin said.

"Whaddya mean, lousy cut. It's a good-enough cut," I replied.

"It's off by a half inch."

"A quarter inch."

"It's still off. You cut the next one like that, you'll have a one-inch gap."

I looked at him with irritation. "I suppose you think you could cut a better line."

"Yeah," he said.

I handed him the saw. "So cut."

He took the saw, bent over the next sheet of plywood and cut a line that didn't deviate from the chalk mark by more than a sixteenth of an inch.

"Where'd you learn to do that?" I said.

"At work. Last summer."

So I did what any dad does at such a point. I handed him the rule and square and smiled sheepishly. "Okay, what do you want me to do next?"

I cannot recall, with Justin, ever having had a quality-time conversation. I have four other children with whom I have had serious conversations, sometimes even at the appointed times—just like those *Leave It to Beaver* episodes where Ward Cleaver joins Wally and the Beav in the bedroom. But Justin and I have had our quality moments, moments every bit as rewarding as the hours I've spent in earnest discussion with the other kids.

What's so terrible about boredom?

Another problem with the urge for quality time is that it tends to eliminate the time children properly spend being bored. In previous generations, the common phrase, "Mom, I'm bored," would be met with the typical, "So find something to do." There was no particular guilt

> Children . . . can learn to handle boredom quite well.

What's Wrong with Quality Time?

1. Quality time follows a parent's timetable, not the child's.
2. It provides an excuse for spending less clock time with our kids.
3. It emphasizes intellectual activity over emotional availability.
4. It encourages parents to intrude and organize a kid's unstructured time.
5. It doesn't allow enough time for "quality moments" to occur on their own.

for mom in her child's boredom, nor was there an immediate expectation that *she* do something about it. Boredom was the child's problem and the solution was put squarely back in the child's hands.

One of the more impressive aspects of children is that they can learn to handle boredom quite well. After a whine or two, a few minutes of sighing and staring out the window at a cloudy sky, most children will invent something to do. In fifteen minutes—as long as the television is turned off—they will be busy building a model or reading a book or redesigning a medieval fort.

For a parent who feels that his time with the children should be of "quality," boredom is a serious problem. He feels guilty that the child is bored, that the moment is unstructured, that no fulfilling activity is underway. And such a parent intervenes. Like Barney, the television dinosaur, such a parent feels he must use his intelligence, creativity and personal magic to make the child's boredom go away. By efficiently eliminating boredom, such a parent intrudes on an important private aspect of his child's life, and he interferes with the child's own powers of dealing with idle moments.

For too many parents, *doing* has replaced *waiting*. This is a shame. There is a wonderful parenting program called *Watch, Wait and Wonder* that helps families who are having difficulties with each other. The premise of the program, according to Elizabeth Muir at the Hincks Centre for Children's Mental Health in Toronto, is that parents should spend more time simply observing their children and waiting until parental interaction is required. The "wonder" of the program name is what parents often feel about the capabilities of their child to be busy and productive—*on the child's own terms.*

Our society does not easily support watching and waiting. In schooling, in medicine and in parenting, we are predisposed to action, but in each case action has its limits of effectiveness. Children certainly *do* profit from parents who are available, who pay some attention to their interests and needs and who make some effort at enriching their lives. But children *do not* benefit from parents who intrude, try to control or shape their lives, or try to substitute material items and intense activity for love and availability.

I find it interesting that so many adults, reflecting on memorable moments in their childhood, recall incidents when they were on vacation with their parents. These are rarely incidents where the parents were trying hard, or specifically engaged in "quality" activities. Rather, they are incidents that occur when parents and children are in each other's company without much that has to be done. This creates a space where, in fact, important things *can* happen. Your child can decide to build her own canoe, or start a spider collection, or write a book of poems—all because the time is available and a certain limited amount of attention can be had from nearby adults.

Linwood Barclay, who ordinarily writes a funny newspaper column, was quite serious when remembering the time he spent with his own father. He describes being in his dad's studio, when his father was a commercial artist, drawing cars at his own easel while his dad was busy working at his. Barclay writes about hours spent cleaning out aluminum boats when his father was running a tourist camp. And he concludes:

> As a kid, you don't realize how important these simple moments are. Later you understand what it meant to have someone this close to you, who wanted to share your company, who spent time with you not because he was your dad and he had to, but because he wanted to. It made you

feel confident, and worthy, and safe. And it made you feel loved.

By and large, children do not need *intensive* parental involvement in their activities. But they do need by-the-way attention. Burton White, in *Educating the Infant and Toddler*, talks about the ways successful parents reared babies who turned out to be reasonably bright. The keys, he found, were not significant intervention by parents in what children do, or providing special one-on-one time, or giving a grueling schedule to the day's activities. No, the keys were talk and attention. The parents who reared bright children talked to their kids about items of interest to the children. This talk was rarely structured, as in a lesson, nor did it go on for long, rarely more than thirty seconds for each exchange. While the parents tended to speak in full sentences and use vocabulary slightly beyond the children's level, they did not make a particular effort to teach or expand vocabulary. To put it simply, the most supportive parents were simply *present*, and paid a small amount of attention to the children every three or four minutes.

> **The keys were talk and attention.**

This isn't quality time, it's quality parenting.

Tough choices

While quality time can't ever replace the hours of dumb time that kids really need, it's probably the only stopgap available for many young families. For most single moms, the choice is really welfare or going to work and providing as much time as possible when the workday is done. For cash-strapped families—that's most young parents—the choices are more complicated. It's rarely possible, any more, for young families to live comfortably on one person's wages. Half of today's dual-income families tell the Gallup poll that they would prefer at least one parent to stay home with the kids, but they don't because "money is an issue."

Indeed, money is always an issue. But just how much money a family needs, at least when the children are young, is a choice.

Increasingly, I meet families who have found an employer that will let them work part-time or from home, or that provides day care at the job site. Or I meet young mothers and fathers who have made a very conscious choice to make the economic sacrifice required for one parent to stay home when the kids are young. Such a call would have been unthinkable in the decades of consumer greed and quality-time apologetics, but many young people today are looking for longer-term rewards.

"I'm only having two kids," said Sarah, only a month away from giving birth to the first, "and I'm staying home with them. Five years. We've decided."

Sarah is a production assistant in television, but hardly makes a large salary. Her partner is a photographer, successful enough, but not with a steady income. I asked her the obvious question: "How are you going to afford it?"

"We're going to be poor," she said proudly.

That's a fair choice. For most of history, young families have tended to be poor, and today's economics have made that lopsided distribution of income and wealth even worse. But babies tend to look quite blank when economic unfairness and middle-class consumer demands are explained to them. They are not particularly interested in our rationales for infant day care, or explanations of how time-off will interfere with promotion, or just why we need a new car rather than an old clunker. Babies are really just like their older brothers and sisters. They just want our time—dumb time. For the early years, especially, we should make sure there's plenty of that available for them.

Raising a Gifted Child

In *Educating the Infant and Toddler,* Burton White describes the way parents raised their bright and gifted children:

1. Parents identified the interests of their child and talked about them.
2. Parents talked to the child fifteen or twenty times each hour, but rarely for more than thirty seconds at a time.
3. Parents rarely "taught" or lectured the kids.
4. Parents spoke in full sentences, using words slightly above the child's apparent level of comprehension.
5. Parents read picture books and stories to the child from infancy.

Chapter 6

When the kids act up:
Distraction is not discipline

Whatever happened to discipline in families? I ask this at the Cincinnati airport as I watch a 10-year-old run the perimeter of the departure lounge at headlong speed. His mother has said, "Johnny, stop!" several times but seems unconcerned that Johnny's operative mode is still "full speed ahead." My fellow passengers, annoyed enough to look up from their newspapers to glare at Johnny and his mother, apparently don't feel that they have the right to say anything. The airline personnel, obviously instructed not to upset either parents or small children, keep their eyes focused on their computer terminals. We are all hoping, perhaps, that Johnny will tire of this game and call it quits. Or perhaps we are secretly expecting that Johnny will run into a pillar so that there will be some real-life consequences to his generally annoying behavior.

None of us seems to expect any discipline to take place. Sometimes I think this has happened because the idea of discipline was besmirched by its connection to the military, an institution that is no longer much honored by society. Discipline has come to mean making your bed one more time or else it's potato-peeling-duty for you, Charlie. There is an arbitrary quality to discipline that conflicts with many of our ideals of an egalitarian, rational society. While we admire discipline when we see it, as in Olympic synchronized swimmers or the Vienna choirboys, we don't much like being at the receiving end of it. Nor do we as parents like the idea of being considered "disciplinarians" ourselves. Better that we should discuss situations with our children, consider alternatives, offer distractions, or somehow avoid that dreadful and final word, "no." We feel that parents must, above all, be nice.

This is a fairly new development. At one time, parents were expected to be highly arbitrary in an effort to give their children "character," a word that was once connected to phrases like "moral fiber." Moral fiber, like a nutritious breakfast cereal, was good for you. The opposite, moral corruption, led to criminality, early death and—in the case of masturbation—blindness. Science ultimately couldn't support the blindness connection, but the other links still stand up reasonably well to sophisticated computer analysis.

There are, it must be admitted, some very real benefits in the arbitrary quality of traditional family discipline. First, old-style family discipline prepares young people for an adult world that can be quite irrational in its behavior and obnoxiously arbitrary in its expectations. A child who ends up working at Sears or K-Mart will be told that she is expected to stand beside the cash register at all times and be pleasant to customers regardless of their sometimes surly dispositions. These are highly arbitrary requirements and only partially rational in terms of making the store function, but it's what our kids might have to do to earn cash. It does them no service to pretend that complaining to me or submitting complaints to the Human Rights Commission are going to produce a more sensible universe.

Second, the very arbitrariness of parental decision making leaves kids free to make their own judgment calls on the deep issues involved. I can tell my son that there's no way he's going to become the next Tiger Woods, so he can just forget about $600 for new golf clubs. But that still leaves the kid free to fantasize about his future career in the PGA and free, as well, to find some way to make the money for the golf clubs of his dreams.

Third, the legal and social structure of our society is such that parents really *are* responsible for a host of actions by the kids—from going to school every day, to repairing windows that errant baseballs have smashed, to making sure the kids don't throw the appetizers while attending Aunt Emily's wedding reception. With responsibility goes power, and parents are still expected to exercise it.

In the 1960s and '70s, however, traditional, arbitrary parenting was challenged by a whole group of psychologists who maintained that it was either fascist or ineffective, or both. "Power assertion," as the psychologists called it, was seen as crude, destructive and suitable only for parents of limited intelligence or creativity. Thomas Gordon, who wrote the popular *P. E. T. (Parent Effectiveness Training)* book, maintained that whenever parents "won" in conflicts with their children there were terrible consequences. Any parent victory ". . . sows the seeds for a continuously deteriorating relationship between parent and child. Resentment and hate replace love and affection." A pretty scary prognosis.

> **Research never suggested that family discipline was unnecessary or that efforts at discipline should be given up altogether.**

At the same time, an increasing amount of research into disciplinary techniques led to a number of fairly solid conclusions about what really works in disciplining kids. Praise, for instance, was shown to work wonders. So does discussion. Research by Sears, Maccoby and Levin back in 1957 showed that praise for good behavior and reasonable discussion of problem areas tended to produce kids who internalized parental values. The flip side of "aversive stimuli"—getting yelled at or hit by a parent—produces an immediate short-term correction in a child's behavior but does little to affect the child's deep value system. The conclusion in terms of discipline was obvious: Don't hit—talk. But such research never suggested that family discipline was unnecessary or that efforts at discipline should be given up altogether.

Researchers find that parents use many, many different techniques in disciplining their children between the polarities of praise and beating. Caroline Piorowski, for instance, recently researched twelve types of interventions by mothers. She surveyed parents on the use of eight "low-power" strategies—discussion, apologies, separating or isolating the troublemaker, distraction, comforting, using reasoning, inducing guilt and consciously taking

no action. Then she asked about four high-power strategies—
yelling, commanding, threatening and physical punishment. She
found that most parents have far more techniques of disciplining
kids than the average artist has colors dabbed on a pallet.

Many writers have pointed out that there are still more
variables in how we discipline children: child's age and
temperament, warmth of the parent, responsiveness to the child,
nature of the misdeed, threats to autonomy of the child, rules of the
parent . . . the list goes on. The various combinations and
permutations of all these categories become factors in determining
just how a parent should deal with a particular situation.

Is it any wonder that parents have become confused?

In the midst of this confusion, many parents found an easy way
out—distraction. If traditional discipline is "bad" and more
sophisticated discipline confusing, time-consuming or just impossible in real life, then it's so much easier not to discipline at all. Distraction was the alternative, at least for little kids. If a kid won't eat his green beans, and we don't have time

> Parents who distract their children all the time fail to teach kids how to contain themselves, one of the truly essential abilities in becoming an adult.

to encourage, wheedle, whine or demand . . . we put Cool Whip
topping on them. Distraction makes the distasteful aspects of
growing up more palatable, it seems, and takes the edge off of
difficulty. We've all used the technique.

"Mom, I want to go home. I'm tired. I don't want to do this
hike any more."

"Yes, you do."

"No, I don't. I want to go home."

"How about I give you a candy bar for energy and then we
finish the hike."

"Okay. Can I have it right now?"

Providing that there is something available with which to
distract (gum, candy bar, toy, video), children can be deflected from
going after what they really want by accepting whatever it is we give

them. The richer the family, the more elaborate such distraction—or bribery—can become.

No one seriously maintains that distraction can replace real discipline, but it is one technique for maintaining order around the house. The only problems arise when distraction is used too often, as I'll discuss more fully in chapters 7 and 8. Parents who distract their children all the time fail to teach kids how to contain themselves, one of the truly essential abilities in becoming an adult. Such containment—the capacity to live a life without *immediate* rewards, mouth-stuffers, praise, entertainment or new consumer goods—is learned best in homes where there is real discipline.

What is real discipline?

Real family discipline suggests that there will be certain basic standards of behavior in a household because—even though there may be adequate rational reasons—that's just how mom and dad have set it up. While such an approach might seem arbitrary to kids practicing now to join the legal profession later, it can be remarkably reassuring for children to know that vast portions of the universe simply are the way they are. No 5-year-old, or 15-year-old for that matter, really wants to be in a position to create or define the universe. It's exhausting. It's scary. And it's fraudulent.

Let's consider 11-year-old Jackson arguing with his mother.

"Why can't I have a soda?" he demands. The day is hot, school was grueling.

"You can't." Mom is working on income-tax forms. This, too, is grueling.

"Why?"

"There's no soda in the house."

"I'll go to the store and buy some." He reaches down for his Doc Martens.

"No."

"What do you mean, no? We've got money. I'll go myself."

"No," mom repeats. "You already had two sodas today. That's enough. Drink water."

"Mo-o-m! Nobody drinks water. You drink soda all the time yourself. You're a hypocrite. You have a double standard."

"No."

There is a pause. Jackson studies his mother's face.

"No," she repeats.

"No?" he asks.

"No."

Jackson looks disgusted, tosses his boots on the floor and proceeds to flop in front of the television. Five minutes later, having forgotten all this, he goes to get a drink of water and asks, "Hey, what's for dinner?"

Jackson's mother could have behaved differently. Some parents, tired, disinterested or unwilling to make a scene, could simply have produced the soda or provided money so the soda could be purchased. An educated, liberal parent, perhaps, would have launched into a lengthy explanation on why soda or its sugar content are evil; she would have explained why pop at 4:00 P.M. interferes with dinner at 5:30; she would have discussed the health implications of Jackson's satisfying his thirst with expensive, commercial drinks as opposed to simple H_2O from the tap.

But Jackson's mother offered two solid explanations and then said no. She repeated no throughout the conversation, until the message got across. In a relatively mild form, she thus inculcated discipline. At age eleven, Jackson is angry—but not terrifically so. At age forty, he may understand why his mother's constancy helped turn him into a reasonable adult.

The idea behind arbitrary discipline is not that we become the "brick wall" parents Barbara Coloroso attacks or that we become so unthinking that our rules become disconnected from real-life needs. The idea is that our external discipline—that container limiting the activities of childhood—becomes internalized so the child grows to have *self*-discipline as an adult. This is what Freud talked about as he describes the development of the superego. In order for this process of creating self-discipline to take place, parents must set some limits on a child's behavior.

Where there are no limits, there can be no testing and evaluation of limits, and a child's time is spent needlessly trying to find where the limits really are. A child who has to spend all his time looking for limits, for the walls of the container, won't have enough time left to explore all the space that's inside.

It would be nice if limits could always be set in a pleasant, cheerful and rational way. It would be lovely, for instance, if the first time a parent said, "Pick up your socks please, darling," a daughter cheerfully replied, "Of course, mom, I'd be delighted." It is far more likely, however, that parents will have forgotten the "please" and the "darling" and that children will barely look up from the television to respond. Ultimately this devolves into orders such as, "Socks— now!" and some grudging action by our children. Social scientists refer to such expressions and the tone of voice that accompanies them as "power assertive" strategies. Such strategies may well lead to resentment and certainly have no correlation with whether your daughter will have a neat house as an adult, but they do get socks off the floor.

Of course, the cheerful but impossible parenting models that we see trotted out in magazine articles on "good" parenting will work with some children, some days. Those wonderful esteem-building charts and heaps of parental praise for kids who pick up their socks may also succeed in keeping our floors relatively neat and tidy. But I suspect real discipline comes from parents who are capable of saying "Socks—now!" and who require some fairly immediate compliance from their children.

Kids often get noisy when limits are set or enforced

A notion seems to be floating around that parents can somehow raise children without conflict, without having to raise their voices and without having any serious discipline problems. I suspect the notion is drawn from television. Television programs often display disagreements between parents and kids, but they're usually resolved with a few jokes, a little talk and a mutually acceptable resolution to the problem. This model of "civilized" parent-kid conflict goes back to the 1960s, when TV's Ozzie Nelson would have had a disagreement with his son David, for example, on whether the kid should have a key to the house. David finally got his key 22 minutes later, but this required only a little discussion and some parental soul-searching. There was nothing approaching an argument.

Similar patterns of civilized disagreement continue to dominate the images of family life on television. If Theo on *The Cosby Show* makes too much noise bouncing his basketball, Dr. Huxtable can resolve the problem with a little humor, a little talk and a little ball-playing of his own. Family members on television situation comedies do not ordinarily raise their voices or get angry unless it's a set-up to a joke. The one popular exception to this generalization, of course, is the husband on *Married . . . with Children*. Al Bundy, like Archie Bunker before him, does get angry, set limits and otherwise attempt to discipline his kids. He is always markedly unsuccessful because Al Bundy is portrayed as a fool; he's sabotaged by his wife; and his children are viciously clever. Nonetheless, if Al Bundy is our only media model for parenting that offers containment and is unafraid of conflict, it's no wonder that parents are getting a skewed image of how normal families operate.

Make no mistake—when we frustrate our children, the conflict will be noisy. Babies have temper tantrums, little kids have snit-fits and teenagers stomp off to stay with their friends. None of this is pleasant, but parents have to withstand the distress if they're going to provide real discipline for the kids.

Real discipline provides a fairly consistent sense of what is a no-go within the family. If a child leaves his socks on the floor, a parent will bug him. If a child hits his brother with a balled-up sock, a parent will say stop. If the balled-up sock bounces off the brother, hits an antique vase at grandma's house and causes it to topple, both the child and his parents will be in deep, deep trouble. Good discipline helps to control sock behavior—both real and metaphorical—before such behavior damages the antique vases of life.

Discipline also provides another terribly important quality in a child's life—predictability. In family life, predictability is probably more important than parents' skills in offering intellectual justifications for their decisions. Judy Dunn's lifelong research into sibling behavior has shown, for instance, that elaborate explanations by parents to children have virtually no effect on how often kids argue with each other. It is parental attention and the structure of the home environment that make a difference.

For parents who cannot impose discipline, or feel the need

to devise a new discipline for each situation, a child faces soul-destroying unpredictability. There is literally no comfort for a child to know that 90 percent of the time he can get away with almost anything if there is the fear that 10 percent of the time his parents will explode into rage or violence. This is the situation frequently faced by the children of alcoholics and drug abusers, a world none of us would wish on our own children.

The creation of discipline—as a container—can involve any number of parenting techniques, from setting an example or making a suggestion to raising one's voice or actually punishing a child who violates the norms of family behavior. In Stephen and Marianne Garber's *Good Behavior*, a book that promises 1,200 solutions to children's problems, there are a number of very clever and sensible disciplinary methods. These include, to keep tossing around my sock metaphor:

- Listening and talking—whereby the virtues of a sock-free floor are discussed, various views are considered and then a parent finally sets down the rules;
- Real-life consequences—whereby socks are left on the floor until the child has no clean socks to wear;
- Over-correction—whereby a kid practices good behaviors (picking up his socks) *ad nauseum*, so that bad behaviors (leaving socks on the floor) do not seem worth the hassle;
- Charts—whereby "sock offenses" are recorded on charts with notations that urge gradual improvement (conversely, more upbeat parents might record "good sock" days);
- Time-out—whereby a child is stuck in an agreed-upon dull place, such as an empty hallway, for two to five minutes so that an awareness is gained that sock habits need improvement;
- Broken-record—whereby a parent repeats a request for sock pick-up often enough to break through the sometimes headphone-blocked ears of the child.

The broken-record technique, often a good strategy for dealing with truculent staff at department-store return desks, is usually seen by kids as nagging. Nagging, of course, is a tried and true parental technique that has been developed into a kind of art form in some families. An enterprising woman in Berkeley, California, has recently begun to sell a CD for parents who are reluctant to nag or who wish to automate the process. The CD, *I'll Say It Again*, contains 24 nags on themes ranging from "Clean your room!" to "Mow the lawn!"— though personally I have nagging doubts about replacing parents with electronics, as I'll explain in chapter 17.

All of these techniques assume that discipline is entirely in the hands of the parents. This ought not to be so. Children who grow up in communities with coherent values—whatever those values may be—are better off than those who face conflicting values at home and in the outside world. That outside world has its own systems for creating discipline. On the side of psychological "reinforcement," there's getting a straight-A report card or a set of Boy Scout merit badges for mastering certain skills. On the "aversive" side are consequences for obnoxious behavior, such as getting sent to the principal's office at school or being sent home from the Boy Scout Jamboree.

> Children who grow up in communities with coherent values . . . are better off than those who face conflicting values at home and in the outside world.

All these examples of a community value system can reinforce what parents are doing at home. One of the many good reasons to get our kids out into the community is so that they can see, in real life, how our home value systems have prepared them for the expectations of the larger world. Earning an allowance, taking music lessons, delivering the daily paper, being on a sports team, going to church, being civilized at dinner, volunteering at a seniors' home and many other activities all help discipline kids. It's not our job alone to help kids grow up to be decent adults. But it is our job to get them started.

And when our kids break the bounds of discipline, it's our job to punish them. That's the next chapter.

A Few Do's and Don'ts about Discipline

Research by Mancuso and Lehrer shows that much discipline is really just communication; hence

1. **Do** be clear about family ground rules and what you expect in particular situations.
2. **Do** be positive when your child does something well. A spoonful of honey . . .
3. **Do** explain, as much as you can, why you expect something to be done. This helps your kid to grow up to be rational.
4. **Do** speak up about what bugs you. Internal fuming is not productive and might push you to "lose it" when you punish.
5. **Do** punish "transgressions." Ignoring or laughing these off helps nobody.
6. **Don't** turn a talk into a lecture.
7. **Don't** bring up ancient history ("This is just like what you did last year . . . ").
8. **Don't** compare the child to his siblings ("If only you were like your sister . . . ").
9. **Don't** generalize about what the child does to include remarks on his character. If you call your kid a slob repeatedly, he just might be a slob for life.
10. **Don't** "lose it" when you punish. The child will only think you're crazy and won't get the real message.

Chapter 7

The bottom line:

How did a simple spank ever get confused with child abuse?

No issue in parenting is as fraught with difficulty as that of punishment—and no single technique generates such heated discussion as that of spanking. Clever parents have several dozen other ways of punishing a child for various offenses against family and social order. There are parents who effectively use a whole variety of withholdings as punishments, ranging from "No, you can't watch *The Simpsons* after speaking to your brother like that," to "That'll cost you 35 cents from this week's allowance." There are parents whose frown and creased brow are so powerful that they can stop a child's errant behavior at thirty paces. There are parents who really do use charts to reward good behaviors and punish bad ones. There are parents whose voices are so fearsome and whose children are so timid that a simple "No!" can reduce a child to tears.

Then there are all the rest of us.

For the rest us, the real-life parents, our capacity to stop a child who is about to hurt himself or someone else, or to restore order for a child who is about to reduce his personal universe to chaos, varies with our mood and energy. Only in the television world can mom and dad remain sensible, clever and psychologically correct at all times.

Five Sensible Ways to Handle Discipline without Spanking

1. Discussion ("Okay, we're going to talk about this . . . ")
2. Time-out ("Go to your chair for five minutes.")
3. Power assertion ("The rule is . . . so stop!")
4. Obvious parental displeasure ("Please do not splash the water."—with *major frown*)
5. Fines ("That'll cost you 25 cents or one load of dishwashing, kid.")

For such fantasy parents, there are no bad days at work, no traumas over the monthly bills, no arguments with a spouse or partner. For the rest of us, we approach parenting with the baggage of real life. There are days when those socks on the floor are charming, when bending over to pick them up is needed exercise, when the children shouldn't be troubled with such trivial matters. And there are days when those socks are one more assault on a harried parent, when cleaning up someone else's mess is an affront to us, God and the universe, when a sock on the floor seems connected to every kind of worldly distress, from Bosnia to the decline of the church. It is at times like these that a kid, after having been told three times to stop bouncing on the sofa, is likely to get a spank.

Is this intelligent or fair? No. But is it a terrible thing—such a loss of control that a parent should be consumed with guilt? I don't think so. In fact, there are times when a spank is really the most effective punishment, one that will both stop the immediate problem and maintain the disciplinary boundary that is so essential for a child growing up.

Spanking and parental guilt

In recent years, among the social groups who would be most likely to read this book, spanking has become a kind of parental no-no. This does not mean it isn't done, but that it is done with increasing amounts of parental guilt and recrimination.

I've been discovering this spanking guilt everywhere—at PTA meetings, in parenting classes, at coffee klatches, in discussions with my own family. Fifty years ago, literally all parents spanked their kids, sometimes without real cause, because they thought spanking was "good for them." Now, a majority of parents still spank their kids, but they do so with increasing regret.

"I spanked my child only once," said one mother. We were at a potluck supper and I had raised the issue. "I felt guilty for months."

"What had he done?" I asked.

"We were in the supermarket by one of those stacked-up can displays. I had told him not to touch it, again and again. But Jeffrey just reached out, grabbed a can, and then the whole display began falling over."

"So you spanked him."

"Yes, and I felt terrible," said the mother.

"You talked to your child beforehand about proper behavior," I said, trying to get the facts straight. "You repeated the instruction and he disobeyed. He might have hurt himself, or you or anybody else nearby. And you feel guilty for a spank?"

She laughed, nervously. "Yeah, I still do."

"Well, it sounds like a pretty reasonable spank to me," commented one of the older parents at the table.

"And me," said another.

"Oh, no," protested a new mom. "That was the wrong thing to do."

"That's right," echoed another young parent. "You should have called 'time-out' and sent him to sit on his chair."

"There was no chair," I pointed out, just for accuracy.

"So what makes you think solitary confinement is more noble than spanking?" someone else shouted.

Then the entire discussion became polarized: The older parents nodded approval of the spanking and the younger parents shook their heads in dismay.

"But spanking is hitting," said one of the younger moms.

"No, it's not," replied an older woman. "There's a big difference between a spank and beating up a kid. It's just not the same thing. Believe me, I *know.*"

Our conversation got sidetracked on one of those basic definition problems. What's a spank, a spanking and a beating? This problem leads to outrage on one side and careful explanations on the other. It's one reason why Benjamin Spock treats the issue of spanking so gingerly in his famous *Baby and Child Care*. In all of the editions until 1992, he wrote that physical punishment should be *avoided* because it often does not stop the child's offending actions, it is a poor model of behavior for children and there's too much violence in America already. But Spock never came out and said *don't spank*.

Similarly, Burton White looked long and hard to find some statistical evidence that spanking, which he personally opposes, somehow resulted in damaged or stunted children. In his 13-year-long Harvard Preschool Project, which produced so many insights for *The First Three Years of Life* and other books, he simply could not find any evidence "that spanking either harms or hurts between seven months and two years of age."

What Spock, White and other pediatricians fear is parents who cannot differentiate between a spank and a beating. There actually are parents out there whose spanking can turn into a physical punishment that brings bruised children into hospital emergency rooms. While the distinction between a spank and a beating seems obvious to me, let me define what I call a spank just for some initial clarity:

1. A spank is a swift application of the parent's open hand to the child's bottom. A spank is virtually useless with infants, who can't understand what it means, and inadvisable with children after the age of nine or so, when a parent should be able to use other punishments to emphasize a point.

2. A spank is done only once or, at most, twice. It follows immediately upon the absolutely egregious behavior that caused the parent to become upset. A spank is *never* used as an everyday form of discipline.

3. A spank inflicts some pain—often both to the parent and the child—but never does the spank inflict long-term physical damage upon the child.

4. The power of a spank is not related to the pain it causes, but to the emotional and moral manner in which it is applied. A real spank is more symbolic than physical.

5. Parents who hit a child with closed hands or fists, parents who assault children with rulers, pieces of wood or other weapons, or parents who feel that spankings ought to be given regularly, regardless of the offense, need serious re-education in parenting.

Is a spank such a highly desirable form of punishment that it should be used with all children whenever they transgress against parental rules? Obviously not. But neither is a spank such a heinous action that parents should feel guilty about it for months afterward. Far crueler things are done to children by well-meaning parents than simply giving them a spank as the physical emphatic of "No!" A survey of published biographies will reveal many accounts of people who suffered beatings, neglect, abandonment, sexual abuse, parental coldness and emotional guilt-tripping as children. These writers rightfully blame their parents for such treatment. But few adults write about, or even much recall, an occasional spank while growing up. It's just not that important. Only in today's charged political climate could a single means of punishment become the subject of so much debate.

Spanking as a political issue

In Canada, spanking has become a hot political issue ever since a visitor from Michigan was charged with assault when bystanders observed him giving a bare-bottom spanking to his daughter. The girl had closed a car door on her older brother's hand and the father apparently "lost it." There was a significant hue-and-cry about the spanking, some applause for the citizens who intervened on the child's behalf, and some response by the political right wing, who seemed to feel the father wasn't entirely out to lunch on the matter.

Ultimately, the charges against the father couldn't be sustained because Section 43 of the Canadian criminal code permits parents and people acting in the place of parents (teachers, daycare workers, guardians) to make use of "reasonable force" in correcting young people. Section 43 used to be a legal shield for school officials who administered the strap to students. These days, the strap has largely disappeared from schools and Section 43 is under fire from people who think it's high time spanking and other forms of corporal punishment disappeared altogether. Joining in the fight against spanking is a powerful book, *Physical Violence in the American Family*, by the United States's foremost expert on disciplining children, Murray Straus.

> [One study found that] kids who are occasionally spanked end up behaving pretty much the same as the small group of kids who are never spanked at all.

All of these anti-spanking advocates tend to lump together spanking, beating children, child abuse and corporal punishment in the schools. This leads to a powerful argument, but one with inherent flaws. To put it simply, a spank by a parent whose child has just darted into a busy street is not the same as a beating that escalates and brings a kid into the hospital. Nor do either of these have that much in common with a strapping or a caning by school officials. All of these items, unfortunately, get lumped together by those who would criminalize spanking.

This same lumped-together confusion has marked almost all the research done into spanking for the last 50 years. When Zvi Strassberg and his colleagues at Vanderbilt University wrote a new academic study on spanking in 1994, he began with a survey of the available psychological and sociological articles on the issue, but he had to conclude that "no study has distinguished between spanking and other disciplinary practices . . . including the extremes of violent discipline." This is a serious problem that calls into question much previous research. Many studies have concluded that spanking is ineffective, that it leads to greater parental violence, that it's done more by uneducated parents, that kids who are spanked are more aggressive in school and grow up to commit more juvenile crime. The trouble is, these studies lump together kids who are spanked—virtually everyone, that is—with kids who are beaten. When Strassberg separated out that data for kids who are beaten, he found that kids who are occasionally spanked end up behaving pretty much the same as the small group of kids who are never spanked at all.

Strassberg's study of 273 kindergarten kids in Tennessee and Indiana was carefully designed to differentiate among kids who were spanked occasionally, those who were spanked a lot and those who were beaten. He also studied 16 kids who weren't spanked at all, at least according to their parents. Strassberg's group set up questionnaires and interviewed parents, then observed the kids in school playgrounds to see if spanking made a difference in how the children behaved. Some of what the researchers found backed up previous studies. For instance, the higher a family's socioeconomic status, the less a child tended to be spanked in the home. As well, children who were classed as coming from "violent" families tended to be much more aggressive and bullying in the school playground.

The surprise in Strassberg's research was that the frequency of spanking by parents seemed to have little effect on the number of playground incidents unless the kids came from "violent" families. More important, children who were spanked occasionally weren't much more aggressive in the playground than kids who weren't spanked at all. Spanking by fathers was particularly unimportant, leading to no difference in the observed number of "bullying" and "instrumental" aggressive acts ("I want your football!") in the playground. I have to admit that spanking by mothers did have a significant effect, especially in bullying on the playground, but no kind of occasional spanking came close to producing the large number of aggressive acts committed by kids who were beaten by their parents.

Strassberg concludes the study by saying that spanking is an ineffective means of discipline and he wishes, frankly, that it would end. In doing so, he joins almost every other psychologist and sociologist who has come out in print on the issue: Spanking is a no-no. But when we look at Strassberg's data, we find that spanking—as opposed to beating—doesn't produce kids who are monsters. In the case of what Strassberg calls "reactive" aggression, it simply produces kids who make a fuss when somebody else tries to take away their ball. Many adults would not consider this unreasonable at all.

Anti-spanking proponents often point out that a growing number of countries around the world have outlawed spanking. This is a movement that began in Sweden in 1979 and has grown to include Denmark, Finland, Norway, Austria and Cyprus. It's possible that Germany and Ireland might have "outlawed" spanking by the time this book sees print. Why shouldn't the United States join such civilized countries?

My answer would be primarily because the legal change doesn't seem to have much real-life effect. In Sweden, public support for spanking has dropped each year since the legislation, but the effect on actual cases of child abuse has been minimal. Ironically, reports of children hitting other children in Sweden have skyrocketed since the legal ban on spanking was introduced, but it's still foolish to make a connection. There are too many other factors—from TV violence to family breakdown—that are affecting rates of aggression among children. For the other five countries, results are simply inconclusive. Cyprus, for instance, never did have much juvenile crime, nor did most parents tolerate their children being "paddled" in school. Day to day, not much has changed there.

This brings us back to North America. Should we outlaw strapping and paddling in the schools? Probably. It never did work very well. In the days when we still had physical punishment in schools where I worked, I recall that most students chose "the strap" because it seemed a far easier punishment than being kept out of class or sent home to their parents. Why should schools maintain a repugnant punishment when far more effective ones are easily available?

But the question of a spank at home is very different. When the Canadian Pediatric Society considered the issue in 1996, the doctors simply refused to rule out parental spanking. "Overall, we are strongly discouraging any kind of spanking in 99 percent of cases," said their spokesperson, Dr. Emmett Francoeur. "But there has to be the 1 percent." The American Academy of Pediatrics conducted a survey of 603 members that found more than half of those surveyed were "generally opposed" to the use of corporal punishment, but that they believe that "an occasional spanking under certain circumstances can be an effective form of discipline." Frankly, I agree. Spanking is not a desirable form of punishment, nor should it ever be used on a regular basis with children. But there are times and situations when parents need to be able to spank their children.

Four reasonable spanks

Let's begin by assuming that good parents do not use a spank as a day-to-day punishment but as one reserved for certain very special and very essential moments of parenting. A spank is obviously not an appropriate response to a child who dirties his jeans or pours jellybeans on the floor. But there is a role for a spank as an *absolute* response—a symbolic gesture that says, "You must not ever do this again!" Most good parents use a spank in this way.

Statistically, almost all parents spank their children at one time or another. In 1986, researcher Barbara Carsen screened a group of 1,000 parents for a study on spanking but could only find 21 who had never spanked their children. Another study, this time based on a written survey, found that 90 percent of parents of children aged three and four said that they spanked their kids, though only 70 percent thought it was a good idea. Some of these parents, without a doubt, spanked too much, in the wrong context or for the wrong reasons. But after considerable discussion on the issue with parents across the country, I suggest there are proper contexts and reasons for giving a child a spank. Here are four of them:

1. **When the child is about to do something so immediately and terribly dangerous that he will be marked or mutilated for life.** Hopefully this spank will occur *before* the child disobeys our much-repeated instruction not to run out in the street. Hopefully, too, it occurs before he connects with the front end of a passing dump truck.
2. **When the child is about to strike a parent or a sibling with an instrument likely to inflict serious pain or permanent bodily damage.** A child about to stick a fork into his brother's ear needs immediate and forceful correction. Discussion should follow, not precede the punishment.
3. **When the child disobeys any ordinary rules of social behavior and does something so offensive, in context, that he and his parents will be shunned for the rest of their natural lives.** When, at grandma's seventieth birthday

party, the child begins tossing pieces of cake at the guests—and ultimately at grandma—he does not need a copy of *Miss Manners*. He deserves to be taken aside from the group, given a quick spank and then a serious talking-to.

4. **When the child violates the family order to the extent that the entire structure of the household is threatened by his disobedience.** The first time the child looks either parent in the eye and suggests in vociferous and foul language that we take a long walk off a short pier, he deserves a spank.

Yes, any of these events could be dealt with by other means of punishment, from earnest discussion to withholding allowance to being sent to the bedroom. But I recommend a spank for one very solid reason: A spank sometimes works better to *contain* the child, especially a young child, and to contain us as parents.

Children are not naturally contained by themselves, either physically or emotionally. They are born as creatures who spit up, pee into diapers and projectile vomit onto our shoulders—activities to which we respond, amazingly, by cuddling, kissing and holding them close. This *containment* of a baby is an essential aspect of parenting. Children who grow up in the absence of such care, those feral children of anthropology or those neglected children of parents addicted to crack cocaine, are psychologically crippled for life. A child does not spontaneously civilize himself; he is civilized within a family and a society.

> A spank . . . is not a gesture to be used thoughtlessly, regularly, or in response to anything but the most extraordinary types of provocation.

As a child becomes older, he requires a different kind of *containment*. A child is not served by parents whose every response is, "Yes, sure, do what you want." A family that seems to have no limits on behavior will simply inspire a child to push hard enough to find whatever limits there are, and then get the attention that comes with testing them. For children, the advantage of parents who provide containment is that there are observable and definable limits to be railed against, subverted and defied. But within those limits is a very safe territory, a realm for all sorts of behavior and experimentation that is both approved and protected.

A spank, I would maintain, marks the edge of the container. It is not a gesture to be used thoughtlessly, regularly, or in response to anything but the most extraordinary types of provocation. For parents who were abused themselves as children, or are given to uncontrollable outbursts of temper, it should not be used at all. But for most parents, an occasional spank is a reasonable punishment to show that the family container is in place, that there are kinds of activity and behavior that are out-of-bounds. In this sense, a spank is symbolic. A spank may never or rarely be used, but it symbolically represents the power of the parents to establish the outside limits of order in the household.

> For most of us, there is a mutual regret that follows a spank that settles both parent and child.

But couldn't parents do something else, something without violence?

Yes and no. We cannot, with young children, turn them out of the house or drop them off at the Children's Aid Society. Even the threat of such action is far more cruel than a spank. Nor are we always in a position to reason with the kids, mark the chart, dock the allowance or send them to their room—and such responses are far too mild for the extreme situations that warrant a spank. While any family ought to be clear about its limits and expectations beforehand, a spank will at least make those clear afterward. A good parent who spanks a child will find an opportunity to talk about the event and her reaction later, when both have cooled down. That talk is important, but the emotional and symbolic aspects of a spank make it effective.

The last virtue of a spank is that it works wonders in calming parents. Invariably, the point at which a child warrants a spank is never very far away from the point at which a parent is going to lose control of his own behavior. A spank, fortunately, stops both the child's behavior and the growing build-up of anger in the parent that can ultimately lash out in terrible emotional and physical ways. For most of us, there is a mutual regret that follows a spank that settles both parent and child.

"But how," asks one mother, "can you love a child and cause physical pain by spanking him?"

Precisely because you *do* love the child.

There is no point in police officers spanking young offenders or teachers spanking students, because such a spank has no symbolic meaning in those relationships. Similarly, a spank is ridiculous with a 17-year-old who is far more worried about the state of his allowance or his driving privileges than whatever pain we might deliver to his backside. Spanking older children is simply humiliating for them—and this is never an effective technique for discipline. Ultimately, our power as parents is in our moral position and the shame our words can engender—and these, too, should be used carefully with children of any age.

Nonetheless, there are good reasons for a parent, at appropriate moments, to spank a young child to show what the limits are. The spank says, "You've gone too far. Come back to where my love can hold you." It is ironic that a spank, hardly a gracious or cool gesture, can somehow be an act of love. But there are many ironies in parenting that happen to be true.

Five Reasons Children Need Us to Contain Their Behavior

1. So they can internalize a solid value system
2. So they can deal with the world outside the family in ways that won't embarrass the family or themselves
3. So they'll learn to stop doing things that are dangerous or socially repugnant
4. So they don't have to keep pushing the boundaries to know that we love them enough to set limits
5. Because correction by someone who loves you is so much better than correction by a teacher, a boss, a cop or a judge

Chapter 8

Children in public:
Little tyrants at restaurants and other public places

It is a perilous enterprise to take our children out to a restaurant. They—and we—are on display, seated at a table with knives, forks and water glasses, at the mercy of waiters who don't understand kids or how useful a set of crayons might be, under the disdainful eye of other adult patrons who want our children to be cute, silent and still. Invariably our children are none of these. They make faces or stick out their tongues at other diners, sing too loud, babble too much, argue with each other, wiggle in their seats and have no qualms about disappearing either under the table or out the restaurant door. We end up angry, irritable and, depending on the food, dyspeptic.

The alternative, of course, is fast food. Is it any wonder that McDonald's racked up more than $15 billion in North American sales last year?

Forty years ago, when Ray Kroc set up the first McDonald's, children did not go to restaurants often. Neither did the rest of us. The remarkable growth of restaurant dining that took place in the 1960s and '70s, which coincided neatly with a marked increase in families where both partners worked, has left us in the 1990s with the average family spending up to a quarter of its yearly food budget on restaurant fare.

Over the same time span, restaurants have become divided into various subtypes. In the 1950s, most restaurants were of the "family dining" variety ("You want gravy with that, honey?") and a few were of the "fine dining" sort ("May I refill your water glass, madam?"). Children were expected at the family restaurants, immediately provided with crayons or dinner rolls, and the whole family was hustled out again in 45 minutes with plenty of time left to watch *The Wonderful World of Disney* on the black-and-white TV. If the children did misbehave, the noise was lost in the ambient background of French fries frying and juke boxes wailing.

At fine dining establishments, children were almost never seen. When they did appear, children were so cowed by heavy-duty lectures on behavior and so starched within their dress-up clothes that they often got through the meal in a state of terror and amazement, which is to say, with considerable decorum.

When restaurants began to proliferate in the 1970s, they also divided into new types: fast food, wings 'n' ribs, steakhouse, pizza and pasta, roadhouse, ethnic, bistro and trattoria. The precise role of children in these many different types of restaurants has become much harder to define. At many fast-food establishments, the menu and the dining experience seem designed expressly for children. The average fast-food meal lasts twenty minutes; the restaurant seats and tables are plastic and can be cleaned with a wipe; and many locations come complete with a playground so that the little ones can wolf down their Real Meal deals and rush off to play.

There are really no expectations on children's behavior at fast-food restaurants except that the kids not throw food at other patrons. Clearly this represents one approach to establishing manners and decorum involving children (that is, don't bother). Provide entertainment, games, coloring books, movies, a jungle gym and other means of amusement that previously would have been more appropriate to a playground than a dining establishment. By cleverly arranging the environment to accommodate children rather than asking children to adapt to the restaurant environment, fast-food joints have given families what they seem to want.

Problems arise only when we take children who are used to the decorum of a fast-food burger joint to dine in a restaurant where expectations are markedly different. The shift in expectations is not the children's fault, who are rarely prepared in any way for a "fine dining" or even a casual-dining experience. The fault lies with parents who expect proper behavior to happen either miraculously or by osmosis.

Recently we were at a fairly upscale Italian restaurant, a style of dining that does not particularly invite children but doesn't discourage them, either. At two other tables we saw families with fairly young kids, a girl about ten years old, a boy about eight.

The girl was dressed up for the occasion and sat with her parents, another couple who might have been an aunt and uncle, and a set of grandparents. It was a party in honor of the grandfather, whose birthday was celebrated at the end of the meal. What was remarkable for us was the way the girl sat comfortably at the table, waited calmly for her food, doodled occasionally on a pad but just as readily entered into conversation. For two hours, she behaved like a polite, intelligent, but very short adult.

The boy at the other table was also dressed up in white shirt and tie. The shirt was somewhat pulled out and the tie askew, but obviously some effort had gone into dressing for this occasion. Again, it was a fairly large family gathering and this was the only child. The parents had come equipped with toys, coloring books and whatever else was in a pack next to mom, but the boy didn't seem interested in those things. He whined, blew straw wrappers at mom, fidgeted, went frequently to the bathroom, headed off to explore at other tables and, as the parents chit-chatted over liqueurs, finally he went outside to play on the sidewalk. All the diners breathed a sigh of relief at this.

> [Children are] rarely prepared in any way for a "fine dining" or even a casual-dining experience.

What was the difference? The young girl obviously had been prepped on how to behave and was seated right beside mom so she could get lots of attention both of the direct and indirect variety. The boy was seated across from his parents and was basically ignored by the adults throughout the dinner, except when he acted up. At a certain level, I think the boy's family expected him to misbehave just as the first family expected the child to act in a reasonable way.

Afterward, while we were all getting our coats, I complimented the parents of the young girl.

"Your daughter was just wonderful," I said. A sentiment echoed by my wife and one other diner as well.

"She's used to restaurants," said mom. "And this was Grandpa's birthday, so she knew how important that was."

Precisely, I thought. Experience and expectation and a few smarts—just the way to help a kid learn to be civilized.

Out in the parking lot, the second family was collecting their son. I saw dad grab the boy and virtually throw him into the back of the car. Then the mom and dad started cursing the kid, in voices so loud they could be heard through the closed windows of our car. He was terrible, they told him, an embarrassment, a miserable kid, a candidate for Girls and Boys Town if he ever behaved like that again. By the way they were handling the "discipline" and the way they conducted themselves through dinner, I had a hunch that future dining experiences in that family would be no better.

Some who have heard this anecdote come back with that ancient gender excuse, "boys will be boys." This antique expression goes back to 1589, but the sentiment is even older, a sense that boys are innately more troublesome than girls. Unfortunately, there's no real research to back up these sugar-and-spice, rocks-and-snails generalizations. Our kids are born either boy or girl, temperamentally difficult or easy, but their real behavior when they grow up is mostly a function of how we treat them and what we expect. The boy, in this case, wasn't a rude little monster because he was a boy; he was a rude little monster because his parents hadn't helped him prepare for the big family gathering.

> Experience and expectation and a few smarts—just the way to help a kid learn to be civilized.

Ready for the Nobel Prize

Traditional standards for decent behavior used to be established by the general public, not just the individual family. The standard was external, not just the notions of mom and dad. An individual family attempting to establish manners, as parents do today, faces serious obstacles.

When my children were young, we made the usual effort to establish decorum for dining at home. There were napkins—they go on the lap. There is a knife, set to the right, and a fork, set to the left. The fork is held like a pencil, not a screwdriver. One does not slurp. One does not chew with the mouth open.

Invariably, the kids would ask why we had to maintain such behavior at dinnertime.

"Because I want you to be ready when you're asked to dine with the Queen," was our reply.

The idea of dining with the Queen worked wonderfully well when the kids were five and six, because fairy-tale queens could, conceivably, show up for dinner at any moment. But by age ten, the Queen had lost her luster.

"I'm never going to dine with the Queen," said Jason.

"All right, then, with the President. The standard is the same."

"Why would the President want to have dinner with me?"

"After you win the Nobel Prize," I'd say. "To get the money, you have to go to dinner at the Stockholm City Hall. You wouldn't want to use the wrong fork, would you?"

The Queen, in the case of our family, provided a kind of external standard that could be used as a lever to raise the behavior of the kids. It would have been far less powerful to answer the basic challenge, "Why should I do this," by saying, "Because your mom and I want you to." Manners and public behavior require some kind of public standard. But that standard is really in trouble these days.

Of course, standards of public behavior are only required as long as we still have public events. If we all end up huddled in front of our television sets or computer screens, we really won't need public decorum because there won't be any public activities. Fortunately, Bill Gates and Microsoft haven't pushed us there yet.

We still have more than a few public occasions that include children—weddings, funerals, church services, school assemblies, plays and concerts. There are also various occasions when entire families are part of the general public—dining, at airports, in movie theaters, shopping, riding a bus, going to a baseball game. How our children behave at these events says very little about the children and a great deal about our parenting and the expectations that society sets.

Public expectations on behavior, increasingly, are set lower and lower.

I have a friend who is principal of an elementary school that for many years has put on a holiday concert by the kids and for the parents. This year, the school gave up.

"What happened?" I asked.

'They were too unruly," my friend replied.

"The kids?" I jumped in. "You mean the kids can't even sing songs or do a little play?"

"No," she said, "the kids are fine. It's the parents. They show up late and won't sit still. They run up to take pictures when their child's class is on stage, but get up and walk around when another class is up there. Last year, I had to deal with one parent who was falling-down drunk."

One more teacher throws up her hands in despair and the holiday concert gets cancelled. Who loses in this? The kids—and it's not their fault.

Until about forty years ago, most social norms and manners were set by the church. By this I don't mean a single denomination, but by the collective needs of all churches, mosques and synagogues that have children at their services. A religious service is, by its nature, relatively long and boring. I've rarely attended one that clocked in at under an hour and have been at some extended holiday services that pushed two. That much time in a cold, drafty environment sitting on a hard pew—a set of physical hardships relieved only by kneeling for prayer and standing for the occasional hymn—hardly measures up to the comforts expected by a television generation when a commercial break comes up at least three times in every half hour.

But for most of recorded history, human beings were expected to appear regularly at church. This entailed a number of advanced social skills: listening carefully to relatively incomprehensible material (both the Catholic Latin service and the Protestant King James Bible were beyond the reach of many); joining with the group for songs, recitations and physical movement; somehow meditating or praying when called upon, and otherwise staying quiet and still. This last requirement has become a major challenge for children today when every kid seems to have the wiggles and an increasing portion are being diagnosed with attention deficit disorder. For the wiggly tendency we blame sugar, the environment, television, electrical transformers, second-hand smoke and virtually anything else except our declining public standards for behavior.

Yet it is the public standard that is falling. At some point, the entire ethos demanded by the church went into decline and an ethos appropriate to a rock concert became a new kind of social standard. Part of this is the church's own choice—attempting to enliven services, offering texts and prayers in understandable English, shuttling the little kids to Sunday school so only adults have to deal with the full length of the service. Rather than expecting a special and distinct behavior for devotion, the churches began to lift the traditional strictures to lure in a more relaxed generation. What got lost in the shuffle was a particular decorum.

The other establishment that required some kind of special decorum was school. Here, too, the demands of the physical environment led to rules and customs peculiar to the location. Teachers are outnumbered by students thirty to one, yet it is the teachers who are expected to be heard and the children who are expected to listen. Because classrooms are small, acoustically loud, and the odds against a teacher are substantial, society created certain behavioral expectations to make teaching possible: Raise your hand to ask a question, be quiet when the teacher is talking, ask when you have to go to the bathroom, line up for going down the hall.

These standards of decorum, of course, were broken frequently. Standards always are—that's the delight of Romeo and Juliet secretly holding hands at church or any kid pulling the hair of little Sue Ann when teacher isn't looking. But standards do not lose their power because they are occasionally or even frequently broken. They become powerless when they are no longer respected and maintained by the groups in charge. Just as many deacons decided to ease up on behavior at church, so many teachers decided to ease up at school. Raising hands was seen as an interference with spontaneity and self-expression; the idea of transmitting knowledge from teacher to student in relative quiet became replaced with group work and activity-based lessons. I suspect that some portion of this change has been a good thing for the wider education of a broader range of students. But what has been lost, unfortunately, is one more location for learning about public decorum.

Without either the church or the school to establish a standard for social behavior, we fall back once again on the family.

Chimpanzee and human manners

Children learn manners and public behavior the same way they learn anything—mostly by imitation. As Desmond Morris points out so persuasively in *The Naked Ape*, human children are significantly more adept than little chimpanzees in learning things because humans imitate exceedingly well. Young chimps have to be hissed at and cudgeled by their parents into behaving as they ought to. Human children will often behave quite well simply by imitating their elders. This assumes that the elders have manners that are worth imitating, however.

A recent article in our local paper reported that a 5-year-old boy had been accused of swearing at his neighbors. His actions were brought to the attention of his mother, who obviously had her own sense of manners and decorum. The mother told reporters, "He might have told her to f— off," she said, "but he wouldn't have called her a motherf——r."

Every family, obviously, has its standards.

Even where families have a highly developed set of manners, children frequently end up at a level approaching that of their peers. A family down the street from me moved here from London, England, a few years back and their children, initially, had such highly polished Oxbridge manners and accents that all the neighbors were astonished.

"How do you do? I'm Stephen Lestition," said the 8-year-old when he was first introduced. "So pleased to meet you." The young man extended his hand, smiled appropriately and made many of us adults in the room feel vaguely uncouth.

Since then, five years in North America have taken their toll. Stephen is now Steve; he no longer shakes hands; rarely looks adults in the eye; and has mastered the two key phrases in a North American child's vocabulary: "yeah" and "like, you know."

This change in behavior has nothing to do with his parents, who are as British as ever, and everything to do with the other kids in our neighborhood and the norms of our local public schools.

The other kids in the neighborhood imitate their parents, a generation who eschewed earlier forms of politeness for the sort of formless, good-hearted camaraderie appropriate to people who wanted to be at Woodstock but mostly didn't get there. These parents, people of my generation (the first middle-class generation to use four-letter words in polite conversation) are naturally upset that their children too often behave like barbarians. We want the kids to behave better than we do, and many of us are looking desperately for some means to make that happen.

Avoidance, bribery and distraction

Writers whose work appears in parenting magazines frequently tackle the task of establishing manners and appropriate public behavior for children. The usual suggestion is simply to avoid the problem, placating the child by whatever works at the moment. In the magazine *Today's Parent*, Ian Cruickshank examined the problem of airline travel with children in "Travels with My Kids." His article mixes practical suggestions, such as getting a decent seat and wearing clothes that can soak up spilled juice, with classic distraction techniques: stickerbooks, crayons, coloring books, puzzles, toys, headphones and "food, glorious food." Cruickshank does not mention that parents should teach the kids manners ahead of time or that there should be special expectations on airplane behavior out of respect for other passengers, but magazine writers rarely do.

In *Parents* magazine, we find articles on manners that suggest humor and role-playing are the best way to manage kids in public because manners of any kind go against the nature of a child "which is to be frank, spontaneous, and . . . self-centered." Manners themselves are defined as meaningless gestures, but something that will make people "like" our kids a little better. We are provided with no reference to external standards or even the public good, only to common sense. "A 5-year-old may not care that reaching for the salt is bad manners, but he may care if you tell him he'll drag his sleeve through the mashed potatoes," says an expert on diplomatic etiquette. But what, we might ask, if there are no mashed potatoes? Then, presumably, the 5-year-old may simply grab at will.

A similar article on "Surviving the Supermarket" talks about how parents can make shopping a fun experience for a child. The authors recommend parents initiate alphabet and counting games, get the kids involved in selecting or grabbing items from shelves, or keep them busy with a pocket calculator. If the children act up in the checkout line, parents are advised to speak to the management about creating a "candy- and gum-free checkout line." Avoidance works wonders. So does capitulation: "To handle the gimmes, you can announce at the start of the trip that your child will be allowed to pick out one treat." Perhaps this treat can be eaten while waiting in the candy- and gum-free checkout line.

Of course, avoidance and distraction do work as ways to get acceptable behavior from our kids in public places. All intelligent parents avoid problems where they can. We put medicines on the top shelf, lock up the bleach bottles, keep the antique vases (or even the good Crate and Barrel dishes) beyond the reach of 3-year-olds. All intelligent parents know that distraction is a powerful tool in working with kids. I personally found that my Medic-alert necklace, cleverly called "daddy-toy" by all my children, kept the babies nicely amused while my clumsy fingers worked with old-fashioned diaper pins and newfangled, why-do-they-always-rip-off disposable diaper sticky tabs.

The problem with too much avoidance and too much distraction is that children can grow up without having to face the N-word. Parental use of the dreaded word "no" suggests that there are certain expected and enforceable limits on a child's behavior. A child who does not have to deal with such limits early in life faces a rude shock when much more arbitrary limits come up later on. As Sara Dimmerman, of the Parent Child Education and Resource Center, says of children who are too often distracted, "The child begins to expect that everything she doesn't want to do has to be made into a fun experience."

Unfortunately, real life has a limited number of fun experiences.

Wealthy parents have a long history of finding ways to balance avoidance and distraction with the demands of real life. One of the advantages of wealth is that it is possible for staff to provide an environment for children where the N-word might never be heard. Ironically, accounts of the way wealthy children are raised almost never describe such an accommodating environment. Quite the contrary. Wealthy families often seek out and create special challenges for their children. Abby Aldrich Rockefeller, for instance, was of the firm opinion that "Too much money makes people stupid, dull, unseeing and uninteresting." To counteract what was obviously too much money in that household, the Rockefeller children were expected to work hard. They swatted insects to earn spending money (ten dead flies earned a penny), stayed strictly in line when father led walks on the estate, and prepared dinner once a week without the assistance of the cooks, maids, butlers and governesses who could easily have done the work for them. The idea behind this was to build the children's "character." In the case of the Rockefeller children, it certainly worked.

We do not often hear the phrase "building character" in reference to children any more. In a world of distraction, it is easier to parent from moment to moment, dealing with each problem and crisis as it occurs by trying to deflect our kids' response into some not-too-objectionable form. The concept of building character, however, is longer-term. The point of manners and proper behavior in different public environments is not simply for the family to survive the airplane flight or dinner out. The point is to prepare our children for dinner with the Queen or the Nobel Prize ceremony or maybe just doing a suitable best man's toast at some future wedding. Manners will also make more pleasant such mundane occurrences as eating together at home and talking together about everyday issues.

They may even encourage kids to show a little respect toward those older folks who pay the bills, drive them to soccer practice and try to be the best parents they can. That won't happen without real family expectations, a little serious instruction and some regular acquaintance with the N-word along the way.

Five Tips for Rearing a Child Who Won't Embarrass Himself when out in Public

1. **Work up and practice a sense of decorum in advance.** It's too late to talk about eating quietly and not climbing under the table after you've been seated at Delmonico's.
2. **Don't take the kids to adult activities before they're old enough to handle them.** Baby-sitters are expensive, but 5-year-olds don't enjoy Mahler symphonies much.
3. **Don't feel you have to rationally explain a set of manners and conventions that predates all of us.** The fork goes to the left of the plate—period.
4. **Distract if you must.** A good, firm "no" can work wonders, especially in the long term, but sometimes a set of crayons and a coloring book will save a formal occasion.
5. **Set a decent example. . . .** I mean, set a decent example, *please*.

Chapter 9

Too much privacy is not a very good thing:

Kids are part of the family whether they like it or not

Recently we were visiting some friends who had bought a new home in one of the new subdivisions north of our city. The house is a sprawling, pseudo-Victorian place with gingerbread on the outside and every convenience known to man on the inside.

"It's like buying a car," the owner-dad explained to me. "The basic house is cheap, but if you want a staircase or a closet, it'll cost you thousands."

Judging from the tour, I'd say the family decided to spend those thousands. Certainly one of the features they bought was quite extravagant: Each of the children had, not just her own bedroom, but her own *suite* of rooms. The suite consisted of a bedroom, a "study" attached to the bedroom, and a private bathroom.

"Of course, the 3-year-old doesn't use her study yet," dad told me.

"Next year," I said. I hoped I was being facetious.

The other child, 5-year-old Janie, apparently did use her study. She also got a chance to use her bedroom shortly afterward when she refused to clean up a particular mess and was sent to her room by mom. I wasn't entirely clear how this punishment presented any particular hardship, considering her bedroom suite had its own television and stereo and as many dolls and other toys as I've seen outside a Toys 'R' Us store. Janie still acted put-upon and went off to her punishment with a scowl.

For dinner, Janie was expected to reappear and join us. The only problem was that she had locked her door.

"Janie, honey," said dad at the door, "open up. It's time for dinner."

"No," replied Janie.

"Janie, this is making me very angry. Now open this door!"

"No."

Down in the living room, the rest of us were doing our best to keep conversation going while, at the same time, listening intently to the drama upstairs.

Five minutes later, dad reappeared. "I guess Janie isn't having supper with us," he said, embarrassed. Janie had refused to open her door.

"Janie won't be having any supper at all," mom declared loudly, perhaps so Janie could hear. The 3-year-old thought this was excellent justice and giggled accordingly.

"Maybe you should change the door handle so it doesn't lock," I suggested.

"Oh, I couldn't do that," replied the dad. "She has a right to privacy."

We all nodded our heads in agreement and went on with dinner. But the father's comment got me thinking. Since when did kids get entitled to so much privacy?

Privacy within families is a relatively recent phenomenon, historically speaking. Until the last century, most families slept together in a single room, often the same room that they lived in during the day. Sleeping was done on straw pallets on the floor that were simply rolled up and put away during the working day. Parents would have one pallet, the various children would share a few others and family members simply put up with the various noises that all of us emit at night. Sex for the adults—not nearly as important before Queen Victoria as it has been since—simply happened when it happened. Back in the days before foreplay became a word in any language, sex was not nearly as noisy or as busy an activity as it is today. Chances are the kids rolled over and kept on sleeping.

The Victorian age provided for the masses what had been previously reserved for the upper classes—the concept of a separate bedroom. Initially, the bedroom provided very little privacy even for the aristocrat fortunate enough to have one. An eighteenth-century duke would snooze on the bed, two or three servants would sleep on pallets on the floor, and anyone suggesting that the duke might want more "privacy" in sleeping would be seen as a lunatic. European nobility expected to use their bedrooms, or chambers, for both entertaining and sleeping. In Puccini's opera *Tosca*, for instance, when the Italian duke Scarpia seeks to seduce the soprano of his dreams, he does so in a room that serves as both an office and a playboy-style bedroom.

The idea of a separate bedroom used just for sleeping came later, but expanded quickly. A middle-class family at the beginning of the nineteenth century would be fortunate to have two bedrooms, one for the adults, one for all the children (and there might well be a dozen kids). By the middle of the century, all the male children would be in one bedroom, all the females in another. By the 1920s, some families were even able to provide each child with a separate bedroom, but this was hardly the norm. In the 1950s, for instance, Wally and the Beav still shared a bedroom on *Leave It to Beaver*, otherwise they never could have had those heart-to-heart talks so central to the show. It wasn't until the 1960s that the idea of a separate bedroom for each kid had any kind of currency for most families.

Intellectually, the idea that a child might want privacy had to wait until children were seen as separate people. This was hardly quick in coming. For thousands of years, children were legally a kind of chattel like cows or timber, and therefore could be reared, sold or exchanged like any other commodity. Boys who were apprenticed out, for instance, would become the child, servant and apprentice-workman to any employer who took them on. The parents would get a cash settlement and have one less mouth to feed; the employer would get cheap labor. Girls suffered an extraordinary infant mortality rate because they represented not so much an economic asset as an ongoing expense. Many of them simply "failed to thrive," as the old medical expression went, or disappeared under unexplained circumstances.

Such truths seem harsh today, but history is rarely as pleasant as our teachers pretended back in the tenth grade. While it might be tempting to remind our kids how lucky they are we don't trade them for a good milk-cow, I've found this information rarely goes over well with the kids. It is still helpful to remember, however, that the exalted position of children as the focal point of the family is a relatively recent phenomenon, made possible only by the explosion and dispersal of wealth in the twentieth century. A child who announces angrily, "I hate you. I'm going to my room," is engaged in a luxury virtually unknown for most of human history and in many parts of the world today. The kid actually *has* a room.

For today's kids, we have enough wealth to provide them not only with relative privacy, but with the physical accoutrements to make such privacy quite attractive. A young man down the street, whom I'll call Charles, has a suite of rooms that take an entire floor in his parents' house. He not only has his own bedroom, but his own bathroom and study area. This is complemented by his own telephone with its own number, his own computer, his own stereo and his own television. The young man will, some day soon, have his own car, but he'll have to wait. Charles is only eleven.

Charles is the envy of every child in the neighborhood, but he seems unaware that the physical luxury in which he lives is such a wonderful thing. Sometimes I see Charles playing on his own, behind his house, and have a hunch that he's a very lonely boy.

The blessing and curse of privacy

If television really were a mirror to our society, then the general absence of children from the television screen would be quite peculiar. Demographically, there are almost as many children between the ages of zero to eighteen as there are adults from the ages of twenty to forty. But it is adults in the twenty-to-forty age group who dominate the tube because children are difficult to put in front of a camera. As the director's truism goes, the most impossible scenes to shoot involve children or animals. Both take direction poorly and respond with irritation to TV lighting, camera people and directors wearing headsets. In the early days, television dealt with these problems by keeping kids off the screen. Danny Thomas's TV kid Rusty was never seen on *Life with Father* except when he ran in and out of the living-room set; Little Ricky was rarely on screen for more than a minute or two; and real babies almost never appear

Five Ways Kids Used to Be Connected to Their Families

1. **One phone.** Everybody could listen in on what was going on.
2. **One television.** The family had to decide which show *everybody* would watch.
3. **A shared bedroom.** Remember how the kids used to talk to each other on *The Brady Bunch* and *Leave It to Beaver?*
4. **No dishwasher.** Parents and kids could actually talk while washing and drying.
5. **Duties.** From milking the cow to cleaning the Model-T, parents had to talk, supervise and inspect the results.

on any weekly television show, although they do appear frequently on TV ads.

Was it television, then, that encouraged parents to locate the children somewhere other than the living room? If television helps define normality, then family normality since 1950 has included children only as bit players.

Or was it wealth that made it possible to separate children from family life? Many older homes had a sufficient number of rooms to give the children their own, but previously those room arrangements had been made with the entire family in mind. There were music rooms, conservatories, libraries, drying rooms, ironing rooms and storage rooms. The idea that children should take over any of these necessary spaces for their own entertainment would have seemed ludicrous in 1930. By 1960, a family room had become the North American norm.

By the 1970s, family rooms in new houses became larger than the traditional living room which, reverting to its function as a Victorian parlor, became a space used for adults and adult guests.

Ironically, the family room stopped being a room for the entire family and, increasingly, became the domain of the children.

Many social and technological trends led to this domain for the kids. Televisions became small and relatively inexpensive. Music for teenagers became distinct from that of their parents (the arrival of rock 'n' roll represented the first time in history that kids and their parents listened to different music) and, thanks to cheap stereos, noisier. By the 1980s, entertainment and television programming for children (*Zoom, Sesame Street*) became very different from that for adults (*Thirtysomething, Miami Vice*). Parents retreated to quieter rooms for quieter activities, such as reading, while children's activities became noisier and noisier. Shared activities such as reading aloud, Monopoly, radio entertainment and Scrabble lost ground to isolated activities such as television viewing and Nintendo.

And children demanded their privacy. After all, television had shown them that they shouldn't be spending very much time with their parents. Children were, by and large, off camera.

An urge for privacy in teenagers, of course, is normal. Since the primary task of adolescence is individuation (separating the identity of the kid from the parents'), privacy is part of that natural process by which our kids become their own people. But when should this process begin? And how much privacy do kids really need at any given stage?

The key problem parents must address and readdress in raising children is that of distance. How close should a parent be without intruding? How far away must we be to allow our children to thrive and grow on their own? Both intrusion and abandonment are psychologically crippling, but defining the desired middle ground is probably the most difficult task for any parent. As our children keep reminding us, we often get it wrong:

"I'm not a baby, Dad. I can do it myself!" and the converse . . .
"Where were you when I needed you?" and the converse . . .
"It's my life, Mom, let me live it for myself," and the converse . . .
"Why didn't you tell me that . . . ?"

The balance we have to define is not easy to attain, nor is it the same for each family and each child. Children sometimes do need privacy, just as sometimes they need cuddling and birthday parties and friendship with the kid next door. But when a child's privacy becomes a "right," then the structure of a family is seriously skewed.

Kids as part of the family

It seems ludicrous to have to say that children are part of the family, but a reminder is in order when an entire society seems to have forgotten this fact. Whenever parents send the kids off to play in the family room, at some remove from any adult presence or supervision, we have isolated them. When we tell our kids that their "rights" supersede any obligations they might have to brothers and sisters, parents and the community, we have cut them off from an essential connection to the larger world. When we encourage our kids to live entirely in their own world, whether it's based on the television set or the Barbie doll, we have made any future connections to adult life more difficult. None of these serve the real needs of our kids.

The real needs of kids are served by five simple and traditional aspects of good parenting:

1. Let there be duties. I'm always amazed that otherwise solid parenting books such as the Garbers' *Good Behavior* will have an index with 40 listings under "rewards" and none under "duties" or the more old-fashioned word, "chores." The more sensible Dr. Spock offers four pages on duties for very young children, but even these are couched with language that suggests duties should be enjoyable. To be truthful, duties frequently are not enjoyable. Nobody has fun cleaning a room, getting ready for school or washing the dishes (actually, washing the dishes with somebody else can be fun, but there are no guarantees). Duties are simply household jobs that must be done on some kind of regular basis, otherwise the place gets overwhelmed with dust bunnies and dirty clothes. Because kids are part of the family, they should be doing some of the jobs.

The actual nature of the duties probably doesn't matter much. My father

> Whenever parents send the kids off to play in the family room, at some remove from any adult presence or supervision, we have isolated them.

maintained that he was obliged to bring bottles of milk two miles every day—or was it five miles? (the story varied over the years)—from the dairy to his parents' house. When I was a kid, I was obliged to mow the lawn and shovel the snow so that the grass stayed under two inches and the snow never got that high. My own kids have duties ranging from setting the table to cooking once a week to programming the VCR and backing up the computer files. Duties change with time and the kids, but duties there should be. They connect children to the family at a very basic level: We're all in this business of life together.

Incidentally, duties are really quite independent of that other good parenting idea—an allowance. A kid gets an allowance to learn about budgeting money and looking after his own needs; an allowance isn't "pay" for taking a share of the responsibility for family life. Nobody should ever pay kids for picking up their own socks.

> To be truthful, duties frequently are not enjoyable.

2. Let there be manners.
Manners are not the be-all and end-all of human relationships, but they are certainly a good lubricant, a social WD–40. Children should learn manners early on, by instruction and example and practice. "Please" and "thank you" will do for starters. Later, other aspects of manners become important at different times. A child who starts answering the family phone should know what to say: "Hello. This is the Jamison family. Ian speaking," rather than "Uh, who are you?" Manners are not automatic or easy or natural—they require prompting and reminding by parents for a child's entire life (for children who get married, a spouse frequently takes over this task)—but they will prove invaluable for your child in many situations. To quote Miss Manners (Judith Martin):

> There are many forms of manners to be learned, which is why thorough child rearing takes as long as it does. If Miss Manners could compress it all, she would have written two bumper stickers and a T-shirt instead of all these volumes and columns.

3. Let there be respect. Respect differs from manners because the former is an attitude and the latter is a form. Lest this seem too philosophical, let me say that respect is the attitude your child should have toward you (even when you don't necessarily deserve it), while manners are a way of behaving that children should show to everyone, regardless of position.

Make no bones about it: We should have our children's respect. The best way to obtain this, of course, is to give our children and our partner heaping portions of respect for who *they* are. On the other hand, if we regularly address our partner with "Hey, babe, move your fat ass," we shouldn't be surprised when the kid says, "Hey, old man, go take a hike." Children learn effectively by example.

Respect, incidentally, is not our reward for being a nice person. It is possible, if not essential, for children to respect parents regardless of our merits or demerits as human beings. A child whose father is a convicted criminal still owes the man some respect as a father, though the child might well dislike other not-so-savory aspects of dad's behavior. Respect comes with being a parent—for taking on that fairly onerous role—and it should be expected of children. It does your child no good for you to smile nicely if the kid decides to "dis" you. As Dr. Spock wrote before the word "dis" came into our current slang, "Some parents who are very polite people themselves allow their children to be surprisingly obnoxious."

4. Let there be rules. Rules connect neatly to duties, manners and respect. As in the other cases, it doesn't matter much what the rules may be. Rule one in our house, as in many others, is that a kid may never curse at a parent. The nice thing about this rule is that it puts a cap on anger and its expression: Sure, kid, you can be mad and you can say what you think, just never refer to mom or dad with the b-word, the s-word, or the f-word or any other new swear words coming down the pike. Or if you do, be prepared to take a long walk around the block and come up with a good apology before you come back.

Rules give kids all sorts of freedom, up to a point, and also the final freedom to break the rules if they're willing to accept the consequences.

The consequences of rule-breaking for both kids and adults is punishment. I wrote at length about punishment for kids in chapter 7. I need only reiterate here that punishment is ineffective unless there is some respect—child to parent, parent to child—to give it some meaning.

5. Let there be connection to adult life. Our ultimate goal in raising kids is not to keep the children as children but to help them grow into adults. If we wanted to keep them as children, stuffing the kids into a large formaldehyde jar would probably do the trick. Since we have higher aims, our kids need to connect with adults, not be shut off from them.

Hence, the problem of the family room.

Whenever we create a world for children that is disconnected from the adult world, we cut our children off from ourselves as models and their own future as adults. We also cut ourselves off from our children. Research shows that casual interchanges between parents and kids are more important in child development than heavily programmed quality time. Dumb time—all the time we spend in vague proximity to our children with no particular agenda—pays wonderful dividends for families. If mom and dad are in the living room and the kids are playing Nintendo in the family room, there is no connection beyond the occasional "Turn it down!" from the adults and a "Can I go to the video store and rent a new game?" from the kids. Sociologists refuse to dignify such interchanges as conversation; rather, they term it *instrumental discourse*. Families engage in a lot of this, but need more conversation.

There are real payoffs to conversation. According to research at the University of Massachusetts, families who eat dinner together and engage in conversation over the meal are more likely to produce kids who read and do well in school. Other studies have found that families who talk together produce kids who are ultimately more cooperative, better adjusted and more successful on most parameters of success.

Unfortunately, much of the apparatus of modern life does little to facilitate conversation. There was a time, for instance, when entertainment was a family affair. All the family members 200 years ago would listen to the "reader" read poetry and fiction out loud; all the family members in Victorian times gathered together around the piano for songs and declamations after supper; all the family members in the 1930s and 1940s gathered around the radio for entertainment; all the family members in the 1950s and early 1960s gathered around the one massive television set for *Ed Sullivan* or *The Wonderful World of Disney*. All of these forms of entertainment were accompanied by criticism, discussion, shared experience and that side banter of jokes, stories and family history that binds families together.

Today, we ask the schools to teach media literacy and we schedule quality time to talk to our kids. We try to institutionalize what was once a part of family structure.

It is not the purpose of this book to wax nostalgic for times past, but we would be foolish to ignore the value of a family simply spending time together. Our children need more time with adults—a great variety of adults—and that cannot be achieved by watching pseudoadults on television or by scheduling a "take your daughter to work" day once a year. Kids need to see what the world will look like after they grow up in order to see that it's worth getting to adulthood. They can't get this playing on their own in the family room.

Five "Private" Items Our Kids Can Do Without

1. Their own telephone line
2. Their own Internet connection
3. Their own stereo
4. Their own television
5. Their own Walkman (at least during meals)

Chapter 10

Paranoid parents:
How the media have made parents and kids too fearful for their own good

Every age has its collective myths and paranoias, and sometimes these affect parenting. In Victorian times, for instance, state-of-the-art medical science made high ceilings a priority for every home and fresh air a priority for every child. As a result, many upper-class children were sent to drafty attics out of an earnest concern for their well-being, but with a mostly negative impact on their health. In the early part of this century, parental faith in cod liver oil for children probably matched adult belief in the virtues of Knox gelatin for healthy fingernails. While such faith made fortunes for the cod-fishing industry and the Knox family, improved information on balanced nutrition would have been better for the children.

Parenting is still shackled by old-and-untrue notions, new-and-untested theories and species of urban myth. Urban myths are the kind of stories ordinarily reserved for supermarket tabloids, but given additional force by being made local. We all fell for these—or passed them on—back in high school with stories like the one-armed lover's-lane rapist. Some teenagers even planted "the hook" to make the myth more real.

In our age, the urban myth that has most affected parenting is not about fresh air, nutritional supplements or dangerous amputees—it's the myth that adult friends, neighbors and family members are a serious danger to our children.

According to your next-door neighbor, your local newspaper or the hyperventilating TV reporter, there is a child molester somewhere nearby who is just about to assault or kidnap your child.

The trouble with myths like this is, we cannot simply label them as hogwash and then go on to important issues of the day. Urban myths are never *entirely* ridiculous. There actually are a few one-armed rapists who prowl lover's lanes, but the chance of such a man prowling *your* town, in *your* lover's lane, is about as remote as your ticket suddenly winning a million dollars in a state lottery. And this, as we know, is about as likely as your being killed this year by lightning (chances are about 1 in 3.4 million for both). Such things happen, but they don't happen much.

Child molesting and child kidnapping do happen—somewhat more now than they used to, it seems—but the incidence is not as high as most parents perceive and nowhere near what children are made to fear. While no one wants to promise that the world is an absolutely safe place for young people, it is simply not as dangerous out there as we are led to believe. What's worse, parental fear of such exaggerated dangers is impinging on the life and growth of our kids.

The myth of the mysterious stranger in the bushes

The first public paranoia about the safety of our kids was that they were in grave danger of being grabbed by strangers and dragged off to the woods, or transported across state lines or sold into slavery. In truth, there has always been some parental fear about the "mysterious stranger in the bushes." There are deep Freudian reasons why these myths can be found in any culture, and our fears certainly go back well before Little Red Riding Hood appeared in print. In the past, such fears did little except give kids appropriate caution in dealing with people they didn't know. But in the 1970s, parental fear of lurking, evil adults began to increase out of all proportion to the real dangers such people present to children. Fear of child kidnapping, especially, mushroomed thanks to hundreds of newspaper and magazine articles, TV news shows and docudramas. This apparently growing danger drew appropriate words of concern from legislators and other public officials and culminated in a campaign that literally took over the continent's milk cartons and grocery sacks.

Was such an escalation of parental fear warranted?

When all the furor dies down, it turns out that the actual North American figures on child kidnapping are these:

- In the United States, figures from the National Center for Missing and Exploited Children say that only 2 percent of missing children might have been kidnapped by strangers.
- In the United States, more than 750,000 children are reported missing to the police each year, but most of these cases are resolved quickly and without serious consequences. The vast majority involve parental custody disputes.
- Very few U.S. children are abducted by strangers, perhaps 200 to 300 per year total, according to figures cited in a report by Eugene M. Lewit and Linda Schurmann Baker.
- According to figures from NISMART, a child is 500 times more likely to be abandoned or "thrown away" by parents than be kidnapped by strangers.

Where *is* the real danger to our children? Without doubt, the greatest danger for North American kids in terms of both mortality and injury comes from automobiles. In the United States, drowning follows as the next most deadly event for youths: 1,696 young people between birth and 24 years of age drowned in the United States in 1996, the latest year for which statistics are available from the National Safety Council.

Accidental death by fires, firearms, poisons and falls are the next most dangerous events for children, in that order, according to the National Safety Council's figures. According to other reliable figures, children are also in some danger from riding bicycles, from scalding hot water and from snowsuit drawstrings. Ten young Canadians have died since 1989 from strangulation by curtain cords, showing that almost anything around the house has the potential to be dangerous.

All of these figures suggest the importance of parental care; none call for protective hysteria. As one insurance lawyer said to me, "Parents who really want to protect their kids should use seat belts, buy the kid a bike helmet and put a lock on the gun cabinet." Simple statistics would indicate that most North American kids are in greater danger from common household perils than they are from mysterious strangers lurking in the bushes or men offering sweets from parked cars.

Nonetheless, parenting magazines have been filled with instructions on improving children's street savvy and entire books have been written on the subject of "streetproofing your child." The book *Protect Your Child* advised parents to designate one evening each week as a family training night and even provides written "safety" tests to be completed by the kids. Some dentists offer microchips that can be bonded to children's teeth for identification. A video-store chain offers to tape your child for later airing on television in the case of abduction. The Sony corporation has produced a video streetproofing set called "Never Be a Victim," which it promotes with the supposed fact that "5 out of 10 children will be molested by age 15." And one electronics company sells a beeper that blasts an alarm if your child is picked up or wanders outside a designated area.

Are these measures warranted when the real risks to children are rarely from neighbors and passersby and almost always from parents themselves?

The rise of divorce in the late 1960s and '70s did lead to an increasing number of ugly parent custody battles over children, fights that sometimes ended with one parent violating court decisions on custody. This is a valid social and legal problem (though statistically it, too, is declining) and the matter deserves attention, but vile custody battles do not affect the security of children whose parents are still together or amicably split up. They only rarely involve the physical kidnapping of children by a parent

The Real Dangers to American Kids

The following figures come from 1996 National Safety Council tabulations of U.S. National Center for Health Statistics' mortality data, the latest year for which statistics were found. In descending order of mortality figures for young people between 0 and 24 years of age:

1. Automobile accidents: 13,591
2. Drowning: 1,696
3. Fire: 976
4. Poisoning (solid and liquid): 629
5. Firearms:539

who feels his or her rights have been interfered with by the courts and the ex-partner.

Teachers and other legal caregivers, however, have become justly worried. Their problem is not so much from the stranger lurking in the woods but from possible lawsuits if little Johnny doesn't come home on the school bus but somehow ends up with his divorced father in another state. While teachers rarely stop to consider this, much of the rationale behind giving kids lessons in "streetproofing" has to do with protecting education districts from legal liability.

But what if a stranger molests the kids?

Of course, abduction is only part of the environment of fear that we have created for our children. The other part is a fear that our children will be molested by the mysterious stranger in the bushes.

Again, this began in the mid-1970s with the popularization of the phrase "child abuse." Before that, library and periodical listings for such crimes were termed "cruelty to children" and consisted of a handful of articles in any given year. In *The Readers' Guide*, we find only one article about child molesters in 1974; 19 articles under the new heading of "child abuse" in 1978; but by 1993—the year Michael Jackson was accused of interfering with young boys—there were two pages of fine-print listings on the topic of "child molesting."

It is possible, of course, that incidence of child molestation somehow expanded astronomically in the 1970s and '80s. But it is more likely that the media simply went to town on such very public figures as Chuck Berry, Woody Allen and Michael Jackson and gave extraordinary attention to events such as the McMartin preschool accusations.

A generation ago, the child abuser was often depicted as a stranger who lured children into a car with promises of candy. That 1950s image was about as reliable as the 1950s idea that children could protect themselves from nuclear attack by ducking under their desks and covering their heads. A positive result of the increased attention given to child abuse in recent years is that the image has become more realistic. Increasingly, the media show us abusers closer to home: clergymen, coaches, teachers, uncles. This depiction at least has some basis in fact. Children have never been in very much danger from strangers sitting in cars with dirty license plates, but kids have always been in some small danger from people they are in contact with in their own community.

The important question is, how much danger?

1. In Chicago, the Catholic archdiocese investigated the personnel files of everyone who had been a priest between 1951 and 1991. Thirty-nine priests of 2,252 clergy were judged, on the preponderance of evidence (a standard lower than criminal courts use), to be guilty of sexual molestation. This amounts to one priest in sixty, not the one priest in five or ten frequently suggested by the press. Philip Jenkins, in his recent book *Pedophiles and Priests*, looks at all the figures and concludes, "The number of 'pedophile priests' has been magnified by a factor of twenty or more."

2. In recent years in Ontario, Canada, about five teachers each year, from a teaching force of 140,000, have had their licenses revoked for "sexual interference" with their

students. With 2,000,000 students enrolled, the chance of a particular child being molested is somewhat greater than being struck by lightning, but considerably less than the chance a child will die in a fire this coming year.

3. According to the Royal Canadian Mounted Police's grisly statistics on child homicide (including victims up to age eighteen), a young person is three times more likely to be killed by his parents than by someone he doesn't know. If it is any consolation, the chance of your child being murdered at all is really about the same as the chance of her being struck by lightning.

Since I keep running these grim possibilities against the chance that a child might be struck by lightning, let me be clear: In a thunderstorm, we don't tell our children it's okay to stand in the middle of an open field or to get under the tallest tree. That's just stupid. Similarly, in a world where there are fewer and fewer adult "eyes on the street," it would be unwise for our children to hang out in dark alleyways with people they don't know. That's good sense.

But irrational fear is turning into a real problem. A recent survey indicates that a majority of American kids seriously believe they are likely to be stolen by kidnappers from their families. How extraordinary . . . and how sad!

In the *New York Times*, former circus clown Bruce Feiler writes of how the business of clowning has changed because of fearful children and their parents. In his first month as a clown, one teenage boy asked if he would sign the back of his hand since the boy couldn't afford the official circus coloring book. Feiler happily signed the kid's hand, but a mother waiting nearby snatched her younger daughter away. "Never let a strange man do that to you," the mother lectured. Is it any wonder, Feiler writes, that clowns are getting depressed? "I tell you, it's no fun anymore," said clown Buck Nolan after giving up the proverbial red nose. "Once you take away the contact with the kids, you take the fun out of clowning."

We also take some of the fun out of childhood. The real dangers to our children are not from clowns, teachers or men walking down the street. No, the real dangers tend to be at home. The likelihood of a child being molested by teachers and football coaches is insignificant compared to the possibility of being molested by a stepparent or other relative. The growing numbers of charges of sexual and physical abuse have some validity—but that abuse is taking place at home, not on the streets of our towns and cities.

Child abuse by parents and caregivers is a problem. With increased awareness by teachers and others, reports of physical and sexual abuse have skyrocketed in the last fifteen years. While we do not have national statistics (not all states or provinces collect them), some information is available. In the United States, a family violence survey published in 1988 found that 1.5 million American children are "very severely" abused each year. "Very severely" was defined to include kicking, burning, scalding and threatening or attacking with a knife or a gun.

An article in *Harper's* by Peter Schneider raises an interesting question: Why do we focus so tightly on the really minimal dangers to children in the larger world and then ignore the very real dangers of abusive and negligent parenting? Schneider suggests that it is far easier to pretend that the dangers are "out there" rather than for us to come to terms with the anger, frustration and possible violence that can happen between ourselves and our kids. It's easy to point the finger at strangers and say "watch out, kids." It's far harder to look at our own homes, or our neighbors, and admit that some parents might be hurting their own children.

Why kids need to play outside

If you watch the streets of neighborhoods and towns across North America in the hour right after school ends, you'll see something quite disturbing. The kids pour out of the school doors at 3:30 or 4:00, they play for a little while or troop along the street in groups, *and then they disappear*. Even in the best weather, in the quietest small towns, the children have disappeared thirty minutes after the end of the school day. By 4:30, the playgrounds and ballfields are empty, uncannily quiet, and those whose homes back onto the parks will not hear childish laughter until after dinner.

Our children, had they been born twenty years before, would be playing tag or dodge ball or hopscotch on the street until just before dinner. Then mom would yell and the kids would grumble and go in for dinner and homework and the piano lesson; but the natural pull was to the street and the culture of kids. As Roch Carrier writes so eloquently about an earlier generation in *The Hockey Sweater*:

> The winters of my childhood were long, long seasons. We lived in three places—the school, the church, and the skating rink—but our real life was on the skating rink. Real battles were won on the skating rink. Real strength appeared on the skating rink. The real leaders showed themselves on the skating rink.

These days the kids are not at the skating rink, they're plopped in front of the television watching cartoons on Fox, music videos on MTV or "real-life" stories of sexual abuse on *Jenny Jones*. Mentally, they are learning to be passive, to hanker after consumer goods and to become cynical miniature adults.

Why? Because the kids' parents are frightened. We are frightened of possible kidnappers and child molesters and drug dealers and a whole world out there that seems more dangerous than ever before. Even as figures for violent crimes decline, our fears increase— fueled by television movies, crime-obsessed newspapers and cheap-shot politicians intent on election or reelection. So we respond to fear with cringing. Two professors wrote *76 Ways to Protect Your Child from Crime* and offer fairly sensible advice, but the book itself adds to public hysteria: "Our children are in jeopardy of becoming victims of crime as never before," say the authors, avoiding only an exclamation point. Yet for the average child, this is simply not true. We do our kids no service by acting as if it were. And we do them no long-term service by making them fearful when they're young.

Psychologically, the problem with children playing inside the house is that too much parental (or caretaker) supervision frustrates a child's development into adulthood. The exploration and experimentation that will permit our 10-year-olds to become happy, successful 20-year-olds cannot take place under our watchful eyes. It has to happen "out there."

If we go back and look at developmental psychology and attachment theory, what we find is childhood described as a process of increasing exploration from a "secure base." The secure base—the mother or other principal caregiver—needs a certain amount of presence (what I've called "dumb time") so the child can confidently move out to the world beyond her view. This kind of behavior can be easily seen in other primates and in human babies. A young baboon, for instance, spends the first month of his life clinging to his mother and begins making excursions from mom about the age of four months—though none of these excursions will be more than twenty yards away. A baboon will play increasingly with peers at about six months, but still sleeps every night fairly close to mom until age two. At that point, scientists observe "human teenage" behavior: squabbling with mom, more and more time hanging around with the other teenage baboons, and mom rebuffing any attempts by junior to act as a baby (no more rides on the back, for instance). But when the young baboon is in trouble with peers or adult males, it's back to mom for protection. It's not until age four that baboons develop quasi-adult independence, and even then a female baboon frequently maintains a close relationship with her mother throughout life.

Our own children are not much different, though the development stretches over many more years. In infants, we frequently see what psychologists call "proximity-maintaining" behavior. Mary Ainsworth has shown that most babies will cry as soon as mom (or another principal caretaker) leaves the room, and that infants who can crawl will try desperately to follow her. Infants who are intensely curious about another person or object will, nonetheless, retreat to the security of mom with a regularity that can be timed by a stopwatch.

> A parent who is a secure base is available but not intrusive.

Yet no mom or dad can be a lifetime protector, friend and confidant to a child. The real sphere of action for children—and, ultimately, adult children—is the world "out there." As parents, we must be a secure base from which they can explore the world. But we are not the world. Sadly, too many parents don't understand what it means to be a secure base.

Let me define: A parent who is a secure base is available but not intrusive. Such a parent provides a still-point of security for the child. But a good parent does not and cannot eliminate or minimize the dangers—and the thrills—of the larger world.

British research on playground behavior has given us a good indication of what growing children really need from us. Researchers found that children neither need nor want adult supervision of the entire playground. This tended to inhibit play and child-organized games. Heavy teacher supervision simply led to more abusive behavior throughout the playground with teachers having to intervene far more often. What the children needed was a "safe place" to which they could run and be protected when the currents of playground life ran too fast or too dangerously. When a single secure place was established, the children themselves would establish a fairly reasonable level of order everywhere else on the playground. There is an honor and an order in childhood play, just as there is among any social group.

What the paranoia has cost our children

Raising children in a climate of fear—especially misplaced fear—not only interferes with normal exploration and development, it robs children of a valuable resource: other adults.

One of the most significant problems in the last forty years of child rearing is the extent to which parents are expected to handle child rearing alone. Due to the breakdown of the extended family, parents have lost access to grandparent time and to the shared experience of their children's uncles and aunts, nieces and nephews. These relatives are now gone from the family home. Thanks to prosperity and changing social mores, grandparents and other relatives are not physically accessible to many children. Compounding this loss is the effect of fear of adults outside the family: We don't trust them. Increasingly, we won't let outsiders have a hand in our children's lives.

Yet the world of a child beyond the age of six or seven is a world much wider than the nuclear family. It traditionally includes a long list of adults who might sometimes serve as mentors, teachers and surrogate parents. A short list includes classroom teachers, lunchroom monitors, school-bus drivers, coaches of school sports, football and Little League, teachers of piano and ballet, choir directors, clergy, neighbors, friends of the family, after-school caregivers, neighborhood store owners, baby-sitters, doctors, public health nurses, public librarians and the little old lady who peeks through her blinds down at the corner.

What do these people have to say to our children? Everything that we can't . . . or everything we're trying to say that our kids won't believe when *we* say it.

Some time after the age of ten, our children don't want to listen to us. That doesn't mean parents are unimportant—in fact, our example and our presence may be very important indeed—but adults outside the home seem so much more reliable in our children's eyes. Such an adult guide or mentor may well be a teacher, coach or club adviser in an effective school. But the odds of your child finding such a person there are no better than 50–50, and in a poor school the odds are worse. Even in the larger world, for a child who plays everything from Chopin to T-ball, there is no guarantee that an adult guide or mentor will appear. Nonetheless, two quasi-mathematical formulas apply:

- Every new, important adult in your child's life increases the odds that your child's life will be changed and enriched by fresh perspectives and insights.
- The more fearful your child is of adults, the less chance your child has to find and place trust in such an adult.

At a dinner party, I asked the group of adults who had been the important people in their lives after age eight or so. Mom figured prominently in the answers, much more so than dad, but for most of us the really influential figures were outside our family homes.

"There was this hockey coach, a priest, who taught me everything I know about how to play the game," said one father. "My own dad was too busy and not very good at sports, but this priest organized whole leagues. I mean, he taught us how to play."

"My school principal," said a mom. "She showed me that a woman could get the top job, not just a teaching position, and not have to take crap from anyone. In fact, she still writes to me every so often to see how I'm doing."

"My uncle put me through college," added one woman. "It must have cost him $20,000. But my own parents had died, so he just offered to do it. Simple as that."

"This business guy next door was the biggest influence on my life," offered another man, the wealthiest of us all. "My family were all academics and had a nose-in-the-air attitude toward making money, but this guy drove me to school for my senior year in high school and I learned that business was okay. It changed my life."

"My piano teacher," said the wealthy man's wife.

"What did she teach you?" I asked.

"It was a he, not a she," the woman said, smiling. "He was gorgeous and cultured and fascinating—everything adolescent boys aren't. And he taught me about unrequited love!"

However wonderful we may be as parents, what we can offer our children is always limited by who we are. My own children can learn from me what it means to be a teacher or a writer, but they cannot learn what it means to be a truck driver, businessman or investment dealer. Yet they can learn such things from the neighbor down the street, or the boss at their first summer job, or the businessman who leads the investment club at school. Too often, parental fear cuts off our children from these contacts.

Even in a more casual way, our children are not served by being fearful of unknown adults. By and large, adult "strangers" do not threaten children; most have a child's best interests at heart. Adults naturally stop to help crying children; we naturally smile and wave at babies; we naturally take lost children to the information desk so their frantic parents can be found. These days, in fact, adult strangers can be very vigorous in protecting children, even from their parents.

Our children grow up in a world where only a tiny fraction of the adults with whom they come in contact present some kind of danger to them. We do them no service by teaching them to be fearful of the vast majority of adults who are on their side. Let the kids go play outside—after all, that's where the world is.

Five Kinds of Child Abuse You'll Never See on TV

1. Parents who can't say no
2. Parents who push their own unfulfilled dreams on their kids
3. Parents who substitute "stuff" for love
4. Parents who don't have time for their kids
5. Parents who have bought into so many feel-good parenting ideas that they're afraid to be parents

Chapter 11

Sibling rivalry:
How come our families aren't like the Brady Bunch?

A minute ago, the kids were playing so nicely together. Then Caitlin grabbed the Lego spaceship and broke off one of the landing gear pieces.

"You're so dumb!" Mark snarls at his sister.

"I am not. It's your stupid spaceship. You didn't put it together right."

"I did too. You're clumsy. You're stupid."

"I'm not. *You* are. You're stupid. You're a poopy-head."

"I am not," Mark shouts, pushing Caitlin in the arm.

"Mom!" Caitlin cries. "Mark hit me."

"She swore at me!"

"I did not. 'Poopy-head' is not swearing!"

"Mom!" they call in unison.

There is one question we parents face in these scenarios: Is it worth climbing out of the bathtub or stopping income tax preparation at line 142 to deal with this? The simple answer is probably not. Unless Caitlin and Mark are about to inflict significant bodily damage on each other, there's not much parents can do about the emotional slings and arrows of sibling rivalry.

One study done by researcher Caroline Piorowski indicates that two preschooler siblings playing in a room together will have an argument about eight times each hour; that's one every 7 or 8 minutes. The average seems to vary widely, however, depending on the temperament of the kids and the situations in which they're involved. Parents can try to intervene in all this, acting as U.N. peacekeepers in the war-torn living room, but only at the price of our own sanity and, it would seem, at some expense to our kids' social development.

How did the kids get to be so nasty?

It is entirely possible that human beings are born with fairly nasty feelings toward brothers and sisters and that they must be "socialized" to get over them. Evidence from the animal world, for instance, does not speak highly of any natural fondness between siblings. "Siblicide" has been observed among a number of species, including such creatures as Galapagos boobies and African hyenas. Apparently when food gets scarce, boobies act aggressively toward younger and weaker siblings in order to get more than their share. Hyenas go as far as to nip the problem in the bud, as it were, by biting younger siblings as soon as they're born.

Human beings, generally speaking, are nicer than this. Older children often respond warmly to the birth of a new baby brother or sister. At least, at first. The trouble begins shortly thereafter.

The classic research on sibling relationships among young children was done by Judy Dunn with a group of families in Cambridge, England, early in the 1970s. Dunn looked at the relationship among siblings when a newborn infant came into the family. What she found says a lot about conventional wisdom and reality in our approaches to parenting:

- Conventional wisdom says that preparing the older child for the new baby will make a big difference in how the older child reacts to the newborn. If so, Dunn couldn't find any evidence of this.

- Conventional wisdom says that the older child's first response to the new baby is a precursor of how the kids will interact for life. If so, Dunn's study couldn't find any evidence of this, either.
- Conventional wisdom says that the older child will be jealous when mom breastfeeds the new baby. Dunn found the opposite. There were twice as many "disturbances" when mom bottle-fed the newborn than when mom breastfed the baby.

Some of Dunn's study-group families had sibling relationships that were marked by acrimony from day one; others had kids who were basically cooperative and friendly to each other for years. On average, Dunn found that "friendly" interactions between siblings occurred twice as frequently as "hostile" interactions when the baby was eight months old and were still 50 percent more frequent when the baby was fourteen months old. If we manipulate Dunn's figures a little, we find that the older kids had a pleasant exchange with the newborn about every 8 minutes and an unpleasant exchange every 11 minutes.

But any average can be deceptive. Dunn found that the *range* of the older child's responses was truly extraordinary. When mom was feeding or otherwise engaged with the newborn, for instance, the older child would be hostile to the baby only 4 percent of the time, on average. This 4 percent figure, however, included some kids who showed no hostility to the baby and some kids who were hostile 24 percent of the time. On the flip side, Dunn found that the average older child was quite friendly 13 percent of the time, but that included some kids who showed no friendliness and some who were friendly almost half the time when mom was devoting her energies to the baby.

Why do sibling relationships vary so much? Dunn, who went on to become a professor at Pennsylvania State University and has twin sons of her own, thinks the difference has to do with a combination of temperament and situation. Some kids are easygoing and cooperative by nature; others aren't. Woe to the parent who's got two or three uncooperative kids. Some combinations, according to Dunn and other researchers, are particularly lousy:

- "Highly active" (aggressive, pushy) older sisters tend to behave more antagonistically toward younger sisters than younger brothers.
- Kids who are similar in personality fight more often than kids who are temperamentally different—but they also spend more time together.
- "Highly active" younger brothers cause more trouble among male siblings. When coupled with "highly emotional" (sensitive, less aggressive) older brothers, the situation gets worse.
- Whenever mother favors the younger child of two, both children fight more with each other. (Conversely, there's no problem if mom just talks a lot to the little one.)

Judy Dunn came back to the entire sibling issue in a later book, *Separate Lives*, based mostly on research she did in Colorado. She was looking for answers to the question, why are siblings so different from each other? Ultimately she found that beyond inherited tendencies for similar size, physical features and susceptibility to disease "siblings generally differ markedly from each other." She cites examples, ranging from the Brothers Karamozov to Tom Sawyer and his brother Sid, that support her solid statistical work: Siblings may emerge from the same womb, but from then on they're very different people. Dunn crunches more numbers and concludes that the "shared environment" siblings have isn't that important. What counts, she says, is the non-shared experience of growing up. This begins with us. As parents, try as we might to treat our kids the same way, we simply don't. Our handling of our first child is very different from our dealings with child number two, three or four.

> Siblings may emerge from the same womb, but from then on they're very different people.

Dunn's conclusion from all this—and she's spent virtually a lifetime studying siblings—is that children are very sensitive to the way we treat them. Any difference or preference we show in affection, interest, expectation or respect is duly noticed by the kids. They use this against each other and sometimes against us, too. Envy and jealousy, it would seem, are at the core of the sibling experience—from Biblical times to our own.

Sigmund Freud, of course, thought that rivalry for parental attention was the source of most family conflict. His entire idea of Oedipal conflict comes from the desire of boys to replace their father as the number-one man in mom's eyes. Father's suppression of this early-adolescent desire, says Freud, leads to adulthood, civilization and all their related discontents. In a way, envy becomes the motivating force behind the last phase of growing up.

Parents are quite nervous about even admitting that envy is going to happen in young children. Invariably we tell the older kids that they're going to love the soon-to-be-born brother or sister. When the older kids express anger or hostility or jealousy, we pooh-pooh their valid emotions. "Oh, why would you say something like that to your baby brother? Of course you love him. Now give the baby a kiss." The older child, internally fuming, will provide the kiss but his grievances will fester.

Some researchers suggest that parents themselves set off conflict among their children because of our own psychological associations. If our daughter, Betty, reminds us of wonderful Aunt Bertha, then we'll be predisposed to treat Betty kindly throughout life. But if our son, Frank, should resemble his ne'er-do-well uncle Francis, the child will be under heavy scrutiny from day one. When parents themselves identify too closely with a child, the result is heavy expectations that the child either has to accept or rebel against. When a parent has difficulty finding an appropriate reflection—say, the jock father with a chess-playing son—the result is friction all along the way. A middling path of interest and indifference is best for kids.

Parents often set rules that, in themselves, lead to squabbling. A rule like "If you ride in the front seat today, your brother rides in it tomorrow" seems logical, but can create all sorts of problems. What if nobody goes out in the car tomorrow? What if you forget who rode in front yesterday? What if both kids have to ride in back because all of you are going out? All of these situations will occur—and each will lead to a sibling argument with parents stuck in the middle.

Conversely, a rule such as "Jennifer rides in front on even-numbered days; John on odd-numbered days; both in back on February 29 in leap years" not only resolves problems ahead of time (providing you know the date), but teaches math and at least one obscure fact about the calendar. The only problem we face is remembering the whole thing.

> Our kids deserve attention; their arguing mostly does not.

In parenting classes, we find again and again that parents raise the level of their own irritation. We try hard to keep the peace, to act as mediator, to be absolutely fair all the time. Better that we should accept a certain level of squabble, insist that kids work most things out themselves and get on with the serious business of raising a family. Our kids deserve attention; their arguing mostly does not.

What do we do when the battle rages?

In any survey of parents, the number-one problem is always the same: "My kids fight all the time!" We have already shown that this is statistically untrue, but a fight every eight minutes or so can still be a miserable problem in anybody's house.

The problem for parents when the sibling wars are raging is keeping our noses out of the fight. We have a tendency to intervene because we think our kids should always love, respect and be nice to each other. Often they do all these things and, because such interactions are quiet, we pay no attention. But even sibs who are each other's best friends will argue and fight—on average, about half as often as they're happy, friendly and supportive of each other. We hear the fights. The kids *want* us to hear them and, at a certain level, want us to intervene. Poorly handled parental intervention answers the question "Which of us does mom love best?" By making enough noise, the kids can force us to show our hand. As ordinary human beings, we usually do love one kid best—or at least a little better on that given day—but we should never admit this.

Hence, the virtue of "benign neglect." If we can possibly let the sibs fight until they resolve it themselves (they always do, sooner or later), everyone is better off. We haven't been forced into the middle. The kids will have advanced their social skills by solving their own problems (studies show that siblings who fight frequently have more highly developed moral reasoning than those who don't). And tomorrow, everybody will once again be sure that we all mostly love each other.

This is easier said than done. The nature of sibling arguments is that they seem to go on forever while our patience has definite limits. One mother, aware that her own fuse is quite short, actually times the kids' arguing to make sure she stays out for a reasonable period of time. Her rule is simple: "Five minutes, then I send them to their corners." She starts timing when she first becomes aware of the fight, then uses her wristwatch ("or sometimes the microwave clock—it's more precise") to make sure the kids have enough time to resolve their own problems. The virtue of such timing, like counting to 10 when angry, is that kids need clock time to resolve their problems. Our emotional time ticks off too quickly.

Of course, "benign neglect" won't keep us out of every sibling skirmish. It shouldn't. Parenting gurus who suggest parents lock themselves in the bathroom when the kids fight do a dangerous disservice to both parents and children. Similarly, psychologists who suggest parents jump into the fray and then make written lists of grievances on both sides, turning the argument into an intellectual discussion worthy of the local Humanist society, are living in some never-never land. Parents can't just hide out; nor can we always expect the kids to solve their own problems. There are valid times for parents to intervene:

Physical harm. When one sibling threatens to do serious physical harm to another, it's time to step in. One study of more than 1,000 families found a few children who actually wanted to murder their siblings. If you have such a child, don't hide in the bathroom.

> If we can possibly let the sibs fight until they resolve it themselves . . . everyone is better off.

Violations of family norms. I have talked throughout this book about the need for family rules and expectations as a container for the children. When one sib goes beyond the norms of family behavior, it's time to step in. For instance, we always felt the kids could argue and refer to each other with the usual set of unpleasant, childish names—but when language went beyond what could be

printed in the daily newspaper, mom or dad would separate the
parties. The offence, then, is not the argument but the vile language.
Other reasonable family norms involve prohibitions on hitting,
taking objects belonging to the other sibling and excessive name-
calling (though the definition of "excessive" might be tricky). Rules
such as "You can't ever make your sister cry" not only won't work,
they are positive inducements to children who can be creatively
nasty all by themselves.

Dangerous outcomes. For the most part, parents should
respect the independence and integrity of their children. But if the
fight concludes with something like, "So if I win, we'll put the
firecrackers in the cookie jar and see what happens," it's time for a
few words of parental wisdom and a little show of parental power.

Pretty clever, those kids

We have observed before that kids are remarkably clever in
manipulating parents: from birth, when they get us talking without
saying one intelligible word; to babyhood, when we go wild over a
smile; to age one and two, when talking and walking become events
that rival the fall of Communism in terms of historical significance.
Kids are smart. Kids together—which is what siblings become—can
be darned smart, but not in ways that will ever be measured on
statewide exams.

Kids together find ways to manipulate us into spaces where we
would rather not be. We don't want to tell one sib that we like her
better than another; we don't want to tell one sib she's great while
another is a goof; we don't want to differentiate among them at all.
As parents, we have a rather industrial model for our children—you
were all stamped out of the same press, you ought to be the same
kind of kids.

Unfortunately, the industrial concept of children doesn't work.
Our kids are unlikely to be interchangeable and sometimes have
little similarity to each other or to us. Every parent has said, "Where
did that kid come from?" upon occasion, even if she was the one
who gave birth to the kid in question. The deep psychological
attraction of "demon seed" and "switched at birth" stories comes
from the fact that our children are sometimes absolutely
unaccountable—at least to us.

When sibs get together, they can find ways to reduce even the smartest parents to tears, anger, irrationality and gross stupidity. This truth is never admitted in parenting manuals that emphasize "rational consequences" or quick fixes to parenting problems, but it remains a truth. Our kids can bamboozle us, and often delight in doing so. All we can do is guard against the patterns:

"Divide-and-conquer." Children will invariably ask for permission on some questionable item from each parent, seeking the slackest answer. Parents who allow such decision making to take place are foolish; the standard line must always be, "Of course, I have to talk to your father/mother about this." But when an argument is underway, it's usually one parent who intervenes. Don't let the kids scam you into taking sides or making rash judgments.

"I'm special." One child will inevitably claim special status in the household, usually with the parents' implicit agreement. "I'm the pianist. My hands are fragile, so I can't do dishes." "I'm the athlete. I should be out practicing, so I can't do dishes." "I'm the star student. I should be studying to get the degree you never got, dad . . . so I can't do dishes." Such special roles are dangerous to families in many ways. They can become self-fulfilling prophecies, lead to lifelong dependencies, or become attached to crippling expectations. The proper response, of course, is to declare that all our children are special so they can all help with the dishes.

Judy Dunn calls the sensible approach "differential appreciation," meaning that each kid should be appreciated for his own merits. The problem comes when we give that kid preferential treatment. There's solid research to show that any perceived differences in how we treat the children (especially by moms) can lead to anxiety, depression, worry and antisocial behavior from the kids. It's terrible but true—the children are always watching us to make sure they get a fair shake.

"I'm sick." One particularly perverse version of the "I'm special" pattern occurs when one child becomes ill or is disabled in a particular way. Without a doubt, such a child deserves special attention from parents. The problem, however, is that too many families completely rearrange their lives as if the "sick" child were at the center of their universe. That one child has special problems does not mean that family rules go out the window, or expectations are forgotten, or that the other children become martyrs to the sick child. It's not the sick child who's making problems in the family—it's the rest of us, when we lose perspective.

We have friends with one child who suffered a serious brain injury in an automobile accident and will be bedridden the rest of her life. Everyone in the family takes a turn helping care for the girl, but there is growing resentment from the other siblings as they get older. Yes, the injured girl needs looking after; no, her sister shouldn't have to give up her date on Friday because there's no one else available to stay at home. Families that try to deal with catastrophic problems by pretending that they can do it all, that no sacrifice is too great, are not going to seek the outside help that's available.

"I'm just like you." Our children—especially our first children—are doomed to carry the weight of our unfullfilled dreams and expectations throughout their lives. Their only compensation is that we have trouble disciplining kids who seem reflections of ourselves. It's easier to side with them and against the child who resembles your spouse or your miserable Uncle Bob. But easy doesn't make it right.

I have one son whose charm and good looks just happen to make me think he resembles . . . well, me. And this is the son who can most easily sucker his old man into an extra twenty bucks for a date, a weekend with the car, or a few hundred dollars when tuition money just happens to run short. It's only when the other kids hear about these special favors—and they always do—that this dad gets the comeuppance he so richly deserves.

Blended families: Real life isn't like The Brady Bunch

The recent popularity of divorce and remarriage—or re-partnership, because so many recombined couples don't marry any more—has led to a remarkable number of blended families. The old pattern of Ward and June Cleaver normality is dying and dying quickly. In New York City, for instance, only 6 percent of households with kids consist of two parents living together with their own children; the other 94 percent are combinations and permutations of parents, partners, stepparents, single parents, grandparents, children, stepchildren, grandchildren and unrelated people. This may not mesh with a white-bread world envisaged by the political right wing, but it is the real world out there—Brady Bunch Plus.

We don't have much research yet on how well this new blended family phenomenon is working out. Formal research studies take time to assemble, measure, evaluate and report. In the meanwhile, we have observations on the families around us.

The good news from my own observations is just how well most blended families get along with each other. The ancient Hansel and Gretel images of wicked stepmothers, distracted fathers and abandoned children have turned out to be as accurate as the depiction of wolves in Little Red Riding Hood. Things aren't that bad. After a reasonable period of adjustment—building up warmth and trust among the kids and the new stepparents—such families seem to function about as well as any others.

Nonetheless, when children and stepchildren get together, they manage to manipulate parents with special tools unavailable in the Cleaver household. These can be devastating to the adults—because recombined relationships are somewhat more tenuous than our first tries at lifelong marriage. The greatest single cause for breakup of second marriages (or partnerships) is friction over dealing with the blended kids. Blended parents are well to be wary of the kids' techniques:

"Well, (stepparent) lets *his* daughter . . . " Parents in blended families often developed their parenting techniques earlier, with other people, and may have become fairly fixed in their approaches by the time they're dealing with a blended family. Kids use a special version of divide-and-conquer to seek out the weakest line of containment. If your partner lets his teenage kids stay out to midnight while your kids have to be home by 10:00, there will be trouble. Consistency is vital, in blended families as well as traditional ones.

In our own blended household, we use the "favored sibling" rule. We find some place to talk where the kids can't overhear (beware frank discussion when you think you're in private—it can hold more power than the Watergate tapes). Then we discuss whatever issue has come up and ask the question, "What if X had asked for that?" X is the favored sibling of the week (with five kids, this position rotates frequently), the one toward whom we are mostly kindly disposed at the moment. What if X had asked for a loan to go to a movie, or to take a week off from school for a special trip, or a pair of new running shoes when the old ones were perfectly okay? Would our answer be yes or no? Then that's the answer for kids Y, Z, A or B, too. We know that ten eagle eyes are watching for every inconsistency.

"If my dad were here . . . " Nasty comparisons are always a good way to encourage parental guilt—and parental weakness. A stepchild's absent dad (sadly, this is too often the case) can be mythologized, demonized and otherwise used to manipulate the custodial parent and stepparent. Wise parents manage to see through this and hold firm to whatever line needs holding.

"You're not my real mom!" Kids in blended families usually carry a fair amount of anger about the earlier breakup, divorce and ensuing mess-up of their lives. In the midst of the furor, their anger is usually expressed in quiet ways—falling grades, strange behavior, ulcers. But sometimes the anger comes right out in the open. Psychologically, this is probably a good thing. The kids are angry about many things, and your rules may just make matters worse. Of course, deep psychological anger like this rarely has much substance in day-to-day reality. You are not Cinderella's stepmother forcing her to clean the house while your own kids go off to the ball. You're just asking her to clean her room like all the other siblings. Fair is fair, after all. If fair isn't fair, then parents had better do some looking at themselves.

When our efforts at dealing with kids in blended families fail (and they do, for everyone), we end up bickering with each other. The emblem of such failure is the phrase: "He's your kid, not mine."

The situation that rips apart families—blended and traditional—is parents who let the kids divide them into arguing halves of an otherwise whole couple. In the households of the last century, where dad's word was supposedly law, such power struggles weren't supposed to happen. But at the end of the twentieth century, when parents are more equal partners, kids can find ways to make us turn our powers against each other.

I've met few parents in blended families who haven't, at some point, reached the level of "the kid does this or I'm out the door." Partners ultimately have to choose each other over the kids—for the good of the kids. At a certain level, the kids know this and give it grudging respect. On a practical level, they'd rather have their blended parents together than end up a divorce casualty for a second time.

As with all children, clear rules work wonders in keeping household order. The parent who tells a noisy child, "Now be nice to your sister," probably deserves to have the fight go on for another twenty minutes. Far better is a simple, direct instruction: "Caitlin can play with the spaceship until 3:05; Mark has the toy from 3:05 until 3:15; any further arguments and the two of you can file complaints to me, separately and in writing." This should get you a few minutes of quiet and might produce some interesting letter-writing as well.

We always told our kids that any serious complaint with our parenting should be handled by writing a letter, in triplicate, to The Commission. About age five they'd begin to wonder who The Commission actually was. By age eight, they'd figure out there was no commission and the line just became funny. Parents should never forget that humor is one of the best survival tools.

Patience is another. For dealing with sibling rivalry, it often works wonders.

Five Smart Things Parents Can Do to Contain the Sibling Wars

Remember, there are no victories, only truces and moratoriums.

1. **Don't force togetherness.** This just brings resentment.
2. **Don't permit physical violence or bullying or persistent emotional put-downs.** You can't stop the wars, but you can limit the weaponry.
3. **Don't get caught in the middle.** It's hard for a parent to be "the judge." Better that you declare a ceasefire and express relative indifference to their grievances.
4. **Accept that the kids are different.** Each sibling should be special, but in his own way.
5. **Don't worry so much.** The kids will fight anyhow, and it's not your fault. Just keep an ear open to make sure that no irrevocable damage is being done.

Chapter 12

Day-care dilemmas:
Most of the options are bad

Sometimes I'm given the privilege of speaking to large groups of people, usually teachers, but occasionally to parent associations and other groups who aren't confined to a classroom 200 days a year. The last part of all these talks is a question period that invariably begins with an awful silence while the first person, the courageous one, makes her way to the microphone to ask a question. Lately I've taken to filling this time by turning the tables and asking a question of the audience.

"Do any of you think full-time day care is a good thing for preschool children?"

The response has been a stunned silence. Sometimes I ask again, adding an "Anybody?" and survey the room. Still, not a rustle.

Now it could be that the silence has something to do with the expression on my face, the nature of groups or the difficulty of being the first person in an audience to raise a hand. So I can ask a second question.

"Well, is there any working parent in this room who didn't have their kids in day care before school age?"

Again, silence. (Only one or two hands in the air.) If both parents work and they have young children, then the kids have to be in some kind of childcare arrangement. We don't let 3-year-olds amuse themselves on their own all day; there are laws about this.

"So if nobody thinks full-time day care is a good thing, and everybody uses it, then what's going on here?"

And then we get discussion. Usually this starts with justification and regret.

"Look, I know it's not the best thing, but we've got a big mortgage and we really didn't have any choice," said one mom.

"We both have careers," explained a father. "I'm not giving up mine. Why should my wife have to sacrifice hers?"

"We don't have the luxury that my parents did," added another woman. "Stay-at-home means starve-to-death for our generation."

While some older members of their audience shake their heads, the talk continues.

"Day care isn't so bad," said one woman. "My kids really enjoy it. They get upset when they can't go to school. I mean, it's not like I farmed them out when they were six months old. Nursery school is a school, that's all."

"And it's good for the kids, isn't it?" someone says.

At which point I stop taking notes and get back into my answer mode. I'm not an expert on day care, but I do my research carefully, and that research is quite clear: For kids from disadvantaged households, there is a net educational advantage for those attending high-quality day care.

"It's good for the kids, isn't it?"

Research at the Perry PreSchool project, by New York University researchers in Harlem, by Jerome Kagan and Burton White in Boston, all show that high-quality day care works well for poor, inner-city kids. It boosts their early school performance, gives them a shot at real achievement in elementary school and apparently improves many measures of success in adult life. The entire Head Start program is based, not on guesswork, but on the proven performance of high-quality early childhood education in boosting kids' learning. Disadvantaged parents need have no qualms about putting their kids in day care at age three or thereabouts.

But what about everyone else? What about day care for middle-class, two-income families who are trying to balance mortgages, car payments, jobs and kids? Governments look at day care as a reasonable and necessary part of raising children (though they're reluctant to fund it), but increasing numbers of children's advocates fear that most day care, as Columbia University sociologist Amitai Etzioni says, is nothing more than "kennels for kids."

The big picture

Any kind of big picture regarding the care of young children has to look at zoology, anthropology and history, not so much for answers, but for a little perspective. It will help us consider just how important mom and (to a lesser extent) dad may be in raising children up to the age of four or five.

To the extent that humans are really heavy-brained, relatively hairless animals, it would seem that the role of mom is pretty central for young children. There is, of course, the nurturing qualities of mother's milk, as important for humans as for any other mammal. Then there is the matter of infant imprinting and bonding. Imprinting is that tendency of some animals to model themselves after the early significant care-giving figures in their lives, whether this happens to be a natural parent or not. In the charming film *Fly Away Home*, for instance, we see the baby geese first imitating a young girl and then, after a little training, an ultra-light aircraft. Biologically, this imprinting has certain limitations—we can't teach geese to talk, however hard we try—but it shows the way in which certain aspects of natural parenting can be replaced by sometimes highly artificial means.

Monkeys and chimpanzees, it would seem, are a little tougher to fool than geese. R. A. Hinde, who has carefully studied the behavior of infants in various species from birds to humans, notes that the infant rhesus monkey establishes a preference for its mother in the first week or two of life. It might, for instance, leave mom and crawl toward another monkey mom, but the baby soon sees his error, turns around and comes back "home." Human scientists who have become foster-parents to monkeys and baboons all point out the persistence of the animal-child's attachment to its human caregiver, an attachment marked by clinging to maintain contact and screaming when the infant (or even mature monkey) is taken away.

Most attachment research has been on the link between mothers and babies, but it's clear that fathers and other caregivers can fill the same role—where society encourages that to happen. When Malinowsky studied the Trobriand Islanders back in the 1920s, he found that the role of caregiver in that Polynesian society was taken by neither the father nor the mother; it was a maternal uncle who reared the babies. These men even developed enlarged nipples so that the babies' urge to nurse could be satisfied by an older male rather than the mother. Because the society was matrilineal, and everyone approved of this arrangement, there seemed to be no particular difficulties for either the infants or their parents in having an uncle fill in for mom.

The importance of adults as an emotional support for children is obvious when families meet a "stranger" on the street. Babies show an initial curiosity about the new person, but they have to check the continuing presence of the parent every 20 seconds or so to continue their examination of the new person. If mom or dad has disappeared, as is the case when the child is left at day care or nursery school, the child's delighted examination quickly turns to crying. Sigmund Freud's distinguished daughter Anna Freud remarked, "It is a known fact that children will cling even to mothers who are continually cross and sometimes cruel to them." A baby needs *somebody* to act like a parent, whether that's mom, dad, grandma or the staff at a day-care center. As Penelope Leach phrases the issue, for infants to thrive, they need someone who not only cares *for* them, but *about* them.

Historically, the care of young children by their natural parents has not really been given a high priority until recent years. For thousands of years, as soon as parents had an income sufficient to cover the expense, actual care of infants was handed to someone else. Probably the first form of day care outside the extended family group was the wet nurse. Such women are mentioned frequently in the Bible, Egyptian papyri and Greek and Roman literature, and they remained popular until the end of the eighteenth century. Their services involved not only physically nursing babies with mother's milk, but also caring for the children until age four or five.

Children were given into the care of the wet nurse, not so much that mothers could engage in "work" either in the house or outside it, but because breastfeeding was seen as distasteful for a woman of a certain social rank. In 1780, the police chief of Paris estimated that 17,000 of the 21,000 children born each year in his city were sent out into the country to be wet-nursed; only one child in twenty was actually nursed by its own mother. In Bavaria, one burgher whose wife insisted on nursing her own babies threatened to stop eating entirely (a significant threat in the days when physical size indicated prosperity) unless she gave up her "disgusting habit." The mother gave in and the husband remained suitably stout.

Back when life was more tenuous, the actual quality of babies' care was not a big item on any family's agenda. Two hundred years ago, when three out of four babies died before the age of five for reasons that were mostly inexplicable and therefore deemed the will of God, no particular baby *could* be that important. If they were, parents would spend their childbearing years drowned in grief.

As we gradually began to understand the nature of disease and the importance of cleanliness, infant mortality declined and babies could become emotionally more important to their parents. Child rearing became the responsibility, not of the wet nurse, but of the extended family. Initially, mom and dad were only two of the parties involved. Even in the growing middle class, there were one or two servants to help in housework and childcare as well as other relatives who could take part of the burden of child rearing.

It wasn't until the 1920s that the burden of childcare was placed almost entirely on the two natural parents. For a little while, this nuclear family model might even have worked. But as women joined the labor force during and after World War II, it became increasingly difficult to maintain a traditional household. In 1940, only 8.6 percent of American moms were working outside the house; by 1958, this figure had grown to almost 30 percent. By 1968, 39 percent of mothers with kids under eighteen were working outside the home. By 1978, when more than half of all moms were working, the stay-at-home mom was still the television model. We have a 25-year lag between what is really happening to families and what television established as ideal.

No wonder working moms felt guilty.

Today, two-thirds of moms with children under eighteen are in the workforce. Slightly more than half of mothers with children under the age of five in the United States are working at least part-time outside the home. All of those moms (and the handful of dads who take on child rearing as their major responsibility) need day care, and all of them feel conflicted about it. On television, of course, babies appear as props that never seem to interfere with any television personality's ongoing activities. But in real life, babies can't just be handed to a stagehand while the show goes on. In real families, babies, toddlers and children make up much of the show—and they need lots of attention.

How do we really feel about this?

"The first day is the worst," one mother said to me. I'd taken a small group out to lunch to talk about day care, jobs and the trials of being a supermom. "I took Jonathan to the day-care center, followed everything they said about getting him ready and explaining everything, and he still wailed. I think walking out that door and driving away was the hardest thing I ever did."

"At least they didn't call you to take him back," added another. "My kid cried so much, and sulked so much and was so bad, they gave up after a week. I think I've got the only kid on earth was expelled from nursery school."

"No, mine too," said mom number three. "But you know what's the worst? It's when they *don't* cry. I got my mother to look after the baby when he was just six months. And my mom did a great job, maybe too great a job. Now Devin can't wait to go to grandma's and doesn't want to spend time with us. We were driving by her house the other day, going shopping, and he wanted to get out of the car. He cried because he was stuck with me."

"That's bad," agreed mom number one.

"You must have felt awful."

There was more commiseration. Then the group moved on.

"You know what else is bad. It's when the kid gets sick. My baby had an ear infection off and on for years. We finally had it operated on last year, and she's fine now. But it seemed like half the time I'd drop her off at mom's, she was sick."

"And nobody understands," said mom number two. "You can tell your boss that your kid's sick one day, but kids are always sick two or three days. Try leaving work early two days in a row."

"I just stayed home the second day. There was no point," chimed in the first mom.

"And they say you can keep a career going with children in day care! What a laugh!"

I decided to venture in. This is dicey territory for men. "What about your husbands?"

"Which husband?" said the first mom.

"Never had one," said mom number two.

"Useless," said the third.

And that would seem to be the consensus of opinion, at least for people looking back a few years. While there is some evidence today that men are more involved with raising children (thanks to high-school parenting courses, the financial importance of women's careers and growing unemployment among young men), it's still relatively slight. Even in the liberal-minded metropolitan area where I live, fewer than one dad in twenty among the people I interviewed had given up his job to look after the child. At-home childcare is still seen as mom's responsibility, just as housework remains something stacked on top of her job while dad gives less than 15 minutes a week to help out. None of this is fair, but currently it's how we live.

Day care, granny care, dad care and mom care

From the baby's perspective, it may not make much difference who's looking after him. We suspect, after research by Jerome Kagan and others, that most infants don't see well enough for the first three months of life to be able to tell the difference between mom's face, dad's face, grandma's face or even a Halloween mask with large eyes. Feeding, rocking and talking—from anybody—would appear to keep infants perfectly content. It's only at five or six months that a child begins forming a secure attachment to a single caregiver.

When children don't have such caregivers, as John Bowlby found in studying British institutional foster care after World War II, infants suffer from what he called "maternal deprivation." The effects of this, according to Bowlby and researcher Rene Spitz, is to rear children who end up listless and apathetic. When two other researchers filmed institutionalized children, they found that deprived infants went from rage to despair to apathy in an appalling progression. Another study has suggested that lack of interaction with a principal caregiver can drop a child's IQ by 10 to 12 points.

And yet—our mortgages are large; payments on the second car have to be made; and careers do count. Even Dr. Spock changed his mind on day care to accommodate the needs of families. In the 1946 edition of *Baby and Child Care*, he wrote: "It doesn't make sense to have mothers go to work and have to pay other people to do a poorer job of bringing up their children." In 1976, the updated text read: "Both parents have an equal right to a career if they want one."

Almost everyone recognizes the importance of a high-quality caretaker for the first three years of a baby's life, and many mothers, given the choice, would choose to stay home and do just that. In some countries, government policy actually encourages parents to stay home and look after their children. In Sweden, two parents can split a leave of fifteen months at 90 percent of previous earnings to care for a new baby; and parents are entitled to an additional eighteen months of "job protected" unpaid leave. In Italy, mothers are *required* to take off two months before and three months after childbirth and most women receive full salaries for the period. In France, at least sixteen weeks of maternal leave is mostly paid for by social security; and mothers are guaranteed an hour a day to breastfeed their child after they return to work. The state also subsidizes a two-year parental leave taken at any time until the child is three.

> More than half of American toddlers are in some form of day care.

But here in North America, our governments haven't done much to permit parents to stay home with the newborn or to make baby part of their work lives. Few union contracts guarantee more than a few months' fully paid leave; only rarely are women guaranteed their jobs back should they be audacious enough to demand three, four or five years off to raise children during the key early years. In the United States, Bill Clinton's family leave bill covers just 5 percent of American companies (though that includes 60 percent of American workers), and provides only for twelve weeks of unpaid leave. In Canada, employment insurance covers seventeen or eighteen weeks of post-pregnancy leave (at 55 percent of average weekly earnings).

Without any real public or policy support, mothers usually go back to work. More than half (55.4 percent) of American women with kids under age three are in the labor force, so more than half of American toddlers are in some form of day care. In Italy, where leave provisions are more generous, only 5 percent of the kids are in day care before attending school. Make no mistake—public policy has a big impact on every aspect of family life.

For many parents who decide to go back to work, the first choice for child care is often grandma. Grandma is seen as a good option because she obviously did a pretty good job with you, she might well live nearby, her hours are flexible and she might not ask for any money to do the job. Besides, few licensed day-care centers will take kids before the age of eighteen months and grandma might, just might, be willing.

Unfortunately, grandma doesn't *always* do a great job. A recent study of child care done by New York researcher Ellen Galinsky looked at kids who were being cared for by relatives and by unrelated childcare providers. Galinsky concluded: "Whether or not Grandma *wants* to be taking care of the kids is critical." Her study found that a licensed day-care provider, someone trained in early childhood education and committed to childcare as a profession, will probably do a better job than grandma.

The problem, of course, is finding and affording licensed day care. Many young families find the expense of licensed day care, or even unlicensed baby-sitting, a considerable burden.

So parents are caught in a double bind. Staying at home to look after our kids means losing a salary, stepping off the career track and certainly taking a step down in material comfort. Going back to work means finding the cash for day care, dealing with the problems of day care and somehow managing all the headaches of a continuing job. Parents lose out either way they turn—and so do the kids.

Choosing day care and what comes with it

Even for parents who manage to take two or three years off from work to look after the kids, nursery schools start to look pretty good after a while. For one thing, they keep us from going crazy.

"My sanity was at stake," to quote a neighborhood mom. "I got sick of listening to Barney and Sesame Street all day long."

"Don't forget the social experience," added another neighbor. "A nursery school means that our kids can meet kids from other neighborhoods. They can mix. Learn to play together."

"And enrichment," said a third. "The staff is trained. I mean, they go to college, don't they?"

Well, sometimes—providing the parents are willing and able to shell out for high-quality care.

The weasel clause in all early day-care studies is "high quality." During the early studies at Yale's Children's House, there was a staff person for every two babies. For Jerome Kagan's research at Harvard, the thirty-three children of the Tremont Street Infant Center were looked after by an array of educated, intelligent and committed staff. There was virtually no staff turnover.

Then there's real life. Former U.S. Commissioner on Child Care Edward Zigler has commented, "We pay our child-care workers less than zookeepers—then we expect them to work wonders."

Sometimes they do. Sometimes intelligent and interested people stay in the childcare profession for years. Bob Munsch, for instance, a best-selling children's author, worked at a university laboratory preschool for nine years. There's no question that his charges got the highest quality of care, and probably a few good stories, too. But then there are all the other scenarios.

The average staff turnover at a U.S. day-care center is 41 percent each year. That's a lot of coming and going for kids who are supposed to have a principal caregiver. Of course, the adjective "principal" is slightly inaccurate because it suggests one caregiver with a couple of helpers. Few real-life day-care centers come close. In the United States, rules for children-to-caregiver ratios vary from state to state. At licensed Maryland preschools, for example, there can be three children for every caregiver up to the age of eighteen months, six children up to age 27 months, and

Disquieting Day-Care Statistics

1. One-third of the kids in group day care are on antibiotics at any given time.
2. There is a 41 percent staff turnover in U.S. day-care centers every year.
3. Licensed day-care educators are usually paid much less than classroom teachers; unlicensed day-care workers often get little more than the minimum wage.
4. Seven out of 10 day-care centers in the United States use TV as part of their program every day.
5. A recent study of 1,300 U.S. families suggests that day care has little effect on the mother-child relationship if the child isn't "vulnerable," if the mother is reasonably competent, if the day care doesn't have high staff turnover, and if the child only spends 10 to 30 hours a week with the alternate caregiver. Four big "ifs."

then ten kids to every childcare worker right up to school age. At unlicensed day-care, the sky's the limit. Throw in the fact that day-care workers get coffee breaks and lunch time, and sometimes have to take sick days, and the real number of kids being supervised will go up higher still.

How do kids respond to such day care? For the lucky ones, whose parents can afford high-quality, licensed day care, the results are pretty good. The children really do learn something about cooperation, and the programs often foster reading and math attitudes (if not skills) that pay off in elementary school later on. But even in ideal situations, there is a nagging problem: The kids get sick more frequently. When one group of researchers looked at 189 families with infants and toddlers, they found that the children in day care got sick much more frequently than children who stayed home. Another study found a third of the kids in group day care are on antibiotics at any given time.

This extraordinary incidence of disease can be partially explained because kids in groups pass germs from one to another. But I have another fear. For kids who are too young to articulate how they feel about day care, I suspect the runny noses, various infections and persistent flus are their way of voting two small thumbs down.

No baby was ever hurt because the parents were poor for a couple years

The real day-care choice isn't made for statistical babies entering into theoretical situations; it's made by us and for our own unique kids. It involves a few specific day-care options and a set of financial parameters that is different for each family. Mom care, for instance, is ordinarily the childcare of choice for most middle-class children, but mom care is hardly desirable for mothers who don't much enjoy their kids or who are more likely to watch afternoon soaps than change a diaper. Dad care—fathers who actually put aside jobs and careers for a few years to raise kids—is still so rare in our society that such fathers are seen as positively heroic when we run across them. Why men should be heroic for doing what most women are expected to do is a dicey question. In Sweden, fathers forfeit a month's leave that is specially designated for them if they don't take time off to look after their babies—not a bad message to dads that their parenting is important. But it's not a message we're sending in North America.

The actual choice families make on child care is complicated by careers, incomes, the presence or absence of state subsidies, and whether or not grandma is willing to look after another generation's babies. Some parents, especially single parents, have no choice at all. But for most people, there are choices—not easy ones, but possible ones.

Part-time work and job-sharing. It's possible to hold down half a job, stay on the career track, make pension fund payments and—thanks to a lower tax burden—only lose a part of one income. Many parents opt for such a scenario for the early years of raising children. They find the financial sacrifice no more than the payments on a second car, and there seems to be nothing wrong for kids at age three going to day care for 20 hours each week.

Work at home. Many companies encourage employees to work at home one day a week. Some parents manage to use this day at home to provide some real parental availability for the kid. Other jobs can be done entirely from home. In publishing, a field where I work, many authors and editors manage to concentrate quite well on their manuscripts despite the fact that kids come bursting into the office regularly to ask why the cereal box is empty.

Take the kids to work. This is difficult if you're a stock trader or do assembly at an auto-parts plant, but people in other occupations can frequently bring babies to work. When I worked at a bookstore many years ago, my firstborn son had a regular spot near the cash register and was much admired by our customers—at least until he learned to walk and his mobility caused problems. Kids have been going to their parents' workplaces for hundreds of years. Many employers today are adopting a more accommodating attitude to make it possible for parents to juggle kids and careers.

Change your job. Some employers are kid-friendly; others are not. Some employers have onsite day care (so you can check in with your child at lunch hour), understand that kids get sick, know that parents need time to take children to the doctor, let parents take leaves and arrange vacations to suit the needs of kids. Other employers are hopeless. The best bet—difficult when jobs are scarce, but possible today—is to find a kid-friendly employer.

Teamwork. If both parents manage to find some flexibility in their job arrangements, it's likely that the kids won't need more than a day or two a week at a day-care center or with an alternate caregiver. That's when day care really can be a good thing for kids—teaching, exploring the world, introducing new kids and adults into their universe.

And last but not least—quit. For fifty years, this is what one parent (usually mom) has done to look after the kids.

We have a friend, call her Jessica, who not only holds down a high-profile and highly paid job, but manages to be a good mother to her two young kids when she's around. The problem for Jessica, though, is that a professional-level job isn't a 40-hour-a-week enterprise, it requires 50- and 60-hour weeks and often calls for travel out-of-town. It was on one of these trips when Jessica ended up sitting beside a retired businessman. They began to talk, as people on airplanes do, about their jobs and families and how airline food had gone downhill after deregulation. Somewhere in their conversation, the businessman asked, "So, you have kids?"

"Yes, two," Jessica said. "A boy and a girl. They're three and one."

"Must be tough," the businessman said, "flying all over, holding down a job like yours with two little kids."

"It is, but my husband helps out, and we have a live-in," Jessica explained. And then she must have felt defensive, so she went on, "And my career is important."

"It is, it is," the businessman agreed. "When I was your age, I thought my career was everything. But it's funny, when you get older. I've been retired five years now, and I never even think of work any more. All those people at my office, the ones who were so important back then, well, sometimes we play golf but I don't see a lot of them. I think that's true for a lot of retired people. You kind of wonder why that old job ever seemed so important."

Jessica waited. She probably knew where this was going.

"You know what does matter, later on," the businessman concluded. "It's your kids. It's family. If you don't have family, well, what have you got?"

It was not this single airline conversation that led Jessica to take a two-year leave of absence from her job. The whole idea of taking time off had been building up ever since she went back to work after the birth of her second child. At a certain level, Jessica knew she wasn't there enough for her children. The kids were growing up and she was only home for a few hours each day to be part of that experience. "With kids," she told a friend afterward, "you don't get a second chance." So she made her decision.

Parents who decide to give up one income to look after a child will certainly make a sacrifice in terms of family finances. The choice often means one less car, a somewhat smaller house, or staying in an apartment a couple more years. It means more macaroni and cheese, and less sirloin. It means that our children will not have a deluxe baby carriage or an extra closet full of toys or more than one Barbie. But no study I've seen has indicated that poor children grow up emotionally worse off than rich ones. In fact, there is some data to indicate that children of the working class get better childcare from their parents than their wealthy counterparts.

Of course, it is possible to trust genetics to frame our children's destiny, to give kids credit for the resilience to overcome early stress, to hope that the day care really will be of high quality and that the caregivers there will really give care. But the gut instinct of moms—and sometimes dads—is to look after their own kids for at least the first three years and maybe for a couple more after that. Parents, it seems clear, should trust their gut.

Alternatives to Week-long Day Care

Because the problems with day care really have to do with how much time kids spend in it, here are some alternatives to being a full-time, stay-at-home parent:

1. **Part-time work:** much-time parenting.
2. **Job sharing:** Twenty hours at work means only 25 to 30 hours of day care for the child.
3. **Day care at work:** Some companies offer on-site day care so you can visit at lunch and on breaks.
4. **Work at home:** Many companies encourage employees to work at home one or more days a week.
5. **Take the child to work:** Tough if you're a stockbroker, but possible if you work at a small boutique or for yourself.
6. **Set up shop at home:** Home-based businesses are growing thanks to Internet connections.
7. **Flex those hours:** Between part-time, flex-time and a good partner, you might not need more than a day or two of child care each week.

Chapter 13

Helping our kids get the most from school . . .

without being *too* pushy

As parents, nothing makes us feel more powerless than trying to deal with our kids' teachers and schools.

"I went in to talk to Blair's teacher yesterday," says one mom.

"Let me guess," replied another. "His teacher was at her desk, in the one good chair, and you had to sit in one of those tiny kid chairs."

"Right. And then she takes out the record sheets and portfolios and starts going on about Blair this and Blair that."

"As if the report card wasn't complicated enough. What were there? Twenty-two different items this time and those categories—'not in evidence,' 'growing competence' . . . I mean, whatever happened to subjects and grades?"

The first mom shakes her head. "Anyhow, after she's finally finished, I just asked her directly—is Blair's reading okay? It's a simple question, isn't it?"

"So what did she say?"

"She said that he's got 'good reading attitude.' What's *that* supposed to mean?"

It's possible, taking a charitable view, to say that teachers and schools simply suffer from an enormous communication problem. Our schools have been laden with such a burden of goals, objectives, initiatives, expectations, outcomes and education-commission recommendations that—in trying desperately to appease everyone from kids to local politicians to the city paper—they manage to please no one. Conversely, it may simply be that too many schools and too many teachers aren't doing the job we need them to do. That's our deepest fear, and it's not without some substance.

Our inordinate faith in the schools

Public opinion polls show a fascinating split in our attitude toward schools. While the vast majority of parents think that *their* kid's school is good or excellent, the same parents have some real misgivings about *other* schools and the education system in general. This kind of wishful thinking is probably necessary so we can continue to send our relatively guileless children to a large, imperfect and sometimes impersonal institution. We expect the six or seven schools our kid will attend to change a basic 5-year-old into an educated, literate, credentialed graduate who's ready to step into a career in business or brain surgery. Sometimes the schools actually accomplish this, but more often there are problems along the way. We blame the school or the teacher; they blame us. Our kid suffers the consequences.

To be painfully honest, our wishful thinking about schools is not entirely supported by such facts as these:

- Probably the single most important learning stage for a child occurs in the preschool years, when the rate of assimilating knowledge and building intellectual connections is extraordinarily high. This is when we put the kids in day care and nursery schools with the lowest-paid teachers, weakest programs and highest staff turnover.
- In the primary grades, when vital groundwork is laid in reading and math, we pack kids into classes that are too large, with teachers who have had perhaps a year of teacher

training and a handful of courses to stay current in their profession. Our governments spend much more on housing a prison inmate than they do educating a child in the first grade.

- Throughout our kid's school career, he's got about a 50–50 chance in any given year of being matched with a good teacher for his particular learning style. He's also going to end up with an incompetent or burned-out teacher at least three times before graduating from high school. Two of these sorry experiences in a row will discourage even the brightest child.
- The average child is going to change schools six times before the end of high school because of family moves and school organization. Despite this, there is little coordination of curriculum or learning expectations from school to school. If you move a lot, your child could end up doing a unit on ancient Egypt three times but miss long division altogether.
- The single most important person in your child's education is not a particular teacher, but the principal. A good principal sets a tone for the whole school, attracts good teachers and gets rid of the bad ones, finds money for programs that count, attracts volunteers like bees to honey, leads and inspires his staff—and then gets transferred or promoted within five years.

Politicians and journalists try to grapple with such facts by proposing a magic-bullet solution that will miraculously return our schools to their supposed days of glory. These magic bullets have included phonics, whole language, "academies," hands-on learning, outcomes-based learning, state-wide testing, "standards," voucher systems, charter schools and decentralization. The problem with magic bullets, of course, is the magic part. What Houdini should have taught us is that magic is really sleight-of-hand. It's not a solution to complex social problems. Nor are the schools an industrial organization whose problems can be solved with a new directive from corporate headquarters (in fact, we've learned this doesn't work too well in business, either). A school is an extraordinarily complex, people-intensive organization that can be improved only through careful application of people skills.

Getting schools to work for our kids

In various publications, I have referred to the traditional connection of parents to schools as the DWP model. DWP is what every mom and dad does on the first day of school: *Drop the kid off, Wave good-bye and Pray.* If we could rely on schools to do a splendid job 100 percent of the time—or maybe if we have real faith in prayer— then the DWP model might be good enough for the twelve to twenty years our kids stay in school. But because schools and teachers are not always splendid, and the results of prayer are iffy in this earthly vale, I suggest a more active model for parental involvement. Not every parent is comfortable with this:

"I don't want the teacher to think I'm a wacko," said one suburban mom with two kids in a so-so school.

I pointed out what she already knew. "Your son says he has a stomachache every day he has to go to school—and you're worried about being called a wacko?"

"That's not it," she protested. "I just feel awkward having to complain."

"So does Jeff," I said. "That's why he's got stomachaches instead of just telling you Mrs. Jones bugs him. Incidentally, have you told Mrs. Jones about the stomachaches?"

"No. I was thinking of calling the principal," she said.

"Well, that's not entirely fair. If Mrs. Jones is the problem, then Mrs. Jones should have first shot at fixing the problem. Give her two weeks and *then* call the principal. Then give *him* two weeks before you call the superintendent."

"You really think I should be that aggressive?"

"I think parents should look after their kids at least as much as the average guy looks after his car. We don't ignore squeaky brakes just because were afraid to call the dealership."

A few years ago, I collaborated with Lynda Hodson to write a book called *The School Solution*, where we combined whatever we knew from fifty years in the teaching profession with basic curriculum information, parent feedback and the kind of research that educators don't usually share with the public. Both of us were clear on the issue of "wacko" parents: For every parent who complains too much (and could perhaps be considered a nut case), there are five parents who don't complain nearly enough. Such parental longsuffering isn't good for the kid, who doesn't create a solution to his problems, nor is it helpful for schools where administrators really do try to weed out or help improve weak teachers.

Exactly how much a particular parent has to be involved depends on circumstances, school systems and the nature of our kid, but involvement is essential to make sure schools and teachers are doing their best for our children. Here are the basics:

Choose the school. We can always send our kids to the neighborhood school, and that might be a good-enough choice for most kids, but it should be a conscious choice rather than just a lazy solution. Many school districts will let parents enrol kids in a different neighborhood school if were willing to handle the transportation, put up with waiting lists (the best schools almost always have them) or line up for several hours to sign up the child.

Then there are other options, depending on our wealth, religion and family circumstances. There are Catholic and other religious schools, ritzy independent schools, alternative schools (both public and private), French immersion schools, Montessori schools, special interest or "magnet" schools (specializing in science, arts, academics or sports) and special-needs schools. I've been in small farming communities where parents of young kids still had four different options for their kid. In a major metropolitan centers, there might well be a dozen.

Choose the teacher. Parents are only rarely asked which teacher they'd like for their child next year (though this trend is growing), but that doesn't mean we can't have a chat with the principal and make a strong suggestion. To do so, of course, we have to know something about the teachers who are handling the next grade level. The best source for this information is nosing around the school as a volunteer. Nothing really beats the evidence of our own eyes. Then there's what we hear from other parents, from our kid's older friends, from the current grade teacher and the principal. All of this is complicated by the fact that our neighbor's kid might have loved Mrs. Jones and everything in her class, but our kid might hate Mrs. Jones' style and be tormented for a full year by little Billy Buffoon who's also going into that classroom. Still, by getting involved in teacher choice we tend to minimize the nagging chance that our kid will end up with a truly terrible or burned-out teacher.

Pay attention to what's going on. Contrary to television myth, kids rarely complain about going to school. One survey says that 74 percent of kids aged eight to twelve would go to school even if they weren't required to do so, and 52 percent of those kids thought their teachers deserved an A. On the other hand, we all know that there are dismal teachers in every school and that sometimes the match of a particular kid with a particular teacher just doesn't work. So parents have to listen. With little kids, we have to listen to their stomachs, or their refusal to get up in the morning, as much as to what they actually say to us. We also have to look carefully at those classroom newsletters and the first report card and every other bit of paper that comes home from school. If our kid is with a great teacher, we'll see that pretty quickly. If not, we've either got to live with the problem or work on getting it fixed before the semester break.

If there's trouble . . . If our kids are hurting in school—either from the teacher or from the other kids in class—we have move fast. The first parents' night often doesn't roll around until October, so a phone call at the end of September is sometimes in order. That's a good time to get out the only tool that can help a parent in tackling a school system: the file folder. Date the phone call, summarize what you and the teacher said, then put that note in the file. If our kid is having a major problem, or we're working with a really obtuse school, the file folder will be pretty thick by the time we're done. The folder gives the parent and the principal "documentation." Without the file folder, you're just a whiny parent with a lousy memory. With it, you have power.

Generally speaking, every link in the school system's chain of command should have a couple of weeks to work on a solution for a child's problem. The teacher gets two weeks, then call the principal. The principal gets two weeks, then call the superintendent. The superintendent gets two weeks, then call the trustee. In our

Five Ways to Spot a Good School in a Five-Minute Visit

1. Look for pictures of kids, project work and posters in the halls and on classroom walls.
2. See if kids are using the halls as an extension of their classrooms. This is good.
3. Peek to see what's going on in classrooms—active learning, or lectures, or just videos.
4. Watch how kids interact with the principal. There should be smiles *and* respect.
5. Don't count the computers. Look for a well-stocked library with a real teacher-librarian.

experience with schools, about 40 percent of problems can be solved by talking to the classroom teacher, 20 percent will need the help of the principal, 10 percent are really problems that we should be dealing with at home and 30 percent just won't be resolved in any satisfactory way. It's sometimes possible to change schools or even move houses (I know people who've done both) to improve a difficult school situation, but that' s pretty drastic. Most kids can survive one bad year in a decent school; the real problem comes when there's going to be two bad years in a row. Then it could be time to call the real estate agent.

How far do we stick our noses in?

As public regard for schools declines, so our sense of what we should be doing at home goes up. After all, everybody knows education is important. If our child comes out of school without having mastered the three R's, spreadsheets and the Internet . . . well, he'll be digging ditches for the rest of his life. To prevent this, good parents stick their noses into their kids' education. We should. If there's a problem, no one is in a better position to advocate for a child than the parents.

But what if there *isn't* a problem? Assuming that the teacher, the school and our kid are all doing what they're supposed to do, just what is the appropriate position for our parental noses?

Answer: close enough to eyeball the work.

Kids who do their work at the table have mom and dad walking around the kitchen, casually making sure that the kids are actually attending to homework, studying or whatever needs to be done for school. These parents are available to reply to the odd question or see that the answer to question three looks a little iffy and might need more work. The marks of kids with this kind of parental supervision and interest are often very high. Some of this is due to teacher attitude. Teachers respond remarkably well to any sign of diligence from students, especially because a fair portion of kids in too many classes can't drag themselves away from the TV to do anything once they leave the four walls of the school. Some of the bonus marks come about because extra time spent at home can easily add 50 percent to the time spent learning in school. But most of the real achievement comes from the fact that parental eyeballing establishes the importance of education in the eyes of mom and dad.

> Parents are the most important study tool for any kid from age five to fifteen.

Some kids have bedrooms large enough that they're outfitted with a separate study area. All the appropriate amenities of modern scholarship are there—computers, dictionaries and encyclopedias, notebooks and office supplies—but mom and dad are somewhere else. The absence of parents, who are the most important study tool for any kid from age five to age fifteen, makes all the other academic hardware virtually useless. There's no way of knowing if the computer is accessing the Microsoft online encyclopedia or Salacious Susie's Sex Site; there's no way of telling if our child is filling the word processor with gems of personal wisdom or whether he's playing Doom on the "D" drive. If we add to this problem the other distractions of a child's bedroom—a telephone, CD/tape player, sometimes a television—the likelihood that our kid is using his bedroom time to master senior algebra or the work of Aristotle is slim indeed.

The role of a parent is never to do the kid's work for him or to attempt to replace the teacher at school. These modes short-circuit the real education that should be taking place in our child's brain and the school's classroom. There is always the temptation for an active and hopeful parent, especially with the first child, to intrude too far. Teachers can easily identify projects completed by anxious parents because their language and presentation is far beyond what 10-year-old Johnny could ever have achieved on his own. In my teaching career, there were many times when I wish I could have given the parents a grade—but instead made the child go back and do the assignment himself.

Nonetheless, there is a valid role for parents in *expanding* the education of their children. Schools today are remarkably narrow in their definition of what constitutes an education. We no longer spend much classroom time on topics that would have been essential in ancient Greece—gymnastics, logic, oratory—nor do we consider grammar, rhetoric, astronomy and music essential subjects, as they were in the Renaissance. We've dropped Latin, a third language and religious education from the curriculum—though there's plenty of time for group work, collaboration, writing process, media awareness, cultural sensitivity and state evaluation units. Many of the choices made about what gets offered in our schools are political, or based on business needs, or only adequate for the mythical "average student." Our kids, regardless of their level of intelligence and the results of state-wide testing, are *always* special—with particular interests, aptitudes and enthusiasms that may not be covered in school curricula.

That's why we should make every effort to expand a child's education outside of school. Probably the single most obvious omission of most school programs is the one that brings the most frequent recrimination from our kids when they get older:

"Mom, why didn't you make me study music when I was a kid?"

When music finally becomes personally important to the kids, about age 12 or so, it's already too late to become really accomplished on any serious instrument. It's always our fault that we didn't "make" them take piano or violin or trumpet early on, and the kids are at least partially correct. No 5-year-old can sign herself up for Suzuki violin and pay for lessons herself; we have to arrange for that, and we should. Kids who study music learn a discipline that has broad application throughout life, which has a payoff in many areas that don't seem to be logically connected. Studies show that children who studied four years or more of music scored 34 points higher on their verbal SATs and children who were part of their school band are 52 percent more likely to go on to college and graduate.

> Kids who study music learn a discipline that has broad application throughout life.

But music is only one obvious addition to the incomplete offerings of our schools. Many other outside activities also broaden the knowledge and experience of kids: going to church, being a Scout, joining a sports team, doing volunteer work, taking dance, karate or ballet lessons, going to summer camp, taking on a paper route or part-time job, enrolling in Saturday classes at a museum or art gallery, traveling to Europe or the Grand Canyon or even Disneyland, going to an opera or a symphony or a monster truck show. Kids are magnificently curious about the world, and even the best schools can show them only a small part of it.

Nonetheless, schools make a big difference

If our kids had many competent and caring adults involved in their lives, then schools wouldn't matter so much. Thinking back, we can all recall the impact that various adults outside our family had on our lives. Priests, ministers, rabbis, camp counselors, football coaches, piano teachers, tae-kwon-do instructors and next-door neighbors can sometimes inspire significant changes in our lives and our life choices.

These days, sadly, few parents allow such outside adults to be as close to our children as we might have in the past. What's left that still seems safe—and really is safe, given all the statistics—are teachers. When I was researching my book on reading, I kept hearing grateful stories from adults who remember a certain teacher, at a certain key time, giving them a particular book. For many, it was that book which began a lifetime of literacy. In my own life, it was probably the influence of one high school English teacher who inspired this young man to abandon a 100-year-old family tradition of engineering and go on to college to study poetry and sociology. School teachers can use their power for good or ill. For every teacher who causes only stomachaches in his pupils, there are two or three who can inspire new excitement about learning and great dreams about life's possibilities. A little parental effort can help make sure our kids get more of the second variety.

Five Ways Parents Can Improve Their Children's Education

1. Remember that real education is bigger than just school. Scouts, sports teams, music lessons and travel all count in the long run.
2. Time you spend reading with your child and examining homework can double the learning that goes on in school.
3. When you change schools, shop for a new school at least as carefully as you would shop for a new car.
4. Volunteer in the school. The information you get will help you obtain the right teacher—next year—for your child.
5. Advocate for your child. Don't roll over and play dead just because your child ended up with a lousy teacher or a weak principal.

matter that we have no cure and few good treatments for psoriasis, or that psoriasis only means "itchy, scaly skin" in Greek; we still feel better with a *disease* than having to face an arbitrary condition of life. It's not us, we can say, it's a *disease*. It's not our fault; we're victims of genetics, the environment, a bacteria or a virus. Increasingly, North Americans would prefer to be victims than simply to carry on, somewhat hobbled, with life as it is.

Without question, doctors and pharmaceutical companies have embraced this concept with considerable success. There is an enormous and profitable industry in North America dedicated to the treatment—though only sometimes the cure—of disease. Increasingly, we look to drugs, treatments and therapies to solve our problems, so it should come as no surprise to find that this trend extends right to our children.

The "new" disorder of ADD

In the days before ADD, back in the 1970s, I taught reading at a boys' vocational school. These almost-extinct institutions were popular at the time for two misguided reasons. First, there was a conventional wisdom that kids who couldn't sit still for an hour-long history lesson might somehow be "good with their hands" and therefore should be at a trade school. Second, there was a notion that boys ought to learn auto body and welding, while girls preferred cooking and sewing classes, and that such studies would be distracted if a member of the opposite sex were anywhere nearby.

The staff at my vocational school would occasionally get together to talk about our difficulties in teaching the kids assigned to us. We noted that some kids were quite content to plod along, day after day, assignment after assignment, and that other kids would quickly turn to staring out the window, bugging their classmates or scribbling on the tabletop. "I guess some of these kids have the attention span of fleas," was the woeful conclusion.

The problem with this simple explanation came from the shop classes. The same kids who quickly started staring out the window and scribbling on tabletops in my reading class were just excellent in auto body, laboriously shaping and painting the cars that they brought into the shop.

Chapter 14

The attention deficit in ADD is probably ours

At one time, when disease was more often fatal than it is today, any state of reasonable functioning was considered healthy. A person in the last century could be considered reasonably healthy while suffering long-term effects from smallpox, tuberculosis, skin cancer and various minor viruses. Just as a beautiful woman in the seventeenth century was any girl lucky enough to have avoided the pockmarks of smallpox, so a healthy man was anyone who wasn't within a week of being dead from disease.

Now we define health much more narrowly. Our society has embraced a medical model of normality that suggests we are either optimal—perfectly healthy in every respect—or we are sick. Since almost no one is *perfectly* healthy, the range of categories for sick has expanded to include a number of other descriptors: syndromes, disorders and chronic problems as well as specific diseases. Only a small portion of these can ever be treated effectively using traditional medical approaches, but failures in treatment haven't caused us to put limits on the entire medical model.

The reason why is simple—the medical model is wonderfully comforting. If a person has itchy, scaly skin, for instance, it certainly feels better to know that one is suffering from psoriasis than to feel he's simply going to be stuck with this condition for life. It doesn't

It took me quite a while to realize that the problem had more to do with how I was teaching reading than it did with the attention span of the kids.

I bring up this story to indicate the norms of an older time, when attention was seen as a more highly variable quality than it is today. We had kids who could devote hours finishing a wood shop project, working on a car or reading the *Penthouse* letters; but these same kids had trouble attending for even a few minutes to a reading assignment, a history project or a French lesson. Conversely, some people who are good at reading, history and French (I'm in this group) can't attend very well to certain repetitive, mechanical tasks. When I was a college student, I once welded automobile front quarter panels as a summer job at a Ford plant; but my concentration and the quality of my work were terrible.

It never occurred to me that my students might have an attention deficit in reading some of the irrelevant material I gave them; nor did it occur to the management at Ford that I might have an attention deficit in welding. We just used to say that our level of attention was connected to what we're interested in, our motivation and our overall physical functioning. Attention varied . . . depending.

In the 1980s, however, we learned that there were "norms" in attention just as there were norms in everything else. Kids who paid attention at levels significantly below the norm weren't just bored, uninterested or unmotivated, they were suffering from attention deficit disorder—ADD.

By that time I had moved on to a more ordinary school and a more ordinary set of students. In education, we had begun to transfer difficult students from special schools, such as the vocational school where I'd taught, to regular schools. Special-needs students were all assigned to a resource teacher whose job was to assist them in particular tasks and serve as surrogate parent, counselor and school system advocate. I recall the first time I was approached by the newly appointed resource teacher about a particularly difficult student.

"Paul," she said, "I know you've been having trouble with Andrew."

"Right," I said, smiling. "He doesn't do homework, skips class, mouths off to everyone and has this tendency to stick straightened paper clips into his classmates. Otherwise, he's a nice-enough kid."

"And you've modified his program, haven't you?"

"Yes," I said. "For our mutual survival." Program modification involves changing activities and assignments to mesh with the learning style of a particular child. In Andrew's case, I had given up on group work (the paper clips were a problem) and changed the reading material (he liked *The Outsiders*).

"I just wanted to tell you that some days he might skip his medication. His mother is concerned."

"Medication?" I raised one eyebrow.

"Ritalin," she said.

"For hyperactivity," I said, using the old-fashioned term.

"No, not hyperactivity. Andrew's got ADD—attention deficit disorder."

"Oh," I said.

"So if he's really antsy in class, just send him to me. I'll check to see if he's taken his pill. Sometimes he hides it under his tongue instead of swallowing."

I nodded, but wondered why Andrew needed a pill. The kid had problems, to be sure, but they didn't seem insurmountable. He was a boy of average intelligence, not much interested in poetry or Shakespearean plays, but quite content to read action novels. Andrew had some fairly serious social problems, mostly of his own making, but he wasn't a total loser in the classroom. In the past, we would have tried to deal with a boy like this by talking to his parents, counseling him, assigning him a student mentor and otherwise trying to talk him into some semblance of normality. But now we were giving him a pill, twice every school day. Even at that time, I wasn't certain that the real benefit was for kids like Andrew.

Antsy and hyperactive and medicated

We have always had kids and adults who could best be described as "antsy": Various parts of their bodies are in motion, their eyes dart about, they can't seem to concentrate on much for very long. Historically, we've kept such kids in school until they flunked out, then sent them off to the frontier or somewhere they could manage to fit. In the days when one could still choose to be a shepherd or a gold prospector or a train engineer, we had room for many different kinds of people with many different spans of attention.

In 1955, however, a drug called Ritalin was developed. It had some peculiar properties. For adults, Ritalin was a stimulant—like caffeine times ten. But for kids, Ritalin worked as a depressant—a full-time downer. In order to justify keeping kids on a drug whose long-term effects were unknown, a disease was required. The disorder was called hyperkinesis in the 1950s, hyperactivity in the '60s. Originally, its diagnosis was limited to a tiny portion of the child population. There had to be major physical signs of hyperactivity—not just difficulty concentrating at school—to justify giving your kid a chemical substance two or three times a day. Doctors would look for fidgeting, inability to sit still for any length of time, inability to attend even to games and toys, sleeplessness, blurting out, excessive and compulsive talking, persistent interruptions—there was a whole range of symptoms that fit less than 1 percent of the child population. Nor did the problem suddenly appear at school age. Hyperactive children show their distress early, usually well before school age, displaying a continuing distractibility and failure to concentrate that drives parents crazy and hampers the child in development and social relationships.

For these kids—and these kids are still around—medication works wonders. Ritalin (methylphenidate) and sometimes dexedrine (dextroamphetamine) or Cylert (premoline) can help some 70 percent of hyperactive kids settle down and get on with something approaching normal kid life. These advantages do not come without side effects—loss of appetite, stomach pain, drowsiness, a sense of disconnection from life. Nor is it entirely clear what long-term side effects come from the early use of serious, brain-operative drugs. But the drugs work. As one of my students reported, "It's like they turned off the static in my head."

Children suffering from hyperactivity are markedly different from antsy or simply spirited children. Hyperactivity starts in infancy or soon thereafter, it affects the child every waking minute, and displays physical symptoms in every context—from home to school to dinner at grandma's. But ADD is a bit more nebulous. The diagnosis is rarely given before school age, and sometimes is a direct result of school recommendation. While it is not impossible for a child to live an entirely successful life with the symptoms of ADD, it's just difficult in most school settings.

Diagnosis of ADD does not involve physical symptoms as much as it does a set of measures on how well a child is adapting to the needs of his environment. We have, for instance, no blood, saliva or brainwave indicators of ADD (though some experimenters using magnetic resonance imaging say the brain's prefrontal lobe behaves differently from normal). Instead, parents and doctors compare notes, get testimony from teachers, try to eliminate other possibilities such as allergies, depression and hearing problems, and then add the checkmarks on their list. The final decision on whether ADD requires treatment is a mix of a kid's behavior and disposition, on one side, and society's expectations and convenience on the other. But many parents have valid questions about whether ADD really is a disorder. Others wonder whether its almost-automatic treatment with Ritalin is the best approach for dealing with the problem—or merely the quickest.

Treating everything with a pill

As the medical model of normality has taken over, North Americans have taken to consuming an astonishing number of pills. Pills can fix our blood pressure, cholesterol level, body fat, nervousness, sleeplessness . . . and restore virtually everything else to a state that doctors call normal. Among these pills are psychotherapeutics, everything from aspirin to major tranquilizers, which have a range of effects on the way our brains function.

It should come as no surprise that the drug companies have pushed the pill solution to emotional and mental problems. There are enormous profits in a drug once it's been developed, and enormous development costs to recoup before it even gets sold. Drug companies have a serious bottom-line reason to push pills, and they do so using a variety of sophisticated techniques.

For a long time, drug marketing was limited to salesmen calling on doctors and hospitals extolling the virtues of whatever new drug had been developed. In the last decade, however, such marketing efforts have increased substantially. Hospital doctors now receive free lunches, samples, pens, notebooks, appointment planners and other goodies for merely listening to a spiel about the latest drugs. Pharmaceutical companies sponsor conferences, buy professional advertising, pay for university-based studies and lately have begun to advertise in consumer publications. The idea here is that a patient/consumer who has done self-diagnosis based on advertising will ask his doctor to prescribe a particular drug; if the doctor refuses, he'll go doctor-shopping until he finds a more amenable physician. Most doctors don't put up much of a fight. A study by the Rand Corporation found the average general practitioner took less than three minutes of listening time before prescribing an antidepressant to an adult patient who complained about feeling down.

The problem of overprescription has finally gotten so serious that doctors themselves have begun to do something about it. Physicians have so overprescribed tetracycline and penicillin that antibiotic-resistant microbes have become a major hospital and health problem. There's only one effective antibiotic drug left for really serious infection, so now doctors are urging each other to be a little more careful before prescribing antibiotic medicines.

Similar caution has yet to appear among doctors prescribing psychotherapeutics.

For children who may or may not be suffering ADD (or ADHD, the more inclusive acronym that restores the word hyperactivity), the trend is ominous. In the United States, the growing trend toward a diagnosis of ADD has led to an *enormous* consumption of Ritalin and generic Ritalin—7.6 million tons of the drug in 1996. The growth has largely come along since 1990. In the 1980s, Ritalin usage doubled from roughly 300 grams per 100,000 people to 600 grams. But by 1994, usage had jumped to 1,400 grams—a truly scary increase. In Canada, where fewer than 1 percent of children were ever diagnosed with old-style hyperactivity, 3 to 5 percent of children are said to be suffering ADD.

The situation even prompted the United Nations Narcotics Control Board to urge "utmost vigilance in order to prevent overdiagnosing of ADD in children." The UN had a sense that American doctors weren't exercising due diligence in prescribing Ritalin, but doctors complained that their refusing to prescribe

Ritalin simply caused parents to shop for another, more accommodating physician.

The pressure on parents to get Ritalin for their "difficult" kids comes from many sources. Schools, increasingly, see medication as a quick fix for kids who are having difficulty in class. It's expensive to lower class size, change teachers, develop a variety of classroom techniques and otherwise accommodate children who need special attention. Ritalin—especially generic methylphenidate (the patent on Ritalin ran out twenty-five years ago)—costs parents on HMO plans next to nothing. It also has a powerful advocacy group. An organization called Children and Adults with ADD (CHADD) has 35,000 members in 650 chapters. Its political clout is so substantial that CHADD managed to convince 140 U.S. politicians to sign up for a campaign that would have cut restrictions on doctors prescribing Ritalin.

> Schools, increasingly, see medication as a quick fix for kids who are having difficulty in class.

CHADD also maintains a sophisticated Internet site, including a set of doctor-heros in its ADD "Hall of Fame."

CHADD, according to the *New York Times*, apparently received $800,000 in 1995 from Ciba-Geigy, the manufacturers of the name-brand Ritalin. For Ciba-Geigy, this was just one more promotional strategy in a campaign that has yielded spectacular results. According to *Newsweek*, U.S. sales of Ritalin topped $350 million in 1995.

But is any of this good for the children who are taking it?

Whose attention problem is it, anyway?

Kids have two problems when we try to improve their attention span by using drugs. The first is that drugs have side effects. Ritalin causes drowsiness, weight loss, stomach distress, headaches and a dissociation sometimes called the "zombie effect." Other antidepressants bring on dry mouth, muscle seizures and repeated nervous movements or facial tics. No one knows what the long-term effects of such drug-taking may be (a cancer scare turned out to be bogus), but dosages have to be carefully monitored for any child. The basic prescription is done using formulas based on age, weight and symptoms, but there are wide individual differences in response and tolerance. Major antidepressants, when they're tried, are sometimes so toxic that an overdose can have very unpleasant physical consequences—nausea, vomiting, dizziness. Additionally, kids who take any of these drugs report a certain lack of connection with life, a loss of zest, that is consistent with taking a downer. For this very reason, some adolescents rebel against their Ritalin prescriptions and hide the pills they were supposed to take.

> It is the child who loses the capacity to develop and change his own personality when the alteration is done chemically.

Second, if we resolve a kid's attention problem with a pill, we stop looking for any other solutions. No one really knows what causes ADD, or what makes one child more antsy than another one. Biological scientists are convinced that it's all in the brain, citing studies of different rates of cortical glucose absorption for kids suffering ADD than for control groups. But this only takes us back one level. Why, then, do some kids have brains that absorb glucose differently from others? Treatment with Ritalin seems to "work" for 75 to 80 percent of ADD children, but it would have a similar effect on any group of kids. Indeed, some perfectly normal high-school students (old enough that Ritalin works not as a depressant but like its chemical sisters, the amphetamines) pop Ritalin pills to get an extra edge in their exam studying.

Some parents and doctors have become skeptical about whether Ritalin treatments have any validity. Dr. Thomas Millar, an outspoken child psychiatrist, says bluntly that ADD is a myth developed to control children.

Basically, a diagnosis of ADD takes the problem of an interface—the place where our kid meets the expectations of the school—and dumps the problem entirely back on the kid. It is the child who suffers the side effects and the long-term consequences; it is the child who loses the capacity to develop and change his own personality when the alteration is done chemically.

Unfortunately, alternatives to drug treatment are costly, time-consuming and parent-intensive. We have friends who explored them all. Marge and Dave have two children, but it was the older boy who had the problem. From an early age, Samuel was very active and easily distracted, but he was also quite curious and creative. Unlike his sister, who was a model of social deportment, Samuel didn't get along with other kids in his nursery school and was often demanding at home. There were temper tantrums, fights, refusals to obey—problems that had an impact on Marge and Dave as well as a succession of live-in helpers.

The Samuel problem seemed controllable, however, until he got to school. Samuel got through kindergarten with only a few problems, but the strict first-grade teacher wouldn't tolerate his temper or his failure to take direction. Years ago, Samuel would have been called "high spirited" and been sent to the office. These days, Samuel became a behavioral problem and was sent for psychological referral. Months later, the school psychologist suggested ADD, the frazzled first-grade teacher concurred and the family doctor went along. The prescription was to be Ritalin.

The parents, however, didn't give in easily. They tried other approaches—eliminating sugar from Samuel's diet, cutting out the TV, even a complicated biofeedback experiment. They considered other schools, private schools that might have smaller classes or more understanding teachers. At one point Marge thought about giving up her job so she could stay home, be there for lunch, provide the proverbial milk and cookies after school. But that would have meant selling their house, moving and enrolling Samuel in a new school. The disruption seemed worse than the vague possibility of a cure.

So the prescription was written and Samuel settled down. He's changed, the parents feel. He's less "off the wall," sleeps better, bugs them less. But something has been lost. Before the medication, Samuel's drawings were incredible, sprawling pictures with lines that zoomed off the page and colors that exploded against each other. Now his drawings are more contained, smaller, mostly in black and white.

Have we gained a Samuel who will do well in life, or have we lost a Van Gogh?

Peter Breggin, who is the director of the Canadian Centre for the Study of Psychiatry and Psychology, says that many kids diagnosed with ADD are simply energetic, creative kids struggling against "an inattentive, conflicted or stressed adult environment." When asked about Ritalin, he feels we're drugging our best and our brightest. Attention deficit disorder, he says, is less about children's attention deficits than it is about "our lack of attention to their needs."

This doesn't mean that every parent who goes along with an ADD diagnosis and picks up a Ritalin prescription is negligent in caring for her kid, but it should give all of us pause before we simply nod our heads and agree to large-scale drugging of our children. Collectively, society is far too interested in keeping kids quiet and compliant, and not interested enough in hearing them speak, encouraging their gifts and tolerating their differences.

Five Ways to Improve a Child's Attention Span without Ritalin

1. Turn off the TV, video and computer games. Three hours at the tube each day is plenty for any boy or girl.
2. Stay close by until your child finishes the project, model or book.
3. Enforce a bedtime and have a breakfast together.
4. Talk to the teacher about what changes could really be made in class—or push to get a new teacher, if you have to.
5. Hold, hug and help—three techniques for any child who's anxious and upset.

Chapter 15

Teenagers:
Adult in size doesn't mean adult in most other ways

If it's any consolation, teenagers weren't always like the way we find them today. For most of human history, kids at age twelve or thirteen were simply incompetent adults who had finished whatever education was available and were deemed ready-enough to apprentice, or farm, or clerk or marry and have kids themselves. Today's extended *angst* of adolescence just wasn't a possibility for an apprentice in the merchant guilds of medieval Europe or any of the Joad kids in John Steinbeck's *Grapes of Wrath*.

We didn't invent the teenager as a separate entity until the 1950s, when a surge of post–World War II money made possible either extended schooling or extended goofing around before taking on a serious job or career. Some historians suggest that the cultural idea of the teenager—as a category distinct from both child and adult—was connected directly to the coining of the phrase "rock-and-roll" by Alan Freed, a New York City radio DJ. Before rock-and-roll, adults and children tended to listen to the same kind of music. Teenage girls and their mothers *both* enjoyed Frank Sinatra and Dean Martin. But when Elvis Presley began gyrating his hips, moms disapproved and teenage girls ended up with a distinct musical taste. Chuck Berry and the Shirelles were a similar demarcation for teenage boys—adults couldn't stand this stuff, so teenagers of both sexes could make rock-and-roll the badge of their independence. When Hollywood added physical images such as James Dean in *Rebel Without a Cause* and Marlon Brando in *The Wild Ones*, we had the cultural ingredients for creating a new demographic group—the teenager.

The economic ingredients developed at the same time. Worried about unemployment with so many soldiers coming back after the war, our various governments decided the easy solution was to keep many young people in school longer than ever before. These young people, temporarily disconnected from the need to get long-term work, still had a certain economic power. They went to movies (when older people were staying home), bought records (45s and 33s, when discs were still vinyl and older people were staying put with their 78s), worshiped cars (though they had to buy them secondhand) and developed a certain kind of attitude that comes with power disconnected from responsibility.

Teenagers still have considerable power and attitude. Their power comes from yearly spending that exceeds $100 billion across North America. Their attitude increasingly derives from a teenage culture that worships material items, embraces any form of non-economic "rebellion," and has a curiously mixed attitude toward sexuality. While it's not true for every teenage subgroup, the middle- and upper-middle-class kids are still mostly disconnected from responsibility because of their affluence.

Parents who accept all this with a shrug that says, "nothing *I* can do," are doing their teenage children no favors.

Why teenagers have to act like teenagers, and why we have to keep acting like parents

The big intellectual and emotional task of any adolescent is to stop being dominated so much by us—mom and dad. It's probably hard for parents to imagine that we dominate our kids that much in any respect, but it's not our perspective that counts. From a kid's point of view, once she's attained the age of moderate rationality (sometime after age 11, if Piaget is right), we've been dominating her life since birth. Enough of that, she thinks, I'm going to become my own person now. Psychologists refer to this as "decathecting parental introjects." For the rest of us, it's teenage rebellion.

To be honest, teenage rebellion tends to be more in the form of attitude—with or without the capital A—than substance. By and large, kids still maintain the same general value system as their parents. One U.S. Department of Education survey says that 73 percent of teenagers agree with their parents on what to do with their lives; 87 percent agree on the value of education; 70 percent on religion and 63 percent even agree on how to dress. In the face of such large-scale agreement, how can the kids declare their independence? By loudly disagreeing on all sorts of *minor* items—from what running shoes they deserve to have on their feet to how late they should stay out at Jamie's party when his parents are off in Florida. Because most parents haven't faced this kind of substantive opposition in the blissful years when the kids are 8 to 11, adolescent attitude can come as a shock.

"I was okay with a lot of Jenn's stuff until the tongue ring," said my friend Marty. There were five fathers in this group, sitting around and having a beer as we sometimes do. Because we're men, it can take hours before we get beyond football scores and business talk to say anything that has any personal significance.

"The tongue ring?" somebody asked.

"Okay, it's not a ring, it's a kind of spike," Marty explained. "I mean, it's a pin that goes through her tongue and then there's a kind of holder at the bottom so it doesn't slip out."

"Sounds painful," I said.

"Probably was," Marty muttered. "I wasn't there. I mean, I was okay when her mom got her ears pierced. That was practical. And I guess I could handle the other five earrings. And the nose ring when she was 16, that was kind of cute."

"Yeah, real cute," grunted somebody.

Marty ignored the comment. "But this tongue thing. I mean, she can barely talk any more."

"You mean, she talks to you at all?" asked one of the other dads. "Mine doesn't. She treats me like a piece of furniture . . . no, a piece of furniture with a wallet."

"At least the tongue thing comes out," said another dad, probably the most cheerful of the group. "It's not permanent. When my kid came home with tattoos on his legs, I was just about ready to kill him."

"That would be permanent," I commented.

"Hey, does anybody know a company working on a quick tattoo-removal thing?" said Bob, our sharpest investor. "I think we could make some money here."

We probably could make money here—that's really what we do best with teenagers. Thanks to part-time jobs, they've got the highest disposable incomes of any segment in the population except seniors, and most seniors won't dispose of their cash nearly as fast as a teenager with a credit card. Economically, our society tends to exploit our teenage kids by shunting them into McJobs that nobody else would put up with, not so much to contribute to the household finances, but so they can buy the pimple creams, motorcycles and compact discs that are pitched to them.

What we don't do well with teenagers is discipline them. The kids are too old to spank, too adult to be treated in an arbitrary fashion and often too smart to be out-argued. We feel powerless. A hundred years ago, a mouthy teenager would have been "turned out of the house," a phrase which now appears only in old movies. Getting turned out of the house back then was a serious business— suddenly a kid would have to get his own Winchester, shoot his own antelope or figure out some way to claim his own 100 acres. Kids might still get mouthy and head off on their own—they've been doing this since the story of the prodigal son in Biblical times—but the parents weren't as wracked with guilt as we are. It's one thing to tell a son to go plow his own field; it's something else to say, in effect, "Get out of here, become a street windshield cleaner and start doing drugs big time."

Three essentials for parenting teenagers

The biggest problem with handling teenagers is that we and they don't talk to each other all that much. A mother and a baby will prattle for many hours a day; parents and an elementary-school kid will still talk for up to an hour; but parents and teenagers seem to engage in grunts more than conversation. One survey says that the total "non-instrumental" conversation of a parent and a teenager comes to four minutes a week. (Instrumental conversation is about mundane items such as "Take your dishes to the sink;" non-instrumental conversation is what made up those bedtime talks between Ward Cleaver and the boys.) The kids, of course, complain that it's us who won't talk to them. We complain that it's the teenagers who won't talk to us. In either event, it's hard to do effective discipline when the two sides aren't talking.

Of the three basic rules for trying to improve life with our teenagers, the first follows from the above.

Talk to your kid, regardless. This is easier to suggest than to accomplish. Too much of modern life conspires to cut into potential conversation time between parents and teenage kids: We don't wash and dry dishes together, we only occasionally watch TV together, we have different tastes in music, we share fewer interests in the outside world. Just as I may find weird my kid's interest in Tibetan chants, so he regards my interest in mutual funds and 401(k)s as bizarre. There is always a gap between generations; successful families have to find time to talk over the chasm.

Parents who still talk to their kids make sure there's some time when conversation can actually occur in the household. This requires a little parental power and organization: eating dinner together, kids doing homework where we can see them, a limit on TV. Creating such situations is a discipline for both sides and is rarely accepted without some grunts of protest from the kids. But unless we preserve some time for it, the talk won't happen.

The second basic rule wouldn't be so essential if we all followed the first, but research puts this close to the top for parents who want to keep their teenagers away from serious grief:

Keep a careful eye on the kid's friends. Starting around age 10, our influence on the kids begins to wane and that of the peer group begins to loom extraordinarily large. Teenagers frequently complain that the only people who listen to them are other teenagers (though this is not true—many teachers and other adult mentors listen very well to teenagers), and generally this tends to be their preference. Since the peer group is where most of the talk is taking place, it's also where most of the values are coming from.

This makes our kids' friends both powerful and potentially dangerous. Judy Dunn notes that "parents' monitoring of adolescent activities with peers"—knowing whom they're with, where they are and maybe what they're doing—works well to reduce problems with teens.

What I find truly remarkable is the number of parents I know who go out of their way to help their kids spend time with other teenagers who might well be dangerous or destructive. While it's always counterproductive to say something like, "Jamie is a bum and he's not allowed in our house," (in fact, such statements would instantly transform Jamie into a radical hero), there's no reason we have to provide transportation to Jamie's house or fork over spending money so our kid can treat Jamie to a night at the local club. Ironically, it's the "good" kids who often seek out a druggie, rebellious Jamie to explore a kind of life they're not prepared to step into themselves. If we've done a fairly good job parenting our kids so far, they'll keep a reasonable distance between themselves and the Jamies out there.

> The most important factor in insulating a teenager from a life on the edge of crime is parents who promote a better group of friends.

At the same time, parents can do much to promote friends who appear to be decent. These are the kids who should get invited along to the cabin, to the beach, or to use the extra ticket to a baseball game. As British research on inner-city kids shows, the most important factor in insulating a teenager from a life on the edge of crime is parents who promote a better group of friends. Improving the peer group is a very valid reason to change a kid's school or, should it be necessary, to change apartments or houses. I've known a dozen parents who've resorted to this, with a better-than-average success rate. They figure that a moving van is cheap compared to the costs of lawyers, drug rehab and psychological therapy. Sometimes they're right.

In terms of discipline, rules and punishments are obviously going to change as a child gets older. We would not let a 5-year-old stay out with his buddies until midnight or fine him twenty bucks for coming in late. But both that rule and the fine would be entirely appropriate for many 16-year-olds. What's important is not that the container of our discipline remains unchanged, but that it continues to exist. Hence, rule three:

Expand the container of discipline, but don't ever abandon it. In the chapters on discipline and punishment, I talked about the way these provide an essential structure—a container—for a kid's life. This is true when a child is two or twelve, or twenty-two, but the size of the container expands. Problems occur when we try to pretend that teenagers are adults who no longer require a container, or our container becomes so rigid that kids have to break it or sneak around it to live their lives.

Some years ago, I asked a group of 16-year-olds to write a manual for parents, a kind of guide to the "care and handling of your teenager." Kids did not want parents to abandon rules altogether, but they did want parents who were "fair" in handling discipline.

"Don't make up a rule after I've done something and tell me that I broke it. I want to know the limits ahead of time."

"Punishment is okay, but don't go bananas just 'cause I finished the last milk in the refrigerator."

"My parents let my little brother get away with anything, but if I do just one thing—*kaboom*. It's not fair."

In talking with the kids and helping them polish their manual, I found it interesting that they rarely compared the rules and expectations of their own families to those of their peers. While parents always hear, "Well, Trevor's parents let him . . . ", the kids themselves didn't make such comparisons to each other. The concept of "fair" was defined *within* their families, not outside of them.

The exact nature of a family's rules didn't matter much, but the kids had to know what they were. That comes back to communication. Again, the kids didn't care much whether their particular parents let them stay up to 2:00 in the morning or whether they had to be in bed by 10:00, but the rules had to be consistent within the household. Sibling rivalry is so powerful that any exception for a brother or sister sends ripples through the whole house. Finally, the kids thought it was essential for them to be punished when they broke the rules ("Like, otherwise, what's the point?"), but the punishment had to be perceived as reasonable.

What's reasonable? Grounding. Virtually every kid thought grounding for a period of time was a fair punishment for a parent to hand out (though the question of how long for a particular offense was debated at length). The second-best approach was losing a privilege like "Friday night I can stay out late" or "Sunday afternoon I get to drive the car" for a period of time. Third best, on their list, was docking an allowance or levying a fine for kids who worked and had outside income.

What did the kids hate in terms of punishment? Yelling (the kids thought we did far too much of this). Hitting (which is what spanking becomes at this age). Shame (getting chewed out in front of friends or siblings). Guilt tripping ("How could you do this to your mother?"). Most transgressions in life, for teenagers and adults both, don't warrant the emotional equivalent of being drawn and quartered. Too often, the kids thought, parents just went wild in handing out a punishment and then refused to back down. Under consumer law, we're all allowed a 24-hour change-of-mind period after making a purchase; parents should give themselves similar leeway to come back to their senses after blowing their cool.

> The exact . . . rules didn't matter much, but the kids had to know what they were. That comes back to communication.

Avoiding Oedipus: Binding, delegating and expelling our kids

When Freud settled on the myth of Oedipus to explain the necessary conflict between parents and children, he had good reasons for doing so. For one, Freud acknowledged for the first time that some of the conflict between fathers and sons, mothers and daughters, had a sexual component. For another, Freud chose a myth where the conflict was necessary, not accidental. In the myth, Oedipus is destined from birth to kill his father and marry his mother. The parents, trying to thwart fate, abandon their baby in

> ## Five Important Principles in Parenting Teenagers
>
> 1. **Be scrupulously fair and consistent.** Our kids' burgeoning intellectual powers are just waiting for evidence of slackness on our part.
> 2. **Keep a wary eye on their friends.** Nobody says you have to drive your kid to a sleepover at the local Hell's Angels clubhouse.
> 3. **Give in slowly to the inevitable.** The kids have to define their independence and autonomy, but smart parents give them ways to do it a little bit at a time.
> 4. **Keep them connected.** Privacy and isolation are not necessarily good things for teens. The kids are still part of the family and ought to be part of the community, too.
> 5. **Ultimately, it's our house.** A teenager does not really want to set his own rules, tyrannize the family and dominate his parents—don't let him.

the hills where the child Oedipus is rescued by a shepherd and raised to adulthood. Unaware of his real parentage, Oedipus goes off to seek his fortune in the world—and ends up killing his father and marrying his mother.

Freud abandoned the Greek emphasis on destiny in examining the myth and looked, instead, to sexual frustration and family structure. It's significant, in the myth, that the parents cannot circumvent destiny. Today, many parents somehow feel that they can get around teenage rebellion—Oedipal or otherwise—by taking some appropriate defensive posture. If parents are just smart enough, or *nice* enough, to avoid confrontation, maybe the kid will turn out just fine. The problem is, this kind of avoidance doesn't work.

Researchers into adolescent separation conflicts such as Helm Stierlin and Kent Ravenscroft of the National Institute of Mental Health have looked at a many cases in which parents tried to get around problems with their teenagers in unsuccessful ways. By trying to avoid the minor blow-ups that occur between parents and teenage children, the families simply created larger problems for the children later on. Stierlin and his colleagues identify three modes of avoidance—binding, delegating and expelling—that might give all of us some idea of how *not* to deal with teenagers.

A *binding mode* occurs when parents try to prevent conflict with their teenagers by spoiling the kids or treating them as if they were still young children. The clichéd parent here is an "intrusive parent" who is invariably butting into a teenage kid's life. The intrusive parent keeps interpreting what happens to the teen for him: "Oh, you're not really hungry. You don't really want to go out Friday. You know how much I hate it when you do that." The trouble with this kind of ego-binding, as psychologists call it, is that it makes separating from such a parent excruciatingly difficult, if not impossible. Psychological binding might forestall conflict in the house when the kids are teenagers, but it does no long-term good for young people who can never become real adults themselves.

The *delegating mode* essentially sends the teenagers out to complete some hidden psychological task of the parent. The kids become so busy with their "mission" that they can no longer find time or energy to question whose mission it is. Shakespeare's Hamlet, for instance, was a delegated teenager. Prompted by his father's ghost, Hamlet sets out to avenge his father's death, destroy his usurping uncle Claudius and restore his mother's honor. Unfortunately, things don't work out quite as Hamlet intended, so the stage at the end of Act V is littered with bodies, including Hamlet's own. The real problem with delegation, unfortunately, is that the kids are not always able to fulfil the mission that's handed to them. We may secretly want our kid to be a brain surgeon or a baseball player, but the kid may not have the diligence or the swing to make these dreams come true.

In another common form of delegation, a parent secretly expects a child to live a wilder life than the parent was able to. The irony here is that a parent might well preach the virtues of good behavior, but tacitly encourage a son or daughter to do the opposite.

The resulting conflict between the voiced "good person" ideal and the secretly applauded "bad person" mission can result in real frustration for the kid. This is one of Biff's problems in *Death of a Salesman*, and it's the problem of my friend Marty's daughter in real life. While the parents might officially express horror at what the kid is doing, secretly they get some pleasure out of the kid's wild life.

Finally, Stierlin writes about the *expelling mode*, where the kids are simply rejected as nuisances by their parents and pushed out to look after their own lives at the time of adolescence. Like any abandoned kids, these teenagers are likely to suffer some abuse from the outside world while, at the same time, developing a certain cunning that enables them to survive. This latter quality can be used for good or ill. Many entrepreneurs, for instance, started looking after themselves at an early age. On the other hand, so did many juvenile delinquents. The emotional cost of being expelled from the family, unfortunately, is a lingering insecurity that won't go away.

I've run through these three scenarios as a set of "cautionary tales," a phrase that used to apply to fairy tales with their simple messages of caution for the child reader. Little Red Riding Hood is a cautionary tale about the importance of being wary of seductive strangers. My stories of intrusive parents, or parents who dump their dreams on their kids, or parents who push the kids away when they get too troublesome, are similar warnings. As parents of teenagers, we've got to be careful.

But we can't be afraid. I have a friend who adopted a child who had come from a seriously disturbed family and had been through a succession of foster homes. Even after some years in Martha's home, the growing teenager was never 100 percent certain that Martha—or anyone—would really care about him. One night he put the matter to a test. The boy stayed out way past his ten o'clock home-time, so Martha went through the usual parental agonies of calling to friends, schoolmates and the local hospital. Just past two o'clock, she remembered having driven past the boy's first apartment, a gutted highrise, and she recalled the look on her adopted son's face. Following her hunch, she decided to drive over. There was the boy, propped in a window three floors up.

"Are you going to send me back to foster care now?" he shouted to her.

"No," Martha said.

"Are you going to come up here and get me?"

"No."

"So what are you going to do?" the kid asked.

"I'm going to wait here until you come down," Martha called up. "Then I'm going to give you a hug. And then we're going to figure out a punishment."

Martha didn't have to wait long. The kid came down and got his hug. He also got a punishment—a long letter of explanation to Martha and a bit of time turning dirt in the garden. Like the hug, the punishment was proof of her love.

"What strange and wondrous creatures"

In talking about teenagers, we always seem to come back to images of Hamlet, the strange and troubled youth who causes grief for everyone around him. I think this is unfortunate, because few teenagers are so difficult. We should remember that Shakespeare also created a teenage character called Miranda, a dutiful and loving child who overcomes a number of difficulties to find true love and become an adult herself. I've taken the opening line for this closing section from her. For Miranda, who has lived all her life on an island with her father, it's her first response on glimpsing the men from the wider world.

Like Miranda, our teenage children are often just innocents who are full of fear and wonder at the looming threat of the larger world. It's easy to forget this simple truth because we are pummeled with images of teenagers on television that have so little connection to the adolescents in our own homes. Television increasingly offers us jaded teenage-adults who seem to have everything under control, including their parents. But real teenagers, the ones we're bringing up, have simply entered a difficult stage in life where they must break free of us to be reborn into the big world out there. It's scary. And it's wonderful. They need help to make this second "birth" successful, just as they needed help coming into the world the first time. That all births are difficult and painful is no excuse for avoiding them; only such pain can bring such joy.

Five More Good Tips for Dealing with Teenagers

1. **Watch the part-time job hours.** Kids who work more than 15 hours a week start having problems in school and actually may begin to think that assembling hamburgers is some kind of lifelong career.
2. **Encourage volunteering.** Helping out at a nursing home or a hospital or a food bank reminds teenagers that they are part of a larger universe.
3. **Watch the computer.** If you have a teenage boy, he will be downloading pornography when you're not around.
4. **Don't push your own frustrated dreams.** Sure, you wanted a motorcycle when you were a kid. But giving a 16-year-old a motorcycle is like handing a 5-year-old a loaded revolver.
5. **Bolster the girls.** There are too many factors "out there" that trivialize and attack the competence of young teenage girls. Make sure your actions at home support their dreams, their achievements and their self-confidence.

Chapter 16

Diapers can be disposable; dads are not

"My sister has decided to come home and live with my parents," says a friend.

"Oh? Won't that drive her crazy?" I ask.

"Probably. Stephanie hasn't got much choice, with the kids and all."

"She's the one who got pregnant a few years ago, wasn't she?"

"Yeah, that was a disaster. Anyway, she found this guy Mike and they sort of settled down. Stephanie had two more kids and then Mike took off."

"'Took off?'"

"Gone. Kept up child support for a while, then disappeared. No way Stephanie could hold down a job and look after three kids. I mean, one of them was sick almost all the time."

"It's tough," I say.

"Single parenting stinks," she replies, shaking her head.

So single-parent Stephanie and her kids apparently beat a strategic retreat to grandma and grandpa's house. This would hardly be a pleasant situation for either mom or the grandparents. Stephanie, who's been an independent adult for 10 years, is suddenly reduced to the status of adult-child-at-home. Not only has she been hobbled by her ex-partner's disappearance and her finances, she faces a further loss of status in her parents' home. The entire question of parenting authority in the combined household also becomes confused. It is not Stephanie who rules this roost, but the grandparents. It is not Stephanie who sets the bottom line, but grandma or grandpa. Children are as adept at locating power and identifying defensive weaknesses as any professional football player.

Nor do Stephanie's parents have much to be cheery about. At age 50-plus, their own kids grown and the house rearranged for the joys of adult-life-without-children, they suddenly have a defeated daughter on their hands and three children, not of their own making, putting jelly fingerprints on the wall and threatening the china. The house, which had seemed too large when Stephanie and her brothers were gone, now seems too small for the six-person extended family. The grandparents resent the fact that Stephanie does not have a job—when both of them still go off to work every day—nor do they like the way she's raising her kids.

And what of the absent dad? His story is never very clear in these situations. There must have been extraordinary frustration and defeat in his life for a man to abandon his own children. There is probably a tale of garnisheed paychecks, denied visitations, failed jobs and maxed-out credit cards—a tale his kids may never hear.

The whole situation is sad. What's worse, it's become entirely too common. Fathers are disappearing from kids' lives at a rate unheard-of in the past. It's easy to blame the fathers themselves, no-fault divorce or tough economic times. But the impact of dads becoming a disposable commodity falls mainly on the kids.

I need your sperm, not you

A few years ago, a friend of our mostly grown kids joined us at our cabin for a weekend and entertained everyone with a remarkable idea.

"I'm going to get pregnant," Catherine said.

"What a wonderful idea," one of my kids said. "You'd be a great mom."

"Do you have any particular man in mind?" I asked. I thought this was whimsical, though my wife shot me one of those looks.

"No, not really," Catherine said brightly. "Any sperm will do."

There was some general laughter over this. The young woman was an intelligent, witty person who worked quite productively as a nurse in a major hospital. Catherine had been through an array of dismal boyfriends, quasi-relationships and quickie sexual encounters, but now she was pushing 35. She wanted a baby, the biological clock was ticking and there was no reasonable man in sight.

"But after the sperm has done its job," I said, "what about the child? I mean, who looks after him?"

"Oh, I will," Catherine said. "And my mother said she'll help. Men aren't any good with babies anyway."

Sadly, her estimation of the value of men as fathers of infants is fairly correct. While the situation must be better now, studies from the '60s indicate that fathers interact with babies about 37 seconds a day. The average father doesn't have much to do with the average baby until the child turns two or so, and even then the interactions often don't improve much until the child can handle a ball or a racquet. Nor are dads, even in post-liberation times, much help around the house. Even in two-income families, surveys say that dad does only 10 percent of household chores. Then there are all those problems with the male personality—tendencies toward aggression, sexism, conflict and sometimes physical violence. In these days of test-tube sperm and in-vitro fertilization, why not eliminate the dad-factor altogether?

This is exactly what the young nurse did. Rather than use a test tube of sperm (a company in California will never sell sperm with credentials—guaranteed donor IQ, hair color, and so forth), Catherine picked up an available man for a one-night stand at the right time of the month. The results appeared eight months later (the baby was premature), a lovely daughter. Under the care of mother and grandmother, the baby thrived, at least until mom went back to work. Then grandma bridled at providing full-time, no-cost day care and got especially irritable when Catherine went back to some of her old habits—casual sex, drinking and drugs. Tensions in the household escalated. Catherine suffered a breakdown from a combination of depression and exhaustion, and ended up in the hospital. Her mother threatened to take permanent custody of the baby for a while, but relented when Catherine got out of the hospital and cleaned up her act.

What about the child in all this? I have only seen the baby once, but my hunch is that she survived this turmoil without terrible emotional scarring. There were, after all, two caregivers—a mother and a grandmother—with whom the child could form a strong attachment. There were two caregivers who could spell each other during times of illness and distress. And there was at least one caregiver when the other threatened to quit or ended up in the hospital. Thank goodness for grandma, in this case, because the child would have been in a terrible situation if Catherine had been without her support.

I tell this cautionary tale because the number of women who choose to be single mothers seems to be increasing. According to the U.S. Census, the number of single mothers has tripled in the past twenty-five years, to 9.8 million such households in 1998, the most recent year for which statistics are available. These households comprised 26 percent of all parent-child families that year, up from 12 percent in 1970. Most of these single parents did not choose their status, but an increasing number of mothers are single "by choice." Increasingly, they have powerful media models.

Murphy Brown's decision to have and give birth to a baby on prime-time television caused a conservative uproar in the United States out of all proportion, considering that Murphy Brown is a fictional character. Other media celebrities have also decided to have children in the absence of men—Rosie O'Donnell tops the list. Of course, famous women like Rosie lead lives where any child is born into a paid-for extended family (indeed, the nannies sometimes have personal assistants), but they still act as models for women leading lives in the much more real world.

In the 1970s, I wrote a book on pregnancy for teenagers back when two-thirds of unwed teenage mothers were giving up their children for adoption. The idea at the time was that adoption was better for the child and that it was important for the mother to get on with her own life. When I came back to the same topic in 1988, I found find that the statistics had reversed. Two-thirds of the young mothers were now keeping their babies, almost always with grandmother's help, and only a third were giving their children up for adoption. Some sea change in attitude had taken place—and is still taking place—regarding our notion of the kind of family that children ought to grow up in.

Technology now permits women to conceive, give birth and raise children without any obvious need for a man beyond the donation of a vial of sperm. But is it any good for the kids?

It takes two to tango, but you can go line dancing all by your lonesome

In the animal world, at least the more complex end of it, the production of children involves a two-creature tango. There are mating rituals, if not courtship, sex when the females are in estrus, birthing and then care for the infants. With the exception of a few species (seahorses, for one), most of the obligations for courtship and sexual performance are on the male and most of the obligations for bearing, birthing and bringing up children belong to the mother.

For human beings, the tango has become an elaborate dance whose movements are dictated by necessity but whose music is set by social convention. In most of history and throughout most human cultures, women were the ones who were designated to tend the infants. This was partially because moms could nurse—an essential item in cultures where formula, stoves and microwaves do not exist—and partially because dad was busy either at farming, hunting or war. Complicating these patterns is the sad truth that a fair number of people, for most of human history, have died quite young. In seventeenth-century Virginia, not even a third of white children would have both parents alive by the time they reached adulthood. In the eighteenth century, the proportion of parents managing to stay alive had climbed to 50 percent; at the start of the twentieth century, the figure had risen to 72 percent.

Staying alive, however, does not necessarily mean staying together. The increase of divorce and relationship split-up in our time is one of the truly massive social experiments in the history of the family. Unhappy marriage has deep social and probably biological roots, but only recently has fleeing from an unhappy marriage or partnership been either possible or socially sanctioned.

The result is that well over half our children today have parents who split up while they are still of school age. Ironically, as a testimony either to the natural attraction of marriage or the real-life failure of divorce to provide the happiness it promises, the vast majority of divorced men and women re-partner fairly soon after parting. Today, the statistics are complicated by partnership arrangements, committed couples who live separately, divorced couples who remain friendly while new partners come and go, and more styles of family relationship than anyone ever saw on the first forty years of network television. These complex patterns of mating, parting and recombining have led to a very complex set of family relationships. Only young people who can manage phrases like "this is my mom's second husband's new girlfriend" seem to be at all comfortable with it.

The net result of all this social upheaval is that a majority of children today will spend some time in a single-parent household. Some social groups, in fact, have so institutionalized single parenting in an extended family structure that having two parents has become exceptional.

Is this a good thing?

The answer is—probably not. For children whose dads are nonexistent or who disappear entirely from their lives, the answer is definitely not.

When divorce statistics hit their peak in the 1980s, the popular wisdom held that a good divorce was better than a bad marriage. Two peaceful parents in separate households were seen as better than two warring parents under the same roof. Appropriate statistics were trotted out to support these contentions, "no fault" divorce lifted some of the moral stigma, and parents took advantage of this opportunity to make graceful exits from what were supposed to be lifelong commitments. After all, life is much longer now than in the past—some changes were in order.

Unfortunately, no one asked the kids what they thought about freewheeling divorce, the prospect of suddenly being hurtled into poverty or the idea of losing access to one parent or another due to squabbling or legal battles. Had we listened, we could have heard the kids saying, "Dumb idea, guys." But we often don't listen to children until they really start howling. In the 1990s, the kids began to shout—at least statistically. As David Popenoe writes in *The Wilson Quarterly*, "The children of divorced or never-married mothers are less successful in life by almost every measure than the children of widowed mothers."

It's fair to quarrel with such blanket statements—after all, *every* measure is a little strong, and some of the consequences of single parenting do relate to the lowered economic status that tends to come with it. Nonetheless, the statistics continue to mount. While more than half of today's kids come from divorced families, better than three-quarters of the students at America's elite Ivy League universities come from *intact* families. U.K. researcher Judy Dunn notes that the absence of fathers from kids' lives correlates highly with teenage boys getting in trouble with the law, with prisoners in penitentiaries, with antisocial behavior in adulthood.

The kids have spoken about divorce in their lives—they don't like it. Indeed, some of their current delay in marrying each other stems from an urge to avoid a divorce such as the one that upset their own lives.

What do dads do, anyhow?

Current social convention holds that, in the event of a fractious divorce, custody of the children goes to mom unless she is manifestly abusive or incompetent. Of course, exceptions to this general rule occur, but the prevailing wisdom is that mothers offer consistent, reliable and solicitous care for a child. Dads are seen as erratic, undependable, career-driven people who don't place kids way up on the "Year's Priorities" list in their daytimers.

This isn't entirely fair. Especially in the 1990s, a few dads have taken over a significant portion of childcare responsibility (one study says 3 percent of stay-at-home caregivers are dads). Increasingly, dads feel they have a responsibility to be a reasonable partner in raising children, though definitions of "reasonable" vary widely. For every dad who actually does half of the dishwashing, diaper-changing, walking-baby-in-the-middle-of-the-night routine, there are probably five who barely raise a finger around the house or with babies. Dads do become more active later on, but are still on the periphery in many families. One study asked teenagers in two-parent families to whom they would turn in times of distress—46 percent said they'd turn to mom, only 10 percent to dad.

Still, dads have certain special functions in families—and they probably perform these better than they do shared tasks.

First, dads help keep mothers on an even keel—and vice versa. In most two-parent families, moms remain the principal emotional caregiver whether they work outside the home or not. Maybe it's something about the brusqueness of dad's conversation, his judgmental appearance or his failure to sympathize at appropriate moments . . . the list of not-so-friendly father qualities could go on. Regardless, kids in most families tend to go to mom for Band-Aids, advice and a shoulder to cry on. Mom, then, is the container for their griefs.

When one of our boys comes in distraught and depressed after a particular job doesn't work out, he doesn't whine to me for two hours—he goes to his mom. After he's gone home, gone to bed or otherwise transferred his grief to mom, she comes to me so I can hear all about it for an hour or so. Sometimes I think of this process in terms of physics—the kid is vibrating like crazy, transfers some of the energy to mom, who then transfers some of it to me. In physics, the emotional soothing is called *damping;* in the emotional life of families we haven't given it a name, but the process works. Probably the single biggest drawback to single parenting is that, emotionally, each parent is trying cope with it alone.

Second, dads tend to be more physical and more daring in their dealings with kids. Just as kids will go to mom for soothing or sympathy, they usually go to dad for aggressive play. It is dads who dangerously toss kids in the air, show kids how to use chisels without safety goggles or push kids too high on the swing so they cry out in mock terror. Kids love it. One U.S. study of kids between age two and three indicates that, given a choice, more than two-thirds will choose to play with their dads rather than their moms.

Third, dads demonstrate the limits of a child's power. It has been observed that when dads engage in rough play with their kids, they are also teaching the children that biting, hitting and punching are outside the limits. Fathers contain the play even as they push the kid. In Freudian terms, it is repression by the father that forces the child to develop socially outside the family unit. The frustration a

Five Important Things Dads Provide Besides Cash

1. **Dads push the child's envelope.** They often demand more than mom, care less about emotional upset and push the swing until it's scary.
2. **Dads make time for different things:** football games, fishing, monster truck shows, roughhousing on the floor.
3. **Dads help make a kid smart.** Not by themselves, of course, but dad's involvement as a parent is a big predictor for the development of all sorts of intellectual skills.
4. **Dads keep teenagers on track.** Maybe Freud was right: Statistically, a teenage boy without a dad is doomed to trouble.
5. **Dads are men.** There's good and bad in this, but a boy needs to have a close-up view of what that means, to decide what kind of man he wants to be.

child feels during this period of conflict may not be nice, but it's necessary for a child to grow beyond the narcissistic world of childhood.

Finally, though my list could go on, fathers open up areas of the world that have traditionally pertained mostly to men. These range from the mundane (fishing, car repair) to the profound (aggression, competitiveness, the urge for worldly achievement). It's not that such things are closed to women any more than sewing and sympathy are closed to men, just that most of us haven't gotten over thousands of years of sexual stereotyping.

There are aspects of the world that a father shows a son, just as a mother shows a daughter, that are important to growth. And there are aspects of caring, love and protection that fathers feel for daughters that mothers may never know. These generalizations are

sexist, but have largely remained true since the Mayan Indians
incorporated them into a glyph:

> For in the new baby lies the future of the world—
> The mother must hold him close
> So he will know that the world is his.
> The father must take him to the highest hill
> So that he can see what his world is like.

Single parenting stinks

"It's not like during the war," says a friend who lost her husband in
World War II and raised two children on her own. "There were a
lot of us, then, whose husbands were off in the war and we looked
after each other and each other's kids. We had family, too. Aunts and
uncles knew they were supposed to lend a hand. It wasn't a question
of money like it is today, it was just helping out."

Times have changed. Frequently the biggest problem for
single parents today is one of money. An adult needs a job to
make money (and recent welfare changes make that job even more
imperative), but having a job means arranging for day care, or
after-school care, or somebody to help out when the child is sick.
Theoretically, reforms in family law should have provided for a
reasonable level of spousal support to ease the financial problems
of divorce, but so far it has only succeeded in transferring the
problems of nonpaying spouses to an incompetent government
bureaucracy.

Even when money is resolved, the problem of time remains.
Kids need a fair amount of parental time—dumb time, I've called
it—and parents should be available for those moments when kids
really need us. But jobs, housework, school committees, ballet
lessons and driving the kids to soccer practice also require time.
Sometimes single parents are daring enough to expect adequate
time to sleep or perhaps go on a date, but that's difficult with all
the other demands. Even though the ex-husbands may seem to
have done little around the house or with the kids, separation and
divorce can show that his small contribution made family life a lot
more bearable.

"Just when I think I've got everything under control, something else happens," says Shirley, a single mom. "My car won't start or the cat gets sick or the TV goes on the fritz. It's the last thing that does you in."

Shirley's situation is much better than that of many single moms. Her soon-to-be-ex husband is a lawyer and his support checks arrive on time. He actually shows up on time to get the kids on his alternate weekend and doesn't fight too much with Shirley over who gets the kids for Easter. Shirley is an illustrator and she can work at home, so she's accessible to her kids more than the moms in most two-parent families.

"But sometimes you just can't cope," she says. "It's enough to make me wonder why I ever did this."

Shirley's problem is that she is without *other* supports. Her ex-husband works, travels and spends long nights at the office. Her parents are a thousand miles away. Her sister lives in town, but is busy with a family of her own. Her neighbors are pleasant enough, but it's a neighborhood of married families and Shirley isn't married any more.

Is it any surprise that Shirley is virtually destined to re-marry or re-partner within three years? Humans may be romantic, idealistic creatures, but at another level we know when we need help.

What families need, it would seem, is a pair of parents. There are advantages if the pair is married (for stability), one of them male (for modeling and the necessary Oedipal conflict) and at least one of them working (for cash). But it may not be necessary for the parents to be a traditional husband and wife. There is no evidence, for instance, that children raised by gay and lesbian couples are at any disadvantage on social or intellectual measures. There are whole cultures where child rearing is done by mother and grandmother as the basic parental unit. Statistically, the mother-grandmother duo doesn't work well for male children, but these results are less than solid because of concurrent problems connected to race and social class.

What seems clear is that families need a mother and a father figure, if

> What families need, it would seem, is a pair of parents.

not a father. What also seems clear is that split-up families need a lot more help from neighbors, friends, extended family and the larger community than they're getting now. These two truths aren't likely to keep rocky marriages together, but they should serve as cautions for all the Catherines who think that men are useful merely for their sperm. Having kids is a serious and difficult business. Keeping a family going after separation and divorce is no easy feat. But it's about time the adults in our society—that's us—gave as much thought to what our kids need as to what we want for ourselves.

Five Reasons Why Single Parenting Is So Tough

1. **There's not enough money.** Paychecks for young people are small, jobs insecure, child support not very reliable.

2. **There's not enough time.** Between jobs, day care and child trade-offs, the available parenting hours can disappear.

3. **There's not enough outside support.** War widows and soldiers' wives got all sorts of community and extended family support; single moms these days do not.

4. **Kids and parents get sick.** It's hard enough being a good parent when we're well and our child is fine; it's a catastrophe trying to deal with illness on our own.

5. **Nobody can be both mom and dad.** Sometimes a kid needs one, sometimes the other. Ultimately, any parent is just one person. Two's better.

Chapter 17

Technology, toys and tough parenting choices

Technology has often been a good thing in the raising of children. To start with, technology tends to keep kids alive longer. Two hundred years ago, three-fourths of the child population died in infancy; even in Charles Dickens's time almost half of all children died before age five. Today we don't worry as much about infant mortality thanks to technology: clean water, immunization and antibiotics. When our teenagers whine about pimples and possible mononucleosis, it's tempting to remind them that smallpox in the nineteenth century left many people pockmarked for life, or to point out that diphtheria, typhus and pneumonia killed off significant portions of the juvenile population right into the twentieth century. Then again, our teenagers would probably just give us that *look*, so perhaps historical perspective is best kept to ourselves.

In the past one hundred years, technology has brought us many other advances that have made parenting a little easier. Some parents would say that the cordless phone has been a major boon because it enables us to look after kids and still answer the phone when the auto mechanic finally calls back. So, too, are baby-monitoring devices. While parents of my generation had to stay close enough to the child's bedroom to hear if the baby were crying in her crib, parents today can at least go wash the car as long as they can sprint back when the monitor tells them the baby is bawling. A small triumph of telecommunications technology has increased the mobility of parents by some three hundred yards—no mean feat for about fifty dollars.

And yet, even as we all admit that technology has made parents' lives easier, a nagging fear remains that such change might not be good for our children in the long run. Throughout history, parents have embraced technological advances that promised some immediate relief from the annoyances of child rearing, but didn't pan out long-term. In the Renaissance, leeches were the treatment of choice for many childhood illnesses but were often a fatal "cure." In the nineteenth century, the original India-rubber nipple and unsterilized glass bottle made a deadly combination for infant feeding. And in my own time, growing up forty years ago, my parents adorned my bedroom with a pair of charming glow-in-the-dark nightlights. These cheap nightlights shone dimly for all the years of my childhood—courtesy of radium-laced paint. Thank goodness I never had the urge to chew on them.

These days, thanks to *Consumer Reports* and organizations such as Good Housekeeping, there's much less chance of finding a truly lethal item for children on the shelves of your local department store. But that doesn't mean every technological advance is entirely for our children's benefit. Consider these morally hideous bits of technology, all readily available in stores or on the Internet:

- The "ADD buzzer." This behavioral-psychology advance outfits the child with a wristband and an electronically controlled buzzer. The parent or teacher has a control box that can activate the buzzer as a reminder to the kid when he's dawdling or not attending to schoolwork. With the touch of a button, the kid gets a zap by remote control that says, in effect, *don't goof off.*
- Household surveillance camera. For a few hundred dollars, surveillance companies will set up your house with hidden cameras to keep an electronic eye on your nanny or your child while you're at work. Just in case you wondered what was *really* going on when you were away, electronics makes it easy to find out.

- Electronic periphery fence. So far only designed for dogs and other animals, the electronic periphery fence gives your pet an electric zap whenever he strays too far from the house. How many years before we see a similar device for 5-year-olds?

Few parents, fortunately, are rushing to embrace technology that violates basic standards of privacy and respect for human dignity. While it is tempting to push our moral boundaries a bit—for the benefit of our kids, of course—we tend to draw the line at actually zapping our kids or spying on them all day long.

But this doesn't mean we're not letting technology affect the way we parent our children. From the VCR to the Internet, technology is part of our lives and therefore part of family life. For parents who are involved with their children, technology can simply add to the fun. But for parents who think they can substitute technology for the basic, day-to-day demands of being the adult-in-residence, technology becomes a dangerous temptation. A microchip is not a mom; nor can a dedicated Internet connection make up for the absence of a dad.

Most technological blessings are mixed

Parents today have access to any number of pieces of technology that can be used for good or ill. The videotape recorder, for instance, can be a wonderful tool for parents. David Suzuki, the well-known ecologist, uses his VCR to record programs for his kids and thereby preview what they watch. Other parents use the VCR to do time-shifting, so our kids can watch that wonderful movie the network insists on broadcasting at 9:00 PM, without interfering with the kids' regular bedtime. Still other parents use the VCR to make sure their kids can watch decent children's programming without having to be pummeled by heavy-duty toy advertising.

But any technology offers other temptations. There are too many parents, schools and day-care centers who use the videotape recorder as an electronic baby-sitter. Television images have a remarkable ability to keep kids quiet, or mostly quiet, and seemingly content. But is this good for them? No one knows what repeated exposure to even good television does over the long term. Robert Bly and Neil Postman regard the television medium as toxic for young people. I will only report that among my gifted creative-writing students, more than half can sing the entire *Gilligan's Island* theme song from memory, while only two have read Dickens.

No factor is more important in building a child's pre-reading and reading skills than having a parent who cuddles and reads or tells stories to the child on a regular basis.

The VCR and the television constitute two very iffy technological advancements for kids. While there is plenty of data to show that kids watching more than three hours of television every day suffer in school and in their general attitude toward life, we also know that 25 percent of 10-year-olds are now watching a TV screen six hours a day or more. For every parent who successfully limits a child's access to TV, another has the tube glowing all day long. Children of the second group are about to become a remarkable social experiment. They'll be the first group in history to spend more time watching television than they do at school, or eating or even sleeping. So far the statistics for these kids don't look very promising.

The child tape recorder, like the TV and VCR, is another example of technology that can be used for good or ill. Fisher-Price made the first one strong enough to resist prying little fingers; now there's My First Sony and a number of cheaper versions. The basic idea behind all of these products is that kids can use the tape recorder to record themselves, work on school projects or listen to a story. But the downside comes when mom and dad, too tired to read a story to their kids, tells them to go pop in a tape instead. It actually doesn't matter that the tape of Bob Munsch reading *Murmel, Murmel* may be excellent; the truth is that the kid is being short-changed in family reading time. No factor is more important in building a child's pre-reading and reading skills than having a parent who cuddles and reads or tells stories to the child on a regular basis. No plastic tape recorder can provide that experience.

When microchips replace moms

The kids' tape recorder is just part of a growing trend to replace the time, caregiving and limit-setting roles of parents with the cheap tricks of technology. Parents, admittedly, have less time for family life than ever before. The elaborate juggling of two jobs, day care, schools and putting breakfast on the table is exhausting for parents and kids, so there's a natural tendency for all of us to say "whew" and let technology give us a few minutes to put our feet up. But when technology substitutes for parenting, our kids end up losing out.

Let's take control of the television, for instance. Everyone knows that kids benefit by having their television rationed: a limited number of hours, set times for viewing, choices made on appropriate programs. All this implies that parents and kids talk about TV choices and that parents supervise the results to make sure the kids aren't cheating or sneaking in shows they've agreed not to watch. Parent supervision not only creates a chance for talking—a very good thing at every age level—but shows the kids that we care about what they do with their time.

However, it is also possible to limit TV viewing with a microchip. The v-chip goes part of the way in making sure that adult programming doesn't show up in front of our 5-year-old, but for $150 a parent can now limit a child's television viewing with a credit-card device. A small box is hooked up to the television set and each child gets a TV credit card programmed with a certain number of viewing hours. The box can also be programmed to delete certain channels, cut out access to adult programs and eliminate late-night viewing altogether. The net result of this cheap technology is to do in a crude way what good parents should be doing all along—limit the amount of TV kids watch and force them to make choices on programming.

What the TV credit card can't do is *everything else* that good parents know is important:

- It doesn't talk or discuss program choices.
- It doesn't allow for exceptions or extensions.

- It doesn't evaluate different types of programs.
- It doesn't make decisions on when kids watch TV instead of doing homework, soccer practice and ballet lessons.

Can the TV credit card replace mom and dad? Obviously not. But the temptation remains to let technology take over parental controls and judgment calls. The much-celebrated v-chip provides an easy, technological way to limit violent programming coming into the home. Programs such as Cybersitter make it possible to put some technological limits on what kids can access through the Internet. But when technology gives parents one more excuse to let TV viewing or computer use go unsupervised, our kids get boundaries without the talk and love that should come with them.

> When technology gives parents one more excuse to let TV viewing or computer use go unsupervised, our kids get boundaries without the talk and love that should come with them.

Toys, too many toys and imagination

In terms of developmental psychology, toys do not usually substitute for parents. Toys are the means children use to explore the universe around them and to fantasize about their role in that world. Psychologist Melanie Klein suggests that a child's play is a projection of the child's psychic reality onto the toys. For this reason, the way in which a child plays with her toys is intensely personal. As a parent, you might be encouraged to pick up your child's new Barbie doll, but when your child says, "No, Mommy, don't just look at her. Play!" you might not have the vaguest memory of what you're supposed to do. The world of toys for children is self-referential, as the psychologists say, which makes it difficult for us to enter in for very long.

The impact of technology on the world of toys, like its impact on parenting, has been mixed. One sure result has been to cut the price of toys substantially. A child of the last century would have perhaps a dozen toys at her disposal, most of them made by hand.

The impact of cheap plastic, new techniques of injection molding and the easy importing of toys from other countries after World War II led to a sharp decrease in the price of toys. It's no accident that Barbie arrived on the scene in 1959. Her development was a combination of improved plastic, new manufacturing processes, improved family income and a new kind of role modeling for children. Today, while the growth of real family income has been stalled for the last ten years, toy prices have continued to fall. The average North American girl, for instance, now owns not one or two but *eight* different Barbies. When we add baby dolls, other dolls, action figures and stuffed animals, many girls will have thirty or more fantasy figures someplace around the house. It's no wonder that when Disney released a new version of *101 Dalmatians*, other companies quickly churned out more than 17,000 licensed products connected to the film.

The nature of children's play has changed as a result of this proliferation of toys. A Victorian child might have a single doll, a ball, a stick for batting and a few metal figurines. To get enjoyment from such a limited number of toys, a child would have to join with other kids in communal play or else make use of her imagination so a single toy could be used in a number of different fantasy scenarios. Since then, the role of fantasy in play has become much less important than the role of toys in padding corporate profit sheets.

The Lego company, for instance, took its name from the Latin word for teaching, which in Danish also meant "play well." The founders of the company, Ole Kirk Kristiansen and his son Gotfried, took the teaching philosophy to heart, originally designing a set of wooden blocks that could stack and adhere to each other in a number of different ways. Their original wooden blocks turned to plastic in 1953 thanks to the company's purchase of one of the first post-war injection molding machines. In 1955, the Lego product line consisted of 28 sets of blocks and 8 Lego vehicles. The initial sets were purposely non-representational so a child could use the finely machined blocks to create virtually anything she could imagine that would structurally hold together. The idea was that kids should use their own imaginations to build the objects of their fantasies. This philosophy managed to produce a group of engineers, artists and designers who went on to apply their Lego skills to real-life professions. If the current tales from Silicon Valley are true, virtually every software designer and computer geek today cut her intellectual teeth on Lego twenty years ago.

But since then, the Lego philosophy has shifted. Pressure grew in the 1960s for the company to offer suggested designs—at least one project a child could assemble from a particular assortment of blocks. After founder Ole Kirk Kristiansen died, the company slowly began giving in to the pressure. In 1964, "model" sets were offered in addition to "block" sets. By 1966, there was a Lego train; by 1970, Lego Technic was in development. In 1974, Lego "people" blocks appeared. By the time the third generation of Kristiansens took control of the company in 1979, sales of Lego models had vastly overtaken those of the free-form blocks. Today, Lego sells about 10 billion individual pieces a year, almost all of them as models—boats, trains, vehicles, planes, landscaped designs and hundreds of others. The "finished" picture is on the box and the instructions are packed inside.

As much as these ships, planes, motorized cranes and blinking space stations are "way cool," they all have a tendency to short-change the free-form fantasy and engineering structures that were encouraged by the simple block sets. It's a long way from the 1950s' attitude of "Here are some blocks. They stick together. Wonder if we could make something?" to the 1990s' "Here's the Lego Starship. Let's find the instructions and see if we can put together all 625 pieces, step-by-step."

Fortunately, children have their own ways of resisting too much adult intrusion into their fantasy lives. In terms of the elaborate Lego kits, they invariably manage to lose the instructions, or leave key pieces under the couch, or simply not bother to rebuild the initial Starship design at all. Instead, they take the individual pieces and create robots or trucks or other devices of their own invention, much as the original block sets encouraged right from the start. I suspect Ole Kirk Kristiansen would be pleased.

The British psychologist D. W. Winnicott observed that children's play was a bridge between the child and world. He writes, "The task of reality-acceptance is never completed, in that no human being is ever free from the strain of relating inner and outer reality." The toy experience, we might say, mediates between the fragile inner world of the child and the harsh reality of the outer world he must live in. Fantasy play allows the inner anxieties and aggressions of our children to be expressed in a relatively safe area. It is far more acceptable for our kids to decapitate G.I. Joe, for example, than it is for them to try to decapitate each other. Apparently, the more parents structure the play area—or structure the usage of toys—the less psychologically effective play becomes in helping a child work through his inner problems.

The difficulty for parents comes when we purchase toys that intrude rather than facilitate our children's development. By and large, they would be better off if we spent our available cash on a decent softball rather than shelling out hundreds of dollars for the half-life-size, two-horsepower, high-torque adventure vehicle.

So where does this leave mom and dad?

I'm at a parenting class, allowed to sit in so long as I don't obviously take notes or otherwise interfere. The discussion is about kids, parents and toys.

"So what should I do?" asks one mother. "My kid has this elaborate gas station thingie and can't put it together, but pushes me away when I try to help."

"Don't bug the kid," says a dad. The dads in parenting classes always seem more assured about what they think they know.

"That's right," agrees the instructor. "When your child says, 'I can do it myself, Mommy,' you've got to let her do it herself."

"But shouldn't I be playing with her?" asks another mom. "Isn't that real quality time?"

"What do the rest of you think?" asks the instructor. Parenting-class instructors are urged to be non-authoritative. Given some of the advice that sometimes floats around out there, this is probably a good thing.

"It depends if you feel like it," says the assured dad.

The rest of the class frowns.

"Well, I don't know if it does any good to get down on the floor and play if I just do it out of guilt," offers another mom, a working single parent.

"Follow the child's lead," says a third.

"That's right. Wait to be invited into the game. Otherwise you're just intruding," adds a mother of three kids.

"I never intrude," says the assured dad.

"We're not saying you do," comes the response, "only that parents shouldn't."

The class seems to reach agreement on the question. Following the child's lead is a big idea in parenting class groups these days, and it is one fairly solid answer to the problem of establishing parent and child distance. It suggests, for instance, that we at least listen to our children—and listening has been shown to be a very good thing.

But if we base our parenting entirely on listening, we'll hear one refrain over and over again: "I want!" If we really feel that parents have no more wisdom than to "follow the kid's lead," then our kids will have their wants and interests defined by television. This does them no favors.

Our children are being raised in a culture that pushes products and entertainments at them on a continual basis. There may be rules on advertising during children's programming time, but there's still 14 minutes of commercials every hour. Even if we somehow insulated our kids from that, they still go to school and play with other kids who want the newest, the latest, the "bestest."

In the face of this overwhelming outside pressure, parents really have to intrude. Neil Postman, writing of childhood and television culture, suggests it is the obligation of parents and schools to provide a countervailing value system. Where commercials shout "Buy! Buy!" parents should be helping their kids enjoy the toys they have. Where television implies "Now! Immediately!" parents and schools have to emphasize history, perspective and slowing down.

Saying "no" in the face of such organized pressure to consume, to substitute electronic time for real time, requires real parental courage. We have to have the strength to say "no" or "no more," even when much of the advice addressed to us urges quite the contrary. Open a parenting magazine and we'll find many ads for formula and

> Saying "no" in the face of such organized pressure to consume . . . requires real parental courage.

Technology and Children: The Good and the Not-So-Good

Five Wonderful Technological Breakthroughs for Kids

1. The disposable diaper
2. The baby monitor
3. Public television
4. Infant car seats and bike safety helmets
5. Baby Snuglis and back carriers (we've finally caught up with Native Americans and Africans)

Five Iffy Technological Items for Kids

1. The television and video recorder
2. Computers and the Internet
3. Kids' tape recorders
4. Any toy that requires new batteries every 20 minutes
5. The v-chip or any other technology that substitutes a microchip for parental supervision

Everything depends on how parents use them . . .

bottles—but no advertising for breastfeeding. Open the newspaper and we'll find articles saying a child without a computer and Internet access is destined for computer illiteracy for the rest of her life—but no mention of how important it is for parents to be looking over the child's shoulder while the computer is on. Turn on the TV to a kid's show and we'll find an incredible number of ads for expensive electronic toys or movie-tie-in action figures—but there are no commercials for simple rubber balls, jacks or skipping ropes.

We and our kids are on the receiving end of a corporate culture that is much more interested in profit margins than in the welfare of children. The result of this is a generation of kids that has more toys than any other in history—but also is more overweight and seems to have a shorter attention span than ever before.

It would be foolish to expect that television itself, or government regulation, or our politicians, are suddenly going to control the corporate agenda and begin offering a better set of values for our kids. That's up to us. No computer, microchip or expensive toy can really substitute for mom and dad. We have to resist the temptation to think that might be possible.

Chapter 18

Grandparents:
Let's lend a hand

When these suburban mothers gather, coffee is the first agenda item. Starbucks is being tested lately, replacing the ground A&P standby, and it's collected generally good reviews so far. The group has been having coffee together since their children were babies. Now, because most of the kids are in school, there's less interruption to the flow of conversation.

"Bill and I are taking two weeks by ourselves," says one mom. Let's call her Gloria.

The others look in admiration. "By yourselves? You mean, alone?"

"Uh-huh," nods Gloria. "My mom is flying in to look after the kids." She smiles proudly while the others look on, amazed.

"For two weeks!" says a friend, incredulously. "She's coming from the coast to look after your kids for two weeks?"

"She must be a saint," says another mom.

"My parents do squat," adds a third. "Of course, they didn't do much for us kids when we were little, either."

"I have trouble getting my mom to look after my kids for a *weekend*. And my dad is hopeless. He looked after the kids one Saturday and I came home to find dog vomit in one corner and dog poop in another. I'm lucky my kids are still alive."

"At least he tries. My mother's too busy playing golf," moans another. "Maybe when the kids get old enough to hit the ball."

"You know what's wrong with our parents," says a quiet woman, looking at the others over her coffee. "They give you the down payment for your house, never let you forget it, and then disappear to Florida."

The others nod. "Well, at least we've got a house. Only Gloria gets a vacation."

Today's families are subject to certain vagaries of demographics, economics and social custom that do little to help them in raising children. Of course, young families have always gotten the short end of these theoretical sticks. When there is economic hardship, the youngest workers are told to sacrifice for their elders or are simply let go first. When there is war, it is the young fathers who go off to fight it. When there is peace, young parents are expected to work hard *and* raise families and do it all without complaining. Many of these long-standing patterns continue to apply today, but to this list we must add a phenomenon that is brand new: the revolt of the grannies.

The revolt of the grannies—and I mean both genders here—is a strikingly modern phenomenon. In the ancient days of extended family, say up to sixty years ago, children, parents and grandparents tended to live together with aunts, uncles and cousins in a single-family home. Childcare was a parental responsibility, but arrangements were loose because so much backup was available. If Mom was sick, Aunt Hilda or Grandma Mimi could step in; if Dad had gone to the city for seasonal work, Grandpa and Uncle Hugh could. Because there were so many caregivers, parents had a certain measure of freedom.

Grandparents in the extended family were considered the heads of the household and supposedly honored by all who lived there. In actual fact, however, they were economically dependent on their children—the parents of working age—and had roles carefully prescribed by the church and tradition. Grandparents were the family conscience, the purveyors of family history and wisdom, the exemplars of spiritual life. In *McGuffey's First Eclectic Reader of 1890*, grandma rates a whole lesson:

See my dear, old grandma in her easy-chair! How gray her hair is! She wears glasses when she reads.

She is always kind, and takes such good care of me that I like to do what she tells me.

This charming school propaganda indicates a wonderfully idealized grandparent role, but life expectancy was such that few adults made it to the age of grandparenting and those who did wouldn't have to do it for long. It wasn't until this century that most grandparents lived long enough to actually get to know their grandchildren.

It shouldn't be surprising that the seeds of the granny revolt were sown in the 1950s. World War II was over; the husbands had come home; the nuclear family reigned supreme in most households and on that new black-and-white television set. For the first time, there was nothing for grandparents to do. They didn't fit in the new, post-war bungalows and they were seldom seen on the new television screen. A look at the popular family television shows of the 1950s—*Father Knows Best, Leave It to Beaver, I Love Lucy, The Honeymooners*—shows nary a grandparent in sight.

Social inertia, however, kept the grandparents of the 1950s tied to historical roles. They still offered to baby-sit the kids, still came in "to look after things" when new babies were born, still took kids when the working parents went on vacation or were going through a "bad patch." Grandparents were still expected to provide a kind of anchor point for the younger nuclear family—a certain amount of wisdom, dependability and honesty.

> It wasn't until this century that most grandparents lived long enough to actually get to know their grandchildren.

The real revolt of the grannies didn't begin until the 1960s. The kids—my generation—were growing long hair, listening to The Beatles and declaring "All You Need Is Love" as an economic and political philosophy. The grannies, a bit smarter, shook their heads at their hippie children and got organized. "Gray power" became a substantial political force, first in Florida and then across North America. The American Association of Retired People (AARP) grew from a small group of retired folks to a powerful lobby group with 33 million members and a $350 million budget. Because the seniors' lobby was organized and knew precisely what it wanted, governments enacted legislation leading to a significant rise in pension income. Social Security checks, originally a limited form of age-specific "insurance," became an inflation-adjusted "entitlement." Perhaps as a result, in a country where some 40 percent of young families have no medical coverage, every senior receives Medicare in a program two-thirds underwritten by general tax revenues.

The result of all this change is striking—while seniors made up the poorest demographic segment in 1930, by 1990 they had become the richest.

For the first time in history, the grannies have become independent. Some have used their newfound independence to leave their large family homes and move to places that are cheaper, more comfortable and—for those who had spent their lifelong winters in the North—warm.

> For the first time in history, the grannies have become independent.

At the same time, their kids became mobile. The average apartment-dwelling young person moves every two years. The average young family changes homes every four years. When downsizing hit in the 1990s, all classes of employees were expected to move with their companies or move to find new jobs. And they did.

Grandparents suddenly had money, unexpected income and the cash proceeds from paid-off houses. The kids were moving around—and moving away—so that relationships between generations were harder to maintain. The traditional social roles of grandparents as family leaders, exemplars, teachers and carvers of the Thanksgiving turkey were being eroded by a television universe where grandparents were either nonexistent or a geriatric problem.

In real life, most grandparents were not a geriatric problem. Regular retirement at age 65 for men and 62 for women still meant leaving work in relative good health. Early retirement—often

Five Reasons Why Grandparents Aren't Around

1. They retired early enough to travel and have fun.
2. Many of them have enough money to live where they want and do what they want—often pursuing goals that were put on hold during their child-rearing years.
3. The importance of their role in raising the grandchildren has been downgraded in the media and often by their own children.
4. Divorce and family moves often make grandparent involvement difficult.
5. Looking after young kids isn't a job most people do on a volunteer basis.

available to teachers, public servants, military people and increasingly to businesspeople—meant leaving work at age 55 or 57. Such young grannies had a good twenty years of active life and no intention of lavishing those years on a younger generation who weren't sure what their role should be.

The grannies saw their opportunity for revolt and seized it. Just when the younger generation was finally admitting that grandparents are a pretty good thing, the not-so-old folks had gone off to Florida and Arizona or finally booked that month-long cruise package to Tahiti.

Of course, there are always exceptions. To be fair, not all grannies are on cruise ships. A number of seniors did not profit from the 1965 to 1988 housing boom. Many are not cashing checks from inflation-protected pension plans and are not receiving much income at all besides Social Security. These folks are not well off—but they are a minority in the demographic group. The poor in the United States, by and large, are no longer seniors but families with children.

To be doubly fair, there is also a growing proportion of seniors who have taken on the role of parents for a second time in their lives. The 1994 census showed that 3.2 million grandparents are offering some kind of care for their grandkids. Almost a million children are being raised *entirely* by their grandparents. These figures have risen by some 40 percent since the 1980s as younger families began to fall apart and grandparents intervened to prevent family catastrophe. The rise of divorce, unemployment, abandonment, drug and alcohol abuse among young parents has virtually forced seniors to come to the rescue. Without them, many single parents would be in far more desperate straits than they are.

Nonetheless, the recent prosperity and relative good health of middle-class retired people is an extraordinary turn in history. The fact that we no longer have a coherent role for grandparents is not their fault. At the turn of the century, only 1 person in 25 was over the age of 65; today that figure is 1 in 8. The number of "elderly" Americans has increased 11-fold in the course of 100 years, and the nature of being "elderly" has changed at the same time. Better eating, better public health, increased income and improvements in medicine mean that many seniors are as healthy as they were during their working years. In 1900, granny was invariably depicted on her rocker—as in James McNeill Whistler's painting of his mother—too infirm to do much beyond scowl at the artist. Today, the seniors we see in advertisements for travel health insurance seem to have just stepped off the tennis court. My own mother, in fact, plays a pretty good game of tennis at age 80 though she hasn't beaten me in a full set since she was 75. "I think I'm slowing down a little," she says.

Judith Waldrop in *American Demographics* breaks the seniors' group into four subgroups. Only 17 percent are the "frail recluses" that were depicted in Whistler's famous painting. Another group, "ailing outgoers" are still getting by pretty much on their own. The remaining 54 percent—called "healthy indulgers" and "healthy hermits"—are all capable of quite active lives. According to a Boston study, 70 percent of retired people report that they are busy volunteering in their communities.

Some retired people are also very involved with their families. There are grandmothers who do prenatal lessons with their daughters, assist with the birthing of their grandchildren and provide child care on a fairly regular basis. There are grandfathers who fill in for parents during vacations, take the grandkids fishing and hiking, make sure there are books and Lego sets in the house and even pay to take the grandkids on that winter ski trip. There are grandparents who manage to keep contact with their grandkids—by letter, audiotape and e-mail—though the kids may be split by divorce and living hundreds of miles away. I know examples of all of these people.

And I know some who never get off golf courses except to get on a cruise ship.

Grandma, come back, we need you

What is the role for grandparents in today's families? Sometimes it seems as if society does whatever it can to frustrate the connection between grandparent and grandchild. Families move; grandparents travel; divorces sever ties; and the media doesn't offer models. Moms are all over the television screen, displaying their genius in commercials, suffering in made-for-TV movies, being witty on sitcoms and emotionally competent on dramas. Dads make it to the boob tube fairly frequently, so we know exactly what image the networks have of fathers—emotionally clumsy and not very bright. This image hasn't shifted much from the days of Archie Bunker on *All in the Family* to those of Tim Allen on *Home Improvement.*

But where are the grandparents? The Golden Girls were usually too busy with their own lives and intrigues to worry about grandkids. When Roseanne Barr's grandma appears, she's neurotic. Bart Simpson's grandfather is senile. Once again, television is offering us a portrait of family life that is at least 25 years out of date with the real world.

One look around the real world is enough to show that grandparents are incredibly important to many families. In psychology, a body of research in a new area called "resilience" basically asks the question, how is it that some high-risk kids turn into healthy, competent adults and others into disturbed unemployables? Researcher E. E. Werner looked at data for some

700 at-risk kids on the island of Kauai in Hawaii and groups of children born to alcoholics and other low-functioning parents to see what the "protective factors" included. His conclusions, bolstered by many other researchers, point to the importance of an adequate substitute caregiver in the second year of a child's life and emotional support from grandparents and other relatives during early and middle childhood. Where the parents are less than adequate, according to research, grandparents are vital.

Single parents don't need multiple regression analysis to know that grandparents are important. Simple experience demonstrates that a single mom or dad needs *somebody* when tempers are frayed, work goes into overtime, a parent or baby-sitter gets sick or life otherwise fails to unfold with the ease and speed of a TV sitcom. It's best for both the kid and the single parent if that "somebody" is a grandparent.

> Where the parents are less than adequate, according to research, grandparents are vital.

"I would never have survived without my grandparents," says Joan, an adult who is not only surviving quite well but is now a grandparent herself. "My mom was an alcoholic, though we never really recognized that, and my dad was away so much. The only stability we had was my grandparents."

"That's nothing," says Paula. "I was raised by my grandparents. My dad was working construction all day and my mother started work at noon, so there wasn't much choice."

"And was there a downside to that?" I ask.

"Just that I ended up caring more about my grandma than my own mother. When she died, I was really thrown. I cried so hard, and my mom—I'll give her credit—at least she understood."

"That's like Winston Churchill," I add, "who cried at his nanny's death but was impassive at the death of his parents."

"But you want to know what's funny?" Paula asks.

We look up.

"My mother is now looking after my sister's kids. She's says it's really like being a mom for the very first time. I guess she realizes now that she wasn't there for us way back then."

When a nuclear family gets into trouble, there's no question that grandparents have an essential role to play for kids. It's why we have millions of grandparents providing free day care, if not life care, for their grandkids. But what about our *successful* nuclear families? We have plenty of data to show that grandparents are vital to low socioeconomic groups and at-risk families. But we have no research literature that measures the importance of grandparents to high-functioning families. As sociologist Robert Coles points out, we do very little research on successful families. But we do have family stories, biography and history to show us that grandparents are important.

In crisis. When my cousin lost his copier-repair job, maxed out the credit cards and finally lost his house, it was his parents who rescued the young family. The grandparents took in both parents and kids, sent dad off to a detoxification program, helped mom find a job and kept the kids fed, bathed and doing homework during the entire mess. The crisis went on for little over a year before the young family was off on their own again, but it was an essential year for those kids to have some kind of stable caregiver.

The role of grandparents in stabilizing families during a crisis isn't subject to research, but it's essential in real life. Surveys on stress and crisis management show that the average four-person family will face a really significant crisis every three to four years. We're not talking about the classic "bad patch" where mom and dad argue and mom stomps off home for the weekend. Significant life crises include death, life-threatening disease, accidents with hospitalization, crime victimization, job loss, bankruptcy, major career change, divorce and separation. These crises can hit parents like a hurricane, so grandparents have a significant role in keeping life on an even keel for grandchildren.

Mentors and models. At some point in their development, children need mentors and models as much as they need decent parenting. The role of the mentor isn't to secure the emotional base of a child's life, it's to increase his reach into the world.

Grandparents can be wonderful mentors. We see this in films, like the charming *Violinmaker's Gift*, or in children's stories like Jo Ellen Bogart's *Gifts* or Bill Martin's *Knots on a Counting Rope*. We see it in real life when grandma teaches our daughter how to make *her* grandmother's special brownies—with the special techniques that never get written down on the recipe card. We see it when grandpa takes our son out for his first hunting trip—the one that we disapprove of but can't forbid—or shows him how to build a kite instead of buying one at Toys 'R' Us. Children need many teachers beyond those in school; grandparents frequently do the instruction with love.

Wisdom. Family wisdom and tradition are both overrated and underrated in our society, but there is certainly a body of wisdom carried by grandparents that can be invaluable for young families. Grandparents know that kids *don't* cry themselves to death, that sooner or later they will eat something, that "no" had better mean "no" or there will never be an end to whining, that a Band-Aid applied almost anywhere is sufficient to solve much childhood distress. Such wisdom is calming for parents who, without it, are invariably grabbing for Penelope Leach and trying to find the appropriate section for the problem of the moment.

Part of wisdom is reminding parents of what they already know, of course. John Rosemond, a family psychologist in North Carolina, writes in his newspaper column of the grandfatherly urge to help the next generation be better parents:

> I know I should keep my mouth shut. I shouldn't tell them [the parents] to keep Jack out of group care until he's at least three years old, and put their television in storage until he's learned to read, and only buy creative toys like Legos and Lincoln Logs, and childproof so thoroughly that he can wander around the house with a minimum of supervision, and never—unless he's sick or going through a major adjustment of some sort—let him sleep with them, and never cater to picky food preferences (except on vacations), and never let him address adults by their first names until they've given him explicit permission to do so, and never let him wear a hat in the house, much less at the dinner table, and

never, ever give in to tantrums but let him throw as many as he wants (except in public, of course), and limit his presence at adult gatherings, and insist that he not interrupt adult conversations, beginning with their own, and begin requiring him to perform chores when he's three, and never pay him for doing chores, and always put him to bed early so they can be just husband and wife for the last few hours of the day.

Then again, grandparents have to remember exactly how much of all this advice any young family wants to hear at one time.

Family legends. Another key role for parents is to inoculate their grandchildren against life's mistakes through appropriate telling of family legends. When I was growing up, stories about my grandfather going off to the Gold Rush gave me a sense that my family had a history of daring and adventure—one that I could live up to. (It wasn't until years later that I figured out that my grandfather could never, historically, have headed off to the Yukon, but by then the impression was made.) Family stories, partially because they're repeated so often, have tremendous power with the young. Grandparents frequently tell them best.

Much has been written about the importance of "roots" since Alex Hailey made it the title of his 1965 book. Adults ordinarily go looking for their family roots sometime after age forty for a whole complex of personal and psychological reasons. But children need roots as well. They need to know where they came from, what kind of people their ancestors were, as part of a process that defines just who *they* are, right now. Grandparents frequently have the time to give this history, and often the pictures and documents to make it physically real to the curious child. A child who knows that Uncle Alex almost won a Nobel prize and Uncle Joe went to jail for forgery is in a position to see how the family history has come down to him, and then decide which model he likes better.

Alternative love. Love puts extra effort into relationships, adds smiles to stern faces and provides a level of acceptance that makes it possible to excuse all sorts of egregious behavior in other people. But parents don't and can't always love their children. First, few of us are saints who can love in a consistent way despite misdeeds, disappointments and the sheer cussedness of many young people. Second, children are often trying to cast us off so they can define their own selves. To do so, they must frustrate our love, reject it or turn it upside down just to break free and prove that they really were the products of miraculous birth rather than the fruit of our loins. This is to be expected.

In these not-so-loving periods of a basically loving relationship, it's certainly nice to have someone else who can look on our children with kind eyes. That's a grandparent. Where mom sees an arrogant hunk of teenage girl with purple hair and too many nose rings, grandma and grandpa still see the sweet 8-year-old who has temporarily lost her way. In the larger family universe, love endures. Our kids need that, whether they know it or not.

Five Reasons for Grandparents to Lend a Hand

1. They've got experience raising kids and can sometimes be a better caregiver than either parent.
2. They frequently have a dollar or two to spend on the grandchildren.
3. They're less likely than many baby-sitters to plop the kids in front of a television.
4. Parents need all the help they can get. Parenting is difficult for that handful of families with one wage earner, exhausting when both parents work and especially hard for single parents.
5. When grandparents do get involved, the grandkids frequently love them madly.

Chapter 19

I've never met an ideal parent . . .

but most of us do a pretty-darn-good job

Over the years I've worked on this book, I've been conducting a simple, nonscientific survey of parents who have been in the business of parenting for a dozen years or more. I asked them two questions: "Looking back at your parenting, what's your biggest regret?" And the second question, connected to the first, "What would you do differently if you had the chance to raise your kids a second time?"

The first result of my survey I should have anticipated—there's no sense asking questions like these of strangers.

In my various kinds of work, I have a chance to travel widely and meet with many different kinds of people. For a while, I tried asking my two questions of these casual acquaintances. Most of them were probably good-enough parents, and most of them were old enough to be able to look back on twelve or twenty years of raising kids with enough dispassion to understand what they had done. Trouble was—they wouldn't talk to me. "Oh, I don't have any regrets." "No, no problems." "Really, I'd just do the same things again." There'd be a little embarrassed laughter and then we'd go on to talk about the weather, movies or how good the corned-beef sandwich was.

I should have expected this. It's the same problem that gives university researchers such headaches when they do surveys on parenting. People clam up. Or they lie. We're all anxious about what we do as parents, all convinced that other people are doing it right while we're goofing up. We watch television and see that everything gets wrapped up just before the final commercial break. We read parenting books and see neat little dialogues where good parents cheerfully resolve any problem with their kids in a few pages of calm discussion. Yet our real lives are messier than this: We lose our tempers, our kids are mean, we get angry, the kids stomp off, we try to talk and it ends up an argument.

But we can't tell strangers about all this. We feel we have to smile and say that, yes, we're really good parents and the kids are just fine. We have to pretend that our family lives are like the Brady Bunch, not the troubled love-hate relationships in *The Glass Menagerie* or *The Horse Whisperer.*

So I went back to my close friends, the twenty or so people I know well enough to get past the initial response of "Well, everything was great," and reach something more substantial, "But if you really *have* to know . . . " The process wasn't easy. I had much less trouble getting stories about reading, schools or teachers for other books I've written. This time, I needed to twist arms a couple of times, or keep calling back on the phone, promising many times that I would disguise everyone's identity. The final answers they gave me aren't all that surprising—mostly they're issues already tackled in this book—but I think the responses offer a good overview of what real parenting is about.

Find time for the kids. Top of the list: Parents felt they hadn't spent as much time with their kids as they should have. My friends are still of the generation when women often took substantial time off from work when the kids were born, so their regret is rarely focused on having missed a child's infancy. Rather, parents talked about missing a later stage, or a whole set of years in a child's life that disappeared because they were busy on careers, personal issues or something else altogether.

"I lost her for about three years," said one mother.

"Lost her?"

"My daughter. When I went back to finish my degree, she was nine, ten. I got so caught up with the course work and all of that, I really just lost her. It was as if she disappeared from my life for three or four years. The next time I looked, she was a teenager."

"You missed some good years," I said.

"You don't have to tell me," she said. "Imagine paying no attention to a delightful 10-year-old only to wake up and find a mouthy 13-year-old in the same place. It was a lousy tradeoff."

Parenting in the real world, of course, is all about tradeoffs. My friend both wanted and needed the university degree, nor did it hurt her daughter to see her mother pursuing her own dream and engaged in serious intellectual work. But there can be a real loss in that special bond between child and parent. The kids always know when were tuned to some other channel, and won't let us forget later on. This doesn't mean we have to sacrifice our lives to children, but it does mean that ignoring our kids is done with peril. According to one survey done by a University of Maryland researcher, parents said they spent an average of 30 hours a week with their kids in 1965. By 1985, that figure was down to 17 hours a week. I suspect today it's lower still among employed parents, and would be lower again if we actually *counted* the hours rather than asked parents how much time they spent. As many of my friends said, it's a shame.

Treat siblings equally, but differently. Most parents feel that they don't do a very good job handling sibling rivalry, so it should come as no surprise that my sampling of parents cited this as a major regret. It was British researcher Judy Dunn who suggested that, regardless of what parents may think, we raise our different children in very different ways. This doesn't always mean we get better at parenting with each new child.

"We didn't get it right until the second one," sighed one mom, "and it shows."

"How's that?" I asked.

"Christie, the first one, had to carry all the weight and all our mistakes. Sometimes I think it's like she got old too soon and never had any fun. And we put all these restrictions on her—don't do this and don't do that. But when Brad was born, it was as if we threw all that out the window. We just didn't pay him that much attention."

"Was that a bad thing?"

"Not for him, so much," she told me. "I think he's stronger than Christie because he was less protected, but I know she blames us. We tried to treat them equally, but, well, we just didn't."

From my observations, I'd say neither Brad nor Christie suffered much because they were raised somewhat differently. Yet somehow parents have got the notion that we must treat every sibling in exactly the same way and, of course, we can't. The kids *are* different—they have different needs, personalities, opportunities, capacities. And we're different—older or younger, more or less assured as parents, more intent on kids or more distracted. Equality is a good *intention* for parents, especially as we try to create the container for our kids' lives, but it's not something we can carve in stone.

When you say no, mean it. Which part of "no" gives us more trouble, the "n" or the "o"? On the contrary, it's the whole word that's the problem, saying it and defining it and sticking by it. Kids are clever in finding ways around the N-word, and we don't do them any favors when we make it easy.

"The kids always found the line of least resistance," said one dad. "Usually, that was me."

"How?"

"Well, they'd want something, or want to do something, or whatever. And Mary would tell them no, and she's good about sticking to her no's. But then Jessica would come to me, or Tom would wait for some second when I'd be by myself, and then I'd get asked. And they were really smart. They'd wait until I was a little relaxed, kind of mellow, maybe had a drink in my hand. So I'd say yes."

"Without checking with Mary."

"Right. I mean, I hadn't seen them all day, I didn't really know what the whole thing was about, and I'm kind of a kid myself."

"That's true." I'd known this dad since we were both in high school.

"So then Mary and I would fight, and maybe I'd win or maybe she'd win, but usually it was the kids who won. It's divide-and-conquer, you know?"

"Too well," I admitted.

"So now Tom's spoiled, a real teenage jerk, and Jessica thinks I'm an idiot and Mary . . . well, that's another issue."

In my small survey, I found only one parent who thought he'd been too tough on the kids when they were growing up. That father, a bit of an adult bully in some respects, probably did dominate his kids and bring about the teenage rebellion the family is struggling with now. But the rest of us, the other 95 percent, look back and admit that we were either too soft, a parent pushover, or too inconsistent. We learned too late that we can simply repeat "no" until the kid gets the message; that explanations don't have to be given 10 or 20 times; that love doesn't mean saying "yes" to everything a kid wants.

Let them grow; let them go. For many of my parents, looking back, there was a sense that they interfered too much in their kids' lives. Sometimes it involved treating one child as if he or she were consistently younger than the kid's real age. This could be a first child, overprotected too much, sheltered too long. Or it could be a last child, forever the baby, infantilized and cuddled for too many years.

"My biggest regret," said one mom, "would have to be my role in our first child's life. I think I did too much for her."

"Like what?"

She stopped to consider. "I really didn't allow her to think for herself, or think critically. I kept jumping in, making decisions, filling in all the blanks for her. We were so busy trying to keep Rachel stimulated that she never had to take control over her own life."

"And now?"

"She can't make decisions. She even has trouble choosing what to eat in a restaurant. For big things, like a career, she's just lost. She's still looking for me to make decisions for her, but Rachel is twenty now."

"So what would you do differently?" I asked.

"I'd have given her more room. Kids need time to be bored, time to do their own thing. I didn't let that happen."

Increasingly, it's difficult for parents to stop sticking our noses into our children's lives. If were not in there providing "stimulation" and challenges, then the TV is on or the Internet is waiting or the

Nintendo is at hand. In every case, our kid's capacity to create his own play—and make his own decisions—is infringed upon by us or by adult technology. Anyone who has seen a bunch of kids with marbles or cardboard boxes from a stove or refrigerator knows that kids don't need our help to create a wonderful world of their own. What they need is for us to create a safe place for them to grow, and then for us to get out of the way.

Divorce . . . sigh. The last major regret isn't one that young parents can do much about. It would be foolish for me to suggest "don't split up" because couples invariably separate and divorce for their own very personal reasons. Nonetheless, of the parents I talked to who had been through a divorce, the response was always regret for its impact on the kids.

"I just didn't know," said one father. "They always used to say that the kids would be better off after a divorce than in a family where the parents fought all the time."

"Did you and your first wife fight all the time?"

"Well, no," he admitted, "not really. But we certainly weren't happy. And the divorce was supposed to be amicable."

"But it wasn't."

"Not after the lawyers," he sighed.

"And the kids took it badly."

"Well, you know how it is. Anger, blame, acting out. I told one kid when he ended up in court, 'This is the first and last bail I'm ever putting up for you.' And I have another son who still won't talk to me and has never met my new wife. I never believed it would be this bad."

Of course, it's not always that bad. Kids who are still young when their parents divorce and remarry seem to handle it better than kids who are teenagers when the split-up occurs. Nor is there much social stigma any more for a child whose parents are divorced—splitting up is the new normality. But the emotional effects of divorce on a generation whose parents have played musical partners still hasn't been adequately measured. All we know for sure is that the current group of kids in their twenties are putting off marriage and partnership for a long, long time. They've learned some kind of lesson from their parents, though I fear it's not a lesson we ever intended to teach.

Most of us are good-enough parents

Much of the professional literature on child development and child psychology is about problems. We read of family conflict, difficulties in growing up, psychological distress, juvenile crime and physical child abuse. From the literature, we'd think that the average child grows up in horrendous family circumstances, rife with everything from physical abuse to neglect to sexual tension. Thanks to sensational news, television docudramas and public fascination with the personal lives of the rich and famous, many people have a distorted image of children and families. One recent poll, for instance, asked American adults what proportion of crime was done by juveniles. The average answer was 43 percent, more than triple the real proportion of crime committed by young people. As a general public, we might have many facts—but we haven't got our facts straight.

Yet when most of us look back on our own upbringing—even those that hardly measure up to television norms—the image is often much kinder. "I guess they did the best they could." "Sure, I got spanked, but nobody ever beat me up." "My parents were nuts, but so are everybody's." And as parents ourselves, we finally gain some understanding of how difficult the job of parenting actually is. Our parents weren't perfect, nor are we, nor will our children be— this is simply the truth.

What struck me most in working on this book was the amount of effort, care and real love that parents shower on their children. In all the families I observed and talked with, only a handful were what anyone could term abusive or negligent. This doesn't mean such families don't exist—after all, we read about them daily in the newspapers—but that we shouldn't all feel guilty about abusing our children.

Of course, many of the parents I observed have done some cruel and stupid things—we all do, occasionally. But mostly they did so in the context of real love and often with the best of intentions. I've never met a parent who wanted his child to suffer, or fail or grow up in a stunted way. I've never met a parent who could see her child hurt without wincing, or upset without sympathizing, or sad without wanting to cheer the kid up. We are such softies, most of us,

> The phrase "family values" is tossed around a lot, but what's needed is family support.

that we're easy targets for smart-ass kids and wise-ass professionals who claim that it's all our fault.

Much of it isn't our fault. Our children come into the world with their own predispositions and their own set of personal and intellectual equipment. We give them the genetics but can't specify the gene combinations, nor can we control the world they're born into. Increasingly, babies are born into families that are economically poor, into societies that don't place much value on either children or families, and into social structures that don't really support the enterprise of child rearing. The phrase "family values" is tossed around a lot, but what's needed is family support. In Britain, thirty years ago, a bus driver would get off the vehicle to help a young mother get on with her baby and then go back out to hang the baby carriage on the front of the bus. Today, a mom in any country putting a baby carriage in front of a bus had better be careful that it doesn't get run over. Ours is not a particularly kid-friendly culture.

It would be better, of course, if we began electing governments that could find intelligent ways to siphon some of the money floating about North America and direct it to our often struggling young families and their children. Hillary Rodham Clinton was right when she used the phrase "it takes a village to raise a child" as the title of her book; but turning that phrase into government policy seems beyond the reach of our politicians.

In the face of all this, and despite the problems we face ourselves, most parents still manage to raise children with remarkable success. Perhaps what impressed me most about the families I spoke with for this book is how hard they *try* to be good parents. Parents wouldn't be buying almost a million copies a year of Dr. Spock's famous *Baby and Child Care* if they didn't care about their children. We wouldn't have millions of parents across the continent enrolled in parenting courses, getting together for workshops or buying books like this one if parents weren't determined to tackle the job of parenting and get it right.

Whenever I see an account of a child neglected by crack-addicted parents, I remind myself of the rural mother who was attacked by a mountain lion while on a morning horseback ride with her children. She did her best to fight off the animal, but when it became clear that the only way to save her children was to sacrifice her own life, that's exactly what she did. She died so her children could live on. To be a parent is to understand that any of us would do the same. To be a parent is to make smaller sacrifices, day in and day out, so that our children can grow and flourish in a difficult world. To be a parent is to undertake the most amazing, trying and rewarding task on the planet—and do it with love. Perhaps with a little reflection, we can do it even better.

If I Could Do It Over . . .

Responses, in order, to Paul Kropp's highly nonscientific but excruciatingly honest survey of twenty middle-class, experienced and mostly competent parents.

1. I'd spend more time with the kids.
2. I'd treat them more equally . . . but differently.
3. I'd be firmer and smarter in saying no.
4. I'd be easier in letting them grow up and letting them go.
5. I'd know that divorce is tougher on the kids than anyone will admit.

Selected Bibliography

You can find whole libraries of books related to families, children and parenting, but here are a few of the most interesting resources.

Best nuts-and-bolts manuals for parents

Leach, Penelope. *Your Baby and Child: From Birth to Age Five* (New York: Knopf, 1989).

Spock, Benjamin (later editions with Michael Rothenberg). *Baby and Child Care* (New York: Pocket, many editions from 1945 on).

On genetics and child development

Bronfenbrenner, Uri. *The Ecology of Human Development* (Boston, Mass.: Harvard University Press, 1979).

Gallagher, Winifred. *I.D.* (New York: Random House, 1996).

Loehlin, J. C. *Genes and Environment in Personality Development* (Newbury Park, Calif.: Sage, 1992).

Nichols, A. R. (ed). *Longitudinal Studies in Child Psychology and Psychiatry* (New York: John Wiley & Sons, 1985).

Rowe, D. *The Limits of Family Influence: Genes, Experience and Behavior* (New York: Guilford, 1994).

White, Burton. *The First Three Years of Life* (New York: Prentice-Hall, 1985).

On the history of children and child-rearing

Aries, Philippe. *Centuries of Childhood* (New York: Vintage, 1962).

Cable, Mary. *The Little Darlings* (New York: Charles Scribner's Sons, 1975).

Marshall, Peter. *Sex, Nursery Rhymes and Other Evils* (Vancouver, British Columbia: Whitecap, 1995).

On the psychology of children

Bowlby, John. *Attachment* (New York: Basic Books, 1982).

Fishel, Elizabeth. *I Swore I'd Never Do That* (Berkeley, Calif.: Conari Press, 1991).

Fraiberg, Selma, Edna Adelson and Vivian Shapiro. "Ghosts in the Nursery," in *Journal of the American Academy of Child Psychiatry*, 14 (1975), 387–421.

Garber, Stephen W., et al. *Good Behavior* (New York: St. Martin's Press, 1987).

Grusec, Joan, and L. Kucynski (eds.). *Parenting and Children's Internalization of Values: A Handbook of Contemporary Theory* (New York: John Wiley & Sons, 1997).

Lamb, Michael. *The Role of the Father in Child Development* (New York: John Wiley & Sons, 1981).

Miller, Alice. *The Untouched Key* (New York: Doubleday, 1990).

Winnicott, D. W. *The Maturational Process and the Facilitating Environment* (Madison, Conn.: International University Press, 1965).

_____. *Through Pediatrics to Psychoanalysis* (London, England: Hogarth, 1987).

On various issues in parenting

Ashner, Laurie, and Mitch Meyerson. *When Parents Love Too Much* (New York: Morrow, 1990).

Bly, Robert. *The Sibling Society* (Reading, Mass.: Addison-Wesley, 1996).

Coles, Robert. *Privileged Ones: The Well-off and the Rich in America* (Boston, Mass.: Little, Brown, 1977).

_____. *The Moral Life of Children* (New York: Random House, 1996).

Coloroso, Barbara. *Kids Are Worth It!* (New York: Avon, 1995).

Clarke-Stewart, Alison. *Child Care in the Family* (San Diego, Calif.: Academic, 1977).

Dunn, Judy. *The Beginnings of Social Understanding* (Cambridge, Mass.: Harvard University Press, 1988).

_____ with Robert Plomin. *Separate Lives: Why Siblings Are So Different* (New York: Basic Books, 1990).

Kagan, Jerome. *The Nature of the Child* (New York: Basic Books, 1984).

Leach, Penelope. *Children First* (New York: Vintage, 1995).

Maynard, Fredelle. *The Child Care Crisis.* (New York: Viking, 1985).

Postman, Neil. *Amusing Ourselves to Death: Public Discourse in the Age of Show Business* (New York: Viking, 1985).

Spock, Benjamin. *Raising Children in a Difficult Time* (New York: Norton, 1974).

Strassberg, Zvi, Kenneth Dodge et al. "Spanking in the Home and Children's Subsequent Aggression toward Kindergarten Peers," in *Development and Psychopathology*, 1994, Vol. 6, 445ff.

Whitehead, Barbara Dafoe. *The Divorce Culture: Rethinking Our Commitment to Marriage and Family* (New York : Vintage, 1998).

Notes on Sources

This book does not pretend to be a scholarly tome, so the text is not dotted with footnotes. Nonetheless, I have leaned heavily on certain works and researchers, and the curious reader might want to ask, "I wonder where he got *that* piece of information?" For those readers, here are a few notes and sources:

Introduction

The Archers and the Zacharies are real, as are all the other children and families referred to or quoted in the book. Since many of these people are friends or family, some specific details have been changed to disguise identities and protect confidences.

I think every parent's bookshelf should have at least four titles. Here are my choices. The two best nuts-and-bolts manuals for parents are Penelope Leach's *Your Baby and Child: From Birth to Age Five* and Dr. Benjamin Spock's *Baby and Child Care*. For understanding a child's early development, I heartily recommend Dr. Burton White's *The First Three Years of Life*, and for looking at the social issues related to child-rearing, Penelope Leach's *Children First*.

Chapter 1

Dr. Spock reminisced ruefully about his supposed approval of permissive parenting in *Raising Children in a Difficult Time* (Norton, 1974). Bernice McCarthy's initial work on learning styles is in *The 4-Mat System: Teaching to Learning Styles with Right/Left Mode Techniques* (Excel, Inc., 1980). Barbara Coloroso's parenting book is

Kids Are Worth It! ; its categories dovetail with those developed by
Diana Baumrind in 1983, but the presentation is far more popular.
Elizabeth Fishel's generally excellent parenting book is *I Swore I'd
Never Do That!* "Ghosts in the Nursery" by Selma Fraiberg, Edna
Adelson and Vivian Shapiro appeared first in the *Journal of the
American Academy of Child Psychiatry*, 14 (1975), 387–421. Their
work on the importance of the subconscious has roots in Anna
Freud's *Ego and the Mechanisms of Defense* (International University
Press, 1936).

Lois Meek Stolz's book *Influences on Parent Behavior* (Stanford
University Press, 1967) discusses many reasons why we parent the
way we do. So does Jacqueline Goodnow and W. Andrew Collins's
*Development According to Parents: The Nature, Sources and Consequences
of Parents' Ideas* (Erlbaum, 1990). Clarence Day's *Life with Father*
(Knopf, 1935) was a set of reminiscences that became a popular play
by Howard Lindsay and Russel Crouse. Television details are from
Charles Panati's *Parade of Fads, Follies and Manias* (HarperCollins,
1991) and various articles in the *New York Times*.

Chapter 2

Two good, readable histories of parenting practice are Peter
Marshall's *Sex, Nursery Rhymes and Other Evils* (Whitecap, 1995) and
Daniel Beekman's *The Mechanical Baby: A Popular History of the
Theory and Practice of Child Raising* (Lawrence Hill, 1977). The now-
standard book on childhood history is Philippe Aries, *Centuries of
Childhood* (New York, 1962).

Probably the most readable discussion of the nature vs. nurture
controversy is Winifred Gallagher's article "How We Become What
We Are" in *The Atlantic Monthly*, September 1994. She expanded
this into a book called *I.D.* (Random House, 1996). The genetics-
first position is expressed in J. C. Loehlin's *Genes and Environment in
Personality Development* (Sage, 1992) and D. Rowe's *The Limits of
Family Influence: Genes, Experience and Behavior* (Guilford, 1994).
David Lykken of the University of Minnesota has become well
known for asserting that our potential for happiness is genetic. His
work, and various rebuttals, are discussed in a good *Maclean's* piece
(September 16, 1996). The developmental position can be found in

Uri Bronfenbrenner's *The Ecology of Human Development* (Harvard, 1979) and in Burton White's *The First Three Years of Life*. Judy Dunn synthesizes data from both sides in *Separate Lives: Why Siblings Are So Different* (Basic Books, 1990, written with Robert Plomin).

Alice Miller's work on childhood trauma and historical figures is in *The Untouched Key* (Doubleday, 1990); her more general work on childhood trauma is *Banished Knowledge* (Doubleday, 1990). Cathy Spatz Widom's research was widely reported in 1996, including *Society* (May-June) 33 (4) 47. Lionel Dahmer wrote *A Father's Story* (Morrow, 1994), an attempt to understand why his son Jeffrey Dahmer turned out as he did. Throughout this chapter, I am indebted to Joan Grusec and her introduction to *Parenting and Children's Internalization of Values: A Handbook of Contemporary Theory* (Wiley, 1997).

Chapter 3

Popular magazines have always liked the family conference idea; for example, the recent article "One Child, One Vote" in *Woman's Day* (March 12, 1996). A balanced view of how parents should be parents can be found in the works of British psychologist D. W. Winnicott, especially *The Maturational Process and the Facilitating Environment* (IUP, 1965). Intrusive parents are studied in Laurie Ashner and Mitch Meyerson's *When Parents Love Too Much* (Morrow, 1990). Kids' post break-up behavior is discussed in many books. See Barbara Dafoe Whitehead's *The Divorce Culture* (Vintage, 1998).

Chapter 4

There are hundreds of volumes and pamphlets on the general topic of self-esteem and more than fifty titles in the Toronto Public Library on how to raise children's self-esteem. I've referred to Jean Illsley Clarke's *Self-Esteem: A Family Affair* (HarperCollins, 1978), Louise Hart's *The Winning Family: Increasing Self-Esteem in Your Children* (Dodd, Mead, 1987) and Vicki Lansky's *101 Ways to Make Your Child Feel Special* (Contemporary, 1991). The alternative view, that kids need a realistic view of themselves and reasonable challenges to build their self-confidence, is a major part of Robert

Bly's *The Sibling Society* (Addison-Wesley, 1996) and his earlier *Iron John* (Addison-Wesley, 1990). It is also a theme in many good books on child development.

Chapter 5

Alison Clarke-Stewart's book *Child Care in the Family* (Academic, 1977) said virtually nothing about quality time, but her comments to journalists seemed supportive of the concept. Spencer Johnson's *The One-Minute Father* and *The One-Minute Mother* (Morrow, 1983) offer help for the time-challenged. He writes, for instance, that a digital watch symbol "is intended to remind each of us to take a minute out of our day, every now and then, and look into the faces of our children."

The problem of declining family and parental time is part of a larger phenomenon of overwork and under-leisure. See Witold Rybczynski's *Waiting for the Weekend* (Viking, 1991) for some discussion of this trend. The view that kids need lots of parental time has been developed by many writers, for instance Jerome Kagan in *The Nature of the Child* (Basic, 1984). The box on page 69 is drawn from Burton White's book, *Educating the Infant and Toddler* (Lexington, 1987).

Chapter 6

The view that kids respond better to reasoned arguments from parents was developed early on by Sears, Maccoby and Levin in *Patterns of Child-Rearing* (Row, Peterson, 1957). It was supported by Martin Hoffman in 1970 ("Moral Development" in P. H. Mussen's *Carmichael's Manual of Child Psychology)* and by many other writers thereafter, reaching a natural conclusion in work by Alfred Adler and Rudolf Dreikurs where reason, by itself, was seen as sufficient to contain children. We all wish it were so.

Stephen and Marianne Garber's book is *Good Behavior* (St. Martin's, 1987). Barbara Coloroso's *Kids Are Worth It!* and Judy Dunn's *Separate Lives* have both been cited previously. Caroline

Piorowski's work is reported in *Today's Parent*. Sarah Johnson's book, *Parents on Parenting* (Vermillion, 1996), offers sensible advice on "Boundaries and Responsibilities" from British parents.

Joan Grusec and Jacqueline Goodnow's "Impact of Parental Discipline Methods on the Child's Internalization of Values" in *Developmental Psychol*ogy, 1994, 30(l) is a wonderful overview of the situation for those who can handle academic prose. Work by J. C. Mancuso and E. E. Maccoby, reported in various academic publications, including *Child Development*, provides a good basis of academic theory on the issue of discipline and family structure. Mancuso's work (used for the sidebars) can also be found in *Parental Belief Systems* (Erlbaum, 1985) and *Thinking About the Family: Views of Parents and Children* (Erlbaum, 1986). Thomas Gordon's *P.E.T: Parent Effectiveness Training* (Wyden, 1970) was into ten printings by 1972 and reissued in 1986, but has been largely forgotten now.

Chapter 7

The new view on spanking is clearly expressed in a *New York Times* article, "Spanking is Becoming the New Don't" by Carol Collins (May 11, 1995). Michelle Landsberg offered similar views in her September 22, 1996, *Toronto Star* column and subsequent articles and television shows. Both writers are indebted to the strong anti-spanking book by Murray Straus called *Beating the Devil Out of Them* (Lexington/Macmillan, 1994), which sums up much historical and sociological information, but makes the assumption that spanking is equivalent to corporal punishment. A more reasonable approach is taken in "Spanking in the home and children's subsequent aggression toward kindergarten peers," by Zvi Strassberg, Kenneth Dodge et al in *Development and Psychopathology* 6 (1994): 445ff.

Chapter 8

Restaurant statistics are from U.S. industry figures and Statistics Canada. Ian Cruickshank's "Travels with My Kids" appeared in *Today's Parent*, September 1994. *Parents* magazine tackled manners in

"Mind Your Manners," November 1994. Camilla Cornell's "The Attraction of Distraction" (*Today's Parent*, May 1996) offers all sorts of distraction ideas but balances them with Sara Dimerman's caution. The life of the Rockefellers is most recently described in Cary Reich's *The Life of Nelson A. Rockefeller* (Doubleday, 1996). Robert Coles's *The Privileged Ones: The Well-off and the Rich in America* (Little, Brown, 1977), offers a number of fascinating portraits of upper-class kids.

Chapter 9

Witold Rybczynski's *Home: A Short History of an Idea* (Viking, 1986) offers a very readable discussion of family living arrangements through the ages. The importance of outside influences on psychological development is considered in Judith Viorst's *Necessary Losses* (Simon and Schuster, 1986). The references in chapters 10 and 18 on resilience are also relevant here. Judith Martin's *Miss Manners' Guide for the Turn of the Millennium* (Simon and Schuster, 1989) has 700 pages on proper behavior for parents who wish an encyclopedic approach to the topic. The Dr. Spock quote is from his famous *Baby and Child Care*.

Chapter 10

J. L. Simmons and George McCall wrote *76 Ways to Protect Your Child from Crime* (Holt, 1992) with a front-cover promise to "reduce your child's risk of being a victim by 90%." Some of the statistics cited are from the *Maclean's* sensible article on this subject, "Perils of Home" (July 24, 1995). U.S. statistics are provided by an article appearing in *Child Maltreatment* (February 2000, Vol. 5, Issue 1, p. 63), an article appearing in *Children and Managed Healthcare* (Vol. 8, No. 2, 1998, pp. 141–151), the National Safety Council, and from NISMART, the National Incidence Study of Missing, Abducted, Runaway and Thrown Away Children. An interesting discussion of how the media have played up abuse by clergy is *Pedophile and Priests* (Oxford, 1996) by Philip Jenkins.

Baboon information is from John Bowlby's *Attachment*, second edition. Peter Schneider's article "Lost Innocents: The Myth of Missing Children" is from *Harper's* magazine, February 1988. Bruce Feiler's *New York Times Magazine* endpaper article is called "Bedtime for Bozo."

Readable material on separation anxiety and the need for psychological individuation by children can be found in chapter 14 of Judith Viorst's *Necessary Losses* (Simon and Schuster, 1986). The importance of adult figures outside the family is also discussed in Norman Garmezy's *Principles of General Psychology* (Ronald, 1974) and Judy Dunn's *The Beginnings of Social Understanding* (Harvard, 1988). The graduate-school work of my stepdaughter Emma Adam was also helpful in summarizing research on the importance of adults outside the family as a resilience factor for at-risk children.

Chapter 11

The classic work on sibling warfare was Freud's *Civilization and Its Discontents* (Vienna, 1930), but the most recent research was by Judy Dunn in *Siblings: Love, Envy and Understanding* (written with Carol Kendrick, Harvard University Press, 1982). Dunn came back to the subject in her *Separate Lives: Why Siblings Are So Different* (Basic Books, 1990; written with Robert Plomin). Elizabeth Fishel also has a thoughtful book of advice: *Sisters: Love and Rivalry* (Morrow, 1979). Patti McDermott's *Sisters and Brothers* (Contemporary, 1992) is an interesting study of adult siblings.

Chapter 12

Zoological information is mostly from John Bowlby's *Attachment*, second edition. R. A. Hinde's work can be found in *Animal Behavior: A Synthesis of Ethology and Comparative Psychology* (McGraw-Hill, 1970) and *Towards Understanding Relationships* (Academic, 1979). For a shocking discussion, not just of wet-nursing, but of how children have been treated and mostly mistreated throughout history, there's a book edited and introduced by Lloyd deMause: *The History of Childhood* (Psychohistory Press, 1974). Malinowsky's classic work is

The Sexual Life of Savages in Northwestern Melanesia (Routledge, 1932).

Alison Clarke-Stewart concluded that childcare outside the family was mostly a good thing in her *Child Care in the Family* (Academic, 1977), as did Ellen Galinsky in *The New Extended Family: Daycare That Works* (Houghton Mifflin, 1977). Fredelle Maynard's *The Child-Care Crisis* (Viking/Penguin, 1985) concluded the opposite. Penelope Leach is also opposed to commercial childcare and makes a convincing case in *Children First* (Vintage, 1995).

Utne Reader ran an entire section on children and childcare called "Who Cares About Kids" in its May/June 1993 issue. Ann Walmsley's article "The Perils of Parental Leave" *(Today's Parent,* February 1997) looks at many of the wrinkles in that option. My description of parental leave legislation is based on newspaper articles in the *New York Times,* as well as data from the National Child Care Information Center.

Chapter 13

Rather than go on at length here, let me refer those interested to the lengthy bibliography for *The School Solution* (Random House of Canada, 1995), which I wrote with Lynda Hodson.

Chapter 14

Some trace the popularity of ADD to Dr. Edward Hallowell's 1994 bestseller *Driven to Distraction* (Pantheon, 1994), though the *20/20* and *Oprah* shows which followed probably reached far more people. The CHADD web site is at www.chadd.org/. *Newsweek* did an excellent overview on ADD called "Mother's Little Helper" in its March 18, 1996, issue. *Today's Parent* did a balanced study of the medication controversy in John Hoffman's "The Ritalin Riddle" (March 1997).

Chapter 15

Newsweek magazine took a careful look at teenage demographics in "Too Old, Too Fast?" (November 16, 1992). The article by Helm

Stierlin and Kent Ravenscroft, Jr. is "Varieties of adolescent separation conflicts" in the *British Journal of Medical Psychology* 45 (1972): 299. Carol Gilligan has written much on the effects of sex stereotyping and girls, especially *Meeting at the Crossroads: Women's Psychology and Girls' Development* (Harvard, 1992). Several articles in Grusec and Kuczynski's *Parenting and Children's Internalization of Values: A Handbook of Contemporary Theory* (Wiley, 1997) were useful in looking at discipline models. Victor Strassburger's *Getting Your Kids to Say No in the 90s When You said Yes in the 60s* (Simon and Schuster, 1993) is far more intelligent than its title suggests.

Chapter 16

The *Utne Reader* feature "Where's Papa?" (Sep/Oct 1996) offers a number of views and statistics on the issue of disappearing fathers. Michael Lamb's *The Role of the Father in Child Development* (Wiley, 1981) is insightful, but its statistics are dated. His more recent "Fatherhood and Father-Child Relationships: Five Years of Research" is in *Fathers and Their Families* by Cath, Gurwitt and Gunsberg, eds. (Analytic Press, 1989). For more on the psychological and mythological roles of men as fathers and sons, see Robert Bly's *Iron John* (Addison-Wesley, 1990) and his *Sibling Society* (Addison-Wesley, 1996). David Popenue's *Life without Father* (Harvard, 1999) offers many insights on the value of having a dad.

Chapter 17

Lego history can be found on its web site, www.lego.com, and other interesting facts are on the Oxford University Lego FAQ site.

Melanie Klein's work on the psychoanalysis of children, including play therapy, can be found in her *Contributions to Psycho-Analysis: 1921–1945* (Hogarth, 1948). Other interesting speculation on the psychological significance of play in infancy is in the work of D. W. Winnicott, especially *The Maturational Process and the Facilitating Environment* (International Universities Press, 1965) and *Through Pediatrics to Psycho-Analysis* (Hogarth, 1987).

There is a whole literature on the history of toys, dolls and dollhouses. Gwen White's *Antique Toys and Their Background*

(Batsford, 1971) is standard; Dan Foley's *Toys Through the Ages* (Chilton, 1962) is more readable. The Barbie phenomenon has recently been looked at in two books: M. G. Lord's *Forever Barbie* (Morrow, 1995) and Ruth Handler's *Dream Doll* (Longmeadow, 1995).

Chapter 18

Statistics are from the U.S. Census, Statistics Canada, reports in *The Report on Business* and the Knight-Ridder/Tribune News Service. Seniors, as a group, are frequently considered in *American Demographics*; see especially Judith Waldrop's article, February 1992. David Foot, in his bestseller *Boom, Bust and Echo* (MacFarlane, Walter & Ross, 1996), maintains that demographics account for two-thirds of everything, and he may be one-third right.

Resilience literature makes an interesting read, though the academic work here is still developing. E. E. Werner's work includes *Vulnerable but Invincible* (McGraw/Hill, 1982) and other studies which can be found in A. R. Nichol's (ed.) *Longitudinal Studies in Child Psychology and Psychiatry* (Wiley, 1985). Other important work in the area, mostly in professional journals, comes from Ann Masten and Norman Garmezy.

Chapter 19

Lengthy discussions of the limitations of academic research into child rearing can be found in the introduction to Fredelle Maynard's *The Child Care Crisis* (Viking Penguin, 1985) and in the introduction to Alison Clarke-Stewart's *Child Care in the Family* (Academic, 1977).

The concept of a "good-enough" parent was developed by D. W. Winnicott and borrowed by Bruno Bettelheim for what is still a good book, *A Good Enough Parent* (Knopf, 1987). John Hoffman wrote a brief article called "Shoulda, Woulda, Coulda: Do Guilt and Parenting Have to Go Hand in Hand?" (*Today's Parent*, August 1996) and concludes, as I do, that they should not.

Index